Careers in Psychology

SECOND EDITION

Careers in Psychology

OPPORTUNITIES IN A CHANGING WORLD

TARA L. KUTHER
Western Connecticut State University

ROBERT D. MORGAN
Texas Tech University

THOMSON
WADSWORTH

Australia • Brazil • Canada • Mexico • Singapore
Spain • United Kingdom • United States

THOMSON

WADSWORTH

Careers in Psychology:
Opportunities in a Changing World, **Second Edition**
Tara L. Kuther and Robert D. Morgan

Publisher: Vicki Knight
Editorial Assistant: Sheila Walsh
Managing Technology Project Manager:
 Darin Derstine
Vice President, Director of Marketing:
 Caroline Croley
Marketing Assistant: Natasha Coats
Senior Marketing Communications Manager:
 Kelley McAllister
Project Manager, Editorial Production:
 Karol Jurado
Creative Director: Rob Hugel

Senior Art Director: Vernon Boes
Print Buyer: Doreen Suruki
Rights and Permissions Manager: Bob Kauser
Production Service: International Typesetting
 and Composition
Copy Editor: Molly Roth
Cover Designer: Andy Norris
Cover Image: Bill Brooks/Masterfile
Cover Printer: Courier Corporation/Stoughton
Compositor: International Typesetting
 and Composition
Printer: Courier Corporation/Stoughton

Printed in the United States of America
2 3 4 5 6 7 09 08 07

Library of Congress Control Number:
2006922145
                    978-0-495-09078-6
Student Edition: ISBN 0-495-09078-6

Thomson Higher Education
10 Davis Drive
Belmont, CA 94002-3098
USA

For more information about our products,
contact us at:
**Thomson Learning Academic Resource
Center 1-800-423-0563**
For permission to use material from this text
or product, submit a request online at
http://www.thomsonrights.com.
Any additional questions about permissions
can be submitted by e-mail to
thomsonrights@thomson.com.

To my family—TLK

To Stacy W. Morgan—RDM

About the Authors

Dr. Tara L. Kuther received her PhD in developmental psychology from Fordham University. She is currently Associate Professor of Psychology at Western Connecticut State University where she teaches courses in child, adolescent, and adult psychology. She is an active member of the Society for Teaching of Psychology, Division Two of the American Psychological Association, and the Council for Undergraduate Research. Dr. Kuther is the author of several books, including *The Psychology Major's Handbook*.

Dr. Robert D. Morgan is Associate Professor and Director of the Counseling Psychology Program at Texas Tech University. He is also Associate Clinical and Forensic Director with Lubbock Regional Mental Health and Mental Retardation Services. He completed his training at the University of Nebraska at Kearney (BS in psychology), Fort Hays State University (MS in clinical psychology) and Oklahoma State University (PhD in counseling psychology). He completed his predoctoral internship at the Federal Correctional Institution, Petersburg, Virginia, and a postdoctoral fellowship in forensic psychology in the Department of Psychiatry at the University of Missouri–Kansas City and the Missouri Department of Mental Health. His research interests include correctional mental health, forensic psychology, and professional development and training. He is coeditor of *Life After Graduate School in Psychology: Insider's Advice from New Psychologists*.

Brief Contents

Contents

Chapter 9

Experimental, Cognitive, and Quantitative Psychology and Psychometrics   120

Chapter 10

Social and Consumer Psychology   133

Preface

Are you wondering what to do with your psychology degree? Many students enter our offices asking the same question: "What can I do with a degree in psychology?" A baccalaureate in psychology is a highly flexible, marketable, and useful liberal arts degree. Psychology offers students insight into human behavior, which is useful in all careers and is perhaps why psychology is one of the most popular undergraduate majors, with about 430,000 undergraduate students and more than 75,000 baccalaureate degrees awarded annually. Graduate degrees in psychology offer additional career opportunities; approximately 13,000 master's and 3,000 doctoral degrees are awarded in psychology each year.

Our goal in writing *Careers in Psychology: Opportunities in a Changing World* is to discuss the broad range of careers that psychology students might choose. Many students are unaware of the breadth of psychology and its many subdisciplines, and this book will introduce you to the wide range of possible undergraduate- and graduate-level careers in psychology. A guiding principle of *Careers in Psychology* is that education in psychology prepares students for careers in many fields; however, students have the onus of determining their career interests and tailoring their psychology degree with additional courses and experiences to round out their preparation and enhance their marketability for their chosen career. This principle holds true for undergraduate as well as graduate degree holders in psychology.

Careers in Psychology is appropriate for a range of students, including prospective and declared psychology majors. It complements a variety of psychology courses, including introductory psychology, careers in psychology, methodology courses, capstone courses, and seminars for psychology majors. We view this book as a resource for psychology students and their advisors, and we encourage students to discuss the career opportunities they find within these pages with their advisors and career counselors.

Careers in Psychology begins by discussing the nature of psychology and the diverse careers available to psychology graduates. In Chapter 1, students are guided through considerations in choosing a major and the benefits of majoring in psychology. Chapter 1 closes with a discussion of tips for succeeding as a psychology student. In Chapter 2, we explore graduate-level careers in psychology that are not discipline specific; psychologists in all fields may seek careers in academia, the military, and publishing, for example.

Each of Chapters 3–11 covers a psychology subdiscipline and presents related careers for baccalaureate and graduate degree holders. Chapters 3 and 4 explore the applied fields of clinical, counseling, and school psychology. In Chapters 5 and 6, readers are introduced to baccalaureate- and graduate-level careers in three popular subspecialties: psychology and law, health psychology, and sport psychology. Chapter 7 covers careers related to biopsychology, cognitive neuropsychology, and clinical neuropsychology. Chapters 8 and 9 discuss careers in industrial/organizational psychology and human factors, as well as careers for students who are interested in experimental, cognitive, and quantitative psychology, as well as psychometrics. Chapters 10 and 11 present career options for students of social, consumer, and developmental psychology. Each of these chapters closes with a checklist to help readers evaluate their interest and aptitude for the field discussed within the chapter.

The Second Edition of *Careers in Psychology* provides updated salary and career information for each subdiscipline of psychology. In addition, two chapters offer advice for students who are graduating. Chapter 12 discusses getting a job after graduation and includes advice on locating positions, writing a resume and cover letter, and interviewing. Chapter 13 examines how to apply to graduate school in psychology and provides an overview of the process, including the various graduate degrees that students may obtain, getting information about programs, the application, and interviewing.

It is our hope that *Careers in Psychology* will help prospective and current students develop and evaluate their interest in psychology and appreciate the myriad career opportunities available with a degree in psychology. We believe that psychology students are well prepared for many careers and that when students think outside of the box, seek out innovative opportunities, and acquire related skills, they will be surprised at the opportunities that await within our changing world.

Acknowledgments

We are most appreciative of the helpful suggestions that we received from reviewers on the first edition: Keith Colman, California State University–Long Beach; Karen Jackson, Texas Lutheran University on the first edition; Cheryl Lynch, University of Louisiana; Colleen Seifert, University of Michigan; Donna Stuber-McEwen, Friends University; Frank Vattano, Colorado State University; Paula Waddill, Murray State University; and Valerie Whittesey, Kennesaw State University. For the second edition, the constructive comments and suggestions made by Andrew Peck, Pennsylvania State University; David Perkins, Ball State University; and Douglas Engwall, Central Connecticut State University have, we feel, improved the book. Our hope is that the reader agrees.

In addition, we thank our editor at Wadsworth, Vicki Knight, for guiding us through the review and revision process and sharing her expertise and insight. Thanks for her assistant, Sheila Walsh; Karol Jurado, Content Project Manager; Kelly McAllister, Senior Marketing Communications Manager; and Natasha Coats, Marketing Assistant. Thanks to Erin McDonald for reviewing and commenting on drafts of the first edition and to Poonam Melwani for her assistance in reviewing and formatting the second edition. Thanks to Judith Johnstone for sharing her copyediting expertise on the first edition of this book and to Molly Roth for her assistance with the second edition. We are also appreciative of the help from Christine Andreasen, Proofreader, and Robert Swanson, Indexer.

Much of what appears in these pages is the result of conversations with students; I (Tara) thank them for asking the questions that prompted us to write this book. I thank my parents, Philip and Irene Kuther—especially my father, who was the first to ask me, "What can you do with a degree in psychology?" and trusted that I would discover the answer. Last, but not least, I thank Larry DeCarlo for his companionship throughout this project and my career.

I (Robert) thank my students for challenging me to explore the boundaries of psychology. I offer special thanks to Robert Ax and Steven Mandracchia for teaching me to think outside of the box. Finally, I thank my family—Stacy, Taylor, Ryan, and Riley—for their unyielding support.

PSYCHOLOGY'S DIVERSE CAREER OPPORTUNITIES

CHAPTER GUIDE

Each time she teaches introductory psychology, one of the authors of this book begins the first class by asking, "What is a psychologist?" and "What does a psychologist do?" Here are some typical student responses:

- "Someone who studies the mind and thought processes of an individual to find the roots of a problem that cannot be explained by physiology."
- "A doctor who does not use medication or drugs to help delve into issues that are causing a person to experience disharmony in life. That disharmony can range from difficulty in personal relations to sleep disruption to behavioral disorders."
- "A person trained in scientific and social analysis who tries to help patients suffering from mental disorders and/or problems by listening."

Are these student responses accurate? Yes and no. Some psychologists are therapists; however, the discipline of psychology encompasses much more than therapy. This book introduces the full range of activities in which psychologists participate. By the time you reach the end of this book, we hope that your perspective on psychology and psychologists will have changed. This chapter introduces the diverse field of psychology and talks about how you can learn more about yourself and your interests in order to help you determine whether psychology is the field for you.

WHAT IS PSYCHOLOGY?

Most of us first become acquainted with the field of psychology informally through our everyday experiences. Turn on the television to see a psychologist on *Oprah* explaining how parents can help their troubled teens. Change the channel to the sitcom *Frasier*, and we see a fictional psychiatrist dispensing advice on his radio show. Open a magazine, and you may find an article, written by a psychologist, about how to love your body. Psychology has ingrained itself into American popular culture. But how much do you really know about psychology and the work of psychologists? You may be surprised to learn that the field of psychology extends beyond therapy, self-help books, and parenting advice.

So, back to one of our original questions—what is psychology? *Psychology* is the scientific study of *behavior*, defined as anything an animal or a person does, feels, or thinks. Topics of psychological study include social relationships, the brain and the chemicals that influence it, vision, human development, the causes of normative and atypical behavior, and much more. Many students are surprised when they discover the broad range of activities in which psychologists engage. Psychologists conduct research with monkeys, study the human brain, and also construct informational surveys. They may work in business settings: developing training programs for employees, conducting interviews, and increasing worker productivity. Psychologists work as administrators, managing hospitals, mental health clinics, nonprofit organizations, government agencies, businesses, and schools. Some psychologists are employed as professors at universities, community colleges, and high schools. Others work as researchers in university, hospital, corporate, or government settings.

Of course, we can't forget the roles that psychologists play as service providers. Psychologists work with people, providing intellectual and personality assessments, conducting therapy, and developing programs to prevent problems or to help people deal with and overcome them. Although the average person is most familiar with this type of psychologist, that is, the practicing clinical or counseling psychologist, only about one-half of psychologists work in these service provider roles (American Psychological Association, n.d.a). Many different careers fall under the umbrella of psychology. Table 1.1 provides a list of all of the discipline subdivisions within the American Psychological Association, the most prominent professional organization for psychologists. As you examine the table, one thing becomes apparent: Psychology is diverse. Each chapter within this book examines one or more subdisciplines within psychology to provide a taste of the many fields in which people like you may find employment. You will learn here about careers in several areas of psychology and at all levels of education.

CAREERS IN TEACHING, RESEARCH, AND PRACTICE

As you can see in Table 1.1, many subdisciplines compose the field of psychology. Within each subdiscipline, some psychologists conduct research to expand the knowledge base, others practice or apply the findings to help people and communities, and many do both as scientist-practitioners. Clearly, psychologists engage in a variety of activities. Broadly speaking, these activities can be categorized into teaching, research, and practice.

A graduate degree, such as a master's or doctoral degree, enables holders to teach at a high school, a two-year college, or, with a doctoral degree, a four-year college or university. A degree in psychology is excellent preparation for a career in research. Graduates with a bachelor's degree may assist with research but will remain under supervision. Research psychologists with a graduate degree conduct basic and applied studies of human behavior and

TABLE 1.1	Disciplines within Psychology: American Psychological Association Divisions

Addictions

Adult Development and Aging

American Psychology—Law Society

American Society for the Advancement of Pharmacotherapy Applied

Experimental and Engineering Psychology

Behavior Analysis

Behavioral Neuroscience and Comparative Psychology

Child, Youth, and Family Services

Clinical Neuropsychology

Counseling Psychology

Developmental Psychology

Educational Psychology

Evaluation, Measurement, and Statistics

Exercise and Sport Psychology

Experimental Psychology

Family Psychology

Group Psychology and Group Psychotherapy

Health Psychology

History of Psychology

Humanistic Psychology

International Psychology

Media Psychology

Mental Retardation and Developmental Disabilities

Military Psychology

Population and Environmental Psychology

Psychologists in Independent Practice

Psychologists in Public Service

Psychology of Religion

Psychopharmacology and Substance Abuse

Psychoanalysis

Psychotherapy

Rehabilitation Psychology

School Psychology

Society for Community Research and Action

Society for Consumer Psychology

Society for General Psychology

Society for Industrial and Organizational Psychology

TABLE 1.1	Disciplines within Psychology: American Psychological Association Divisions (*Continued*)

Society for Personality and Social Psychology

Society for the Psychological Study of Lesbian, Gay, and Bisexual Issues

Society for the Psychological Study of Social Issues (SPSSI)

Society for the Psychological Study of Ethnic Minority Issues

Society for the Psychological Study of Men and Masculinity

Society for the Psychology of Aesthetics, Creativity, and the Arts

Society for the Psychology of Women

Society for the Study of Peace, Conflict, and Violence

Society for the Teaching of Psychology

Society of Clinical Psychology

Society of Clinical Child and Adolescent Psychology

Society of Consulting Psychology

Society of Pediatric Psychology

Society of Psychological Hypnosis

Theoretical and Philosophical Psychology

may participate in research programs sponsored by universities, the government, and private organizations (Bureau of Labor Statistics, 2004). Some work in military research programs, while others act as research and development officers at biotechnological and pharmaceutical companies (Lloyd, 2000). Many psychologists conduct research and teach in medical schools (Pate & Kohout, 2004). As fields such as anatomy, biochemistry, physiology, pharmacology, and microbiology merge, interdisciplinary study plays an increasingly important role in university life and is leading to more research and teaching opportunities for psychologists outside of psychology departments (Balster, 1995; Berry, 2005). Many research positions are available to master's degree holders, but the doctoral degree offers more flexibility, opportunities for advancement, and opportunities to serve as the primary investigator of federal grants (Lloyd, 2000).

Psychology degrees, particularly graduate degrees, open the door to a wide variety of careers besides teaching and research. For example, many graduate degree holders in psychology engage in service delivery. Mental health professionals with graduate degrees, including clinical and counseling psychologists, engage in a variety of practice activities. Some of these activities include the following: (1) conducting psychotherapy with people who have psychological disorders, crises, or problems of living; (2) administering and interpreting psychological tests of personality, intellect, and vocational aptitude; (3) facilitating psychoeducational and psychotherapy groups;

(4) giving talks or workshops on specialty areas; (5) directing and administering mental health programs; (6) supervising the clinical work of other therapists; and (7) responding to crises or emergency situations (Bureau of Labor Statistics, 2004; Himelein, 1999). For more information on careers in clinical and counseling psychology, see Chapter 3.

Despite the ubiquity of the service-provider role, students of psychology can choose from many other types of roles in applied careers. Graduates of psychology programs manage and administer research and applied activities in hospitals, mental health clinics, government agencies, schools, universities, businesses, and nonprofit organizations (Bat-Chava, 2000; Bruzzese, 2005). Degree holders in psychology often are hired as consultants by organizations to provide services such as designing marketing surveys, organizing outpatient mental health services, conducting individual assessments, providing expert testimony to the court, and designing web pages (C. K. Andrews, 2005; Kuther, 2004, 2005; E. D. Taylor, Dobbins & Woodruff, 2005; Van Haveren, Habben, & Kuther, 2005). Many psychology graduates obtain careers in business, where they select and train employees, engage in human resource development, and develop employee assistance programs (Kasserman, 2005; Williams, 2005). This is just the tip of the careers-in-psychology iceberg.

CHOOSING A MAJOR AND CAREER

Now that you've had a brief introduction to the broad field of psychology, let's talk about you. Lots of students find career planning stressful. If you feel that way, you're not alone. How do you decide what you want to do with your life? How do you determine your college major? How is it that some students know what they want to do, but others have a much more difficult time? Understanding your career goals doesn't involve magic, innate abilities, or luck—just hard work and introspection.

Understand Your Interests, Skills, and Values

Your first step in developing career goals and choosing a major involves understanding yourself. What are your interests? If you can understand yourself and choose a major that reflects your interests, you'll find succeeding in your classes easier. Sometimes students choose a major without considering their interests. For example, they might choose a major that they think is marketable, take a few classes, and then realize that they are bored and need to explore their interests after all. Don't complete this task backwards. Instead, consider your interests before you choose a major.

How do you determine your interests? Try this exercise: Write about all of your accomplishments—any times you can think of when you encountered a problem and took action to solve it. Write freely, letting all of your achievements flow onto the page. The problems that you've solved don't have to be huge. Even learning to play a song on your guitar or managing your annoying roommate are accomplishments. In other words, the accomplishments that you list can be small and unacknowledged by others. List as many as you can. Don't stop when it becomes difficult; instead, probe further. When adding to your list becomes more difficult, write whatever comes to mind, without censoring or editing. Even writing about the difficulty of thinking about additional accomplishments might jog your memory.

Once you have completed your list, take a close look at it. What skills does each of your accomplishments entail? List each skill on a separate page. As you consider your accomplishments and their associated skills, your list of skills will grow. Once you have considered all of your accomplishments and listed the related skills and abilities, look at your list. Which skills do you prefer using? Which of these skills are most interesting to you? Do any of your skills need more development? Are there any that you would like to develop further? Which are most important to you?

Now go back to your list of accomplishments. Which are most personally relevant to you? Why? Which have brought you the most satisfaction? Which do you value most highly and why? This exercise is important because by understanding which achievements you cherish you'll get a better idea about your interests and values, which is helpful in determining a major that will hold your interest. Understanding your skills, identifying strengths and areas in need of improvement, and identifying the skills you most enjoy using will also shed light onto possible careers. Finally, as you evaluate potential careers, consider how they fit with your values about work. For example, how important is salary? Do you want to work from 9 to 5 or more varied hours? Do you want to work with the public or alone?

Understand Your Personality

Understanding your unique personality will help you to choose a major and career that are right for you. In one of the most widely used models of career development, Holland (1959) identifies six personality types and relates them to specific career choices. The six categories are presented in Table 1.2. How do you determine your type? Read the descriptions. Most people find that they are a combination of types—that one or two descriptions seem to fit them well. You can also take the Self-Directed Search (Holland, 1994), a formal assessment based on the categories listed in Table 1.2. The career development office at your university can provide you with more

TABLE 1.2	Holland's (1959) Personality Types
Realistic	Someone with a realistic personality type is athletically or mechanically inclined. He or she would probably prefer to work outdoors with tools, plants, or animals. Some of the traits that describe the realistic personality type include practical, candid, a nature lover, calm, reserved, restrained, independent, systematic, and persistent.
Investigative	The investigative type enjoys learning, observing, problem solving, and analyzing information. Traits that describe the investigative type include curious, logical, observant, precise, intellectual, cautious, introspective, reserved, unbiased, and independent.
Artistic	Imaginative and creative, the artistic personality type likes to work in unstructured situations that allow for creativity and innovation. Personality characteristics of the artistic type include intuitive, unconventional, moody, nonconforming, expressive, unique, pensive, spontaneous, compassionate, bold, direct, and idealistic.
Social	The social personality type enjoys helping and training others. Characteristics that describe the social type include friendly, cooperative, idealistic, perceptive, outgoing, understanding, supportive, generous, dependable, forgiving, patient, compassionate, and eloquent.
Enterprising	The enterprising personality type likes to work with people in persuasive, performance, or managerial situations to achieve goals that are organizational or economic in nature. Characteristics that describe the enterprising type include confident, assertive, determined, talkative, extroverted, energetic, animated, social, persuasive, fashionable, spontaneous, daring, accommodating, and optimistic.
Conventional	The conventional personality type is well organized, has clerical or numerical ability, and likes to work with data and carry out tasks in detail. Characteristics that describe the conventional type include meticulous, numerically inclined, conscientious, precise, adept, conforming, orderly, practical, frugal, structured, courteous, acquiescent, and persistent.

Source: Kuther, 2006, pp. 20–21.

information about this tool, or you might take the online version, which you can complete for a fee at http://www.self-directed-search.com. A free quiz based on the Holland personality types is available at Career Key (http://www.careerkey.org).

Understanding your personality type can help you choose a major, because some majors are better suited to particular personality types. Table 1.3 lists college majors organized by personality type. Note that not all possible majors are listed and that the categories are flexible; some majors appear in more than one category because they reflect a variety of skills.

Understand the Difference between a Major and a Career

Choosing a college major is a stressful experience for many students because they believe that their college major will determine their career. This isn't true. Your major is simply a starting point; it will not limit you

TABLE 1.3 Holland Personality Types and College Majors

Realistic	Investigative	Artistic	Social	Enterprising	Conventional
Agriculture/Forestry	Animal Science	Advertising	Audiology	Advertising	Accounting
Criminal Justice	Anthropology	Art History	Counseling	Agricultural Economics	Business
Engineering	Astronomy	Art Education	Criminal Justice	Broadcasting	Computer Science
Health and Physical Education	Biochemistry	Architecture	Elementary Education	Communications	Economics
Animal Science	Biological Sciences	Classics	History	Economics	Finance
Biosystems Engineering	Chemistry	Communications	Human Development	Finance	Mathematics
Plant and Soil Sciences	Computer Science	English	Human Services	Industrial Relations	Statistics
Architecture	Engineering	Foreign Language	Library Sciences	Insurance	
Recreation and Tourism Management	Forestry	Graphic Design	Occupational Therapy	Journalism	
Environmental Studies	Geography	History	Nursing	Law	
Geology	Geology	Interior Design	Nutrition	Management	
Medical Technology	Mathematics	Journalism	Philosophy	Marketing	
Exercise Science	Medical Technology	Music	Political Science	Political Science	
Sport Management	Medicine	Music Education	Recreation and Physical Education	Public Administration	
Aerospace Engineering	Nursing	Speech/Drama	Psychology	Speech	
Civil Engineering	Nutrition		Religious Studies		
Electrical Engineering	Pharmacy		Sociology		
Industrial Engineering	Philosophy		Social Work		
Mechanical Engineering	Physical Therapy		Special Education		
Nuclear Engineering	Physics		Urban Planning		
Radiological Technology	Psychology				
	Sociology				
	Statistics				

Source: Kuther, 2006, pp. 20–21.

to one career choice. Many people end up working in careers that are not closely tied to their majors; rather, they work in careers that are closely tied to their skills. Therefore, the current emphasis in career planning is skill based: What skills of yours will entice an employer? Employers care about communication, computer, writing, speaking, and problem-solving skills. Because development of skills is part of the overall goals of a college education, you have the opportunity to develop these skills in a variety of majors. So, don't worry that your choice of major will pigeonhole you or determine your lifelong career. It can, but it doesn't have to.

Make Informed Decisions

Self-assessment is a process, so it may take time to understand yourself well enough to choose a major. What do you do in the meantime? Don't pressure yourself. Allow yourself opportunities to explore:

- Take a range of introductory classes. You'll fulfill your college's general education requirements and learn about areas in which you might want to major.
- Talk to others about potential majors and get feedback. Talk with other students and ask why they chose their majors. Talk with graduates, parents, and professors to learn about how they chose their careers. Ask questions to learn what you can do with various majors, what each entails, and what skills you need to develop.
- Visit your college's career center to speak with a career counselor who can recommend assessment instruments to help you learn about careers that are suited to you, as well as provide individualized attention and advice.

Remember that although you will seek input and advice from parents, friends, and professors, ultimately the decision is your own. Choose a major that interests you, because passion will make difficult classes and endless term papers seem more manageable. Also, remember that you can change your major—it isn't set in stone.

WHY MAJOR IN PSYCHOLOGY?

With over 76,000 baccalaureate degrees awarded each year (National Center for Educational Statistics, 2003), psychology is consistently one of the most popular college majors. Why? The knowledge and skills that you'll develop as a psychology major apply to a variety of careers. The psychology major is a general liberal arts degree that teaches you how to think and solve problems and prepares you for lifelong learning (McGovern, Furumoto, Halpern, Kimble, & McKeachie, 1991). Psychology majors gain experience in critical thinking and analytical skills, learn how to think independently, and understand how to learn. The skills and knowledge that you develop as a psychology major are generalizable outside the classroom and are desired by employers. Consider the range of skills and abilities that undergraduate programs in psychology seek to promote (American Psychological Association, 2001; Hayes, 1996; McGovern et al., 1991):

- **Knowledge of Psychology** Students of psychology gain knowledge of psychological theories, facts, and modes of inquiry. Psychology is a broad discipline encompassing biology, development, perception, thinking, emotion, and more. As such, students of psychology develop a comprehensive conceptual framework about the human condition that serves as a foundation for lifelong learning about human behavior.

- **Critical Thinking and Analysis** Psychology students are exposed to multiple perspectives on behavior. They quickly learn that any phenomenon is addressed by many, often conflicting, theories. Psychology students learn to think flexibly and accept ambiguity: Often no one knows the "right" answer to questions about a given phenomenon; however, research supports several theoretical perspectives or explanations. Considering diverse perspectives helps psychology students hone their thinking and analytical skills. Critical thinking and evaluation skills are part and parcel of reasoned decision making, which is valuable in today's complex world.

- **Communication and Presentation** Psychology students learn how to communicate verbally and in writing. They learn how to substantiate arguments with evidence and communicate arguments from a psychological standpoint. Psychology students' experience with writing and presenting the results of empirical research provides them with unique skills that set them apart from other liberal arts majors.

- **Information Gathering and Synthesis** Psychology students learn how to gather information through a variety of means: library, computerized databases, Internet, and data collection. They learn how to synthesize and summarize information into a coherent and persuasive argument. Given the speed of technological development and knowledge growth, information gathering and synthesis are skills critical to today's employer.

- **Research Methodology and Statistics** Psychologists pose questions about and devise procedures to shed light on the mysteries of human behavior. Undergraduate students in psychology gain a basic understanding of research methodology and statistics and learn how to interpret data summaries. These skills in asking and answering questions make psychology graduates unique and serve them well in business, marketing, management, and program development careers.

- **Computer Literacy** Psychology students gain familiarity with computers. They understand how to use statistical, word-processing, e-mail, web-browsing, and spreadsheet programs, and they understand how to seek out and learn how to use new computer software.

- **Interpersonal and Intrapersonal Skills** Psychology students learn interpersonal skills; they are aware of and sensitive to issues of culture, class, race, and ethnicity. They learn how to work in groups and can work effectively with others. Psychology students also develop intrapersonal awareness, or self-knowledge. They learn how to monitor and manage their emotions and behavior.

- **Adaptability** Our knowledge base in psychology is constantly growing. Psychology students learn that the perfect research study is unattainable; their aim is to conduct the best research possible, given limited resources. Students of psychology, therefore, learn to be adaptive and flexible, skills that are valuable after graduation.

These skills, emphasized by most undergraduate psychology programs, will help you grow into a well-rounded and educated person who is marketable in a variety of fields. Psychology is unique because it provides a blend of statistical, analytical, research, writing, and interpersonal skills. The broad education that you'll gain as a psychology major is the spirit of a liberal arts education and will prepare you well for life after college (Kierniesky, 1992).

Tips for Success

We've seen that the psychology major offers students the opportunity to develop well-rounded skills. How do you take advantage of the opportunity? How do you ensure that you're prepared for your future after graduation, whether you'll be entering the career world or graduate school? First, plan your career goals. As we've already seen, this is a difficult but essential task. Think about where you would like to be in a few years. The counseling center or career development center at your school can help you to select your goals through personality, aptitude, and vocational-interest assessments and counseling. The career development center may also offer alumni contacts who can tell you about their experiences and offer advice.

After you've considered what types of careers interest you, take a few elective courses outside psychology that are specific to your goals. For example, if you plan to enter the business world, a course in management or accounting would be useful. If you would like a job in human services, take courses in social work, communication, criminal justice, sociology, or anthropology. Regardless of your career plans, classes and experiences that enhance your communication skills (for example, courses in writing, speech, and communications; writing for the campus newspaper) offer a good investment because employers view communication skills favorably (Edwards & Smith, 1988; Grocer & Kohout, 1997; Lloyd & Kennedy, 1997; MSU Career Placement and Services, 2005b; National Association of Colleges and Employers, 2001). Throughout this book we discuss tips for students interested in careers related to specific areas of psychology, so check out the chapters in this book that relate to your goals for more-specific training advice. The following tips are intended to help psychology students regardless of where their interests lie.

Get to Know Professors

Most students see their professors only in the classroom. If this is true for you, then you're not taking advantage of your college's most valuable resource—the faculty. There's much more to learn from professors than content knowledge. Get to know your professors, and you might get involved in their research, learn about professional development, learn about special opportunities such as internships, and see what it's really like to work in the field. How do you get to know professors? Talk to them after class. Stop by during office hours. Ask content-related questions and demonstrate your interest in their subject. Remember, professors are people too: Smile and be friendly, and you'll be surprised how easy it is to get to know faculty.

Get Involved in Research

Seek research experience by assisting professors with their research or by developing an independent research project. Research experience demonstrates your ability to work independently and sharpens your analytical and critical-thinking skills. You'll develop important skills, learn what it's like to generate new knowledge, and gain experience that will impress employers and graduate school admissions committees. Research experience provides employers with evidence of your motivation, initiative, and willingness to go beyond basic requirements.

How do you seek research opportunities? Perform well in class and be motivated and visible in your department. Approach faculty during their office hours and ask who might be looking for research assistants. If you're interested in a particular faculty member's work, approach him or her and ask if you can help.

Seek Internships and Practica

Secure an internship or a practicum for hands-on experience. A *practicum* is a field experience taken for course credit, whereas an *internship* is a paid or unpaid learning position at a workplace, with or without school credit given. Practica and internships provide wonderful opportunities to apply what you've learned in the classroom to the real world, to have learning experiences that you'd never obtain in a classroom setting, and to explore potential careers. They also let you sample a potential career. Do you really want to work with people? Your real-life experiences may surprise you. In addition, internships and practica can provide contacts in the field, offers for employment after graduation, and a reference or recommendation that reflects your ability to apply your knowledge of psychology in the real world. Learn about these opportunities by asking faculty in your department. Also visit the career development center at your college to learn about additional opportunities for hands-on experience.

Get Work Experience

Work experience is invaluable. There are plenty of part-time and summer jobs that allow you to hone your interpersonal skills and explore potential careers. Try a job as a camp counselor, residence hall advisor, child-care worker, or human services worker. According to the Collegiate Employment Research Institute, over four-fifths of employers rate career-related employment as extremely important for prospective hires (MSU Career Placement and Services, 2005a), so your time will be well spent.

Engage in Extracurricular Activities

Extracurricular activities can help you develop useful skills and enhance your marketability. Like internships and work experience, extracurricular activities can provide you with opportunities to test career paths, develop contacts, and work on your communication skills. In addition, employers value volunteer work for campus and community organizations, because it shows that you are a good citizen. Extracurricular participation provides employers with evidence about your leadership skills, your ability to work effectively in a group, and your initiative and motivation.

As a final piece of advice, be open to new possibilities. Flexibility is an important life skill critical to coping and development throughout adulthood. Employers rate adaptability as highly desired in new employees (National Association of Colleges and Employers, 2005). Adaptability and tolerance for ambiguity are important characteristics for graduate students because science, like life, isn't always clear cut. As you read through the chapters in this book and explore various career opportunities, practice being open to new possibilities. Actively consider each subdiscipline and career opportunity to determine if it's a good fit for your interests and aspirations. Above all, keep an open mind and explore multiple possibilities. This will increase your ability to find a job and career that you will love.

SUGGESTED READINGS

Halonen, J. S., & Davis, S. F. (Eds.). (2001). *The many faces of psychological research in the 21st century.* Retrieved September 19, 2005, from the Society for the Teaching of Psychology website: http://teachpsych.lemoyne.edu/teachpsych/faces/facesindex.html

Kuther, T. L. (2006). *The psychology major's handbook* (2nd ed.). Belmont, CA: Wadsworth.

Sternberg, R. J. (1997). *Career paths in psychology: Where your degree can take you.* Washington, DC: American Psychological Association.

WEB RESOURCES

Psychology: Scientific Problem Solvers . . . Careers for the 21st Century
    http://www.apa.org/students/brochure/index.html
Eye on Psi Chi
    http://www.psichi.org/pubs/search.asp
Careers in Psychology
    http://www.psywww.com/careers/index.htm
Pursuing Psychology Career Page
    http://www.uni.edu/walsh/linda1.html
Career Key
    http://www.careerkey.org
American Psychological Association
    http://www.apa.org
American Psychological Society
    http://www.psychologicalscience.org
State Psychological Associations
    http://www.apa.org/practice/refer.html

Psi Chi
   http://www.psichi.org
Psi Beta
   http://www.psibeta.org
Eastern Psychological Association
   http://www.easternpsychological.org
Midwestern Psychological Association
   http://www.midwesternpsych.org
Rocky Mountain Psychological Association
   http://www.rockymountainpsych.org
Southeastern Psychological Association
   http://www.sepaonline.com
Southwestern Psychological Association
   http://www.swpsych.org
Western Psychological Association
   http://www.westernpsych.org

CHECKLIST: IS PSYCHOLOGY FOR YOU?

Do you:
- ☐ Have an interest in how the mind works?
- ☐ Want to learn how to think critically?
- ☐ Have an interest in research?
- ☐ Feel comfortable with computers?
- ☐ Have an interest in biology, the brain, and the physiology of behavior?
- ☐ Have an interest in mental illness?
- ☐ Like mathematics?
- ☐ Have an interest in how we grow and change over the lifespan?
- ☐ Have an interest in personality and what makes people unique?
- ☐ Wonder how we perceive stimuli in our environment?
- ☐ Want to learn how to work well with others?
- ☐ Want a well-rounded education?
- ☐ Have the ability to be flexible and deal with ambiguity?
- ☐ Want to help people?

Scoring: The more boxes you checked, the more likely it is that you're a good match for the psychology major.

GRADUATE-LEVEL CAREERS IN PSYCHOLOGY

CHAPTER GUIDE

Although television and movies often depict psychologists as therapists, graduate education in psychology opens the door to an array of careers that extends far beyond the therapist's couch. In this chapter, we examine career options available to graduate degree holders across the sub-specialties of psychology. As you know, many psychologists work as professors. However, did you know that, in addition to staffing psychology departments, psychologists are also professors in schools of business, medicine, and education? Similarly, research training in psychology prepares graduate degree holders for careers as researchers outside of academia; for example, they might work for the government, foundations, business, or research groups. Some psychologists seek careers in the military and engage in a variety of activities ranging from assessment and counseling to research and human factors. Others pursue publishing or writing careers. This chapter highlights these careers as a sample of the diversity your degree in psychology offers; however, as you will learn throughout this book, you are by no means limited to the careers we summarize here.

THE IVORY TOWER: PSYCHOLOGISTS AS PROFESSORS

Aside from the therapist, perhaps the most familiar career path for those with graduate degrees in psychology is that of college professor. Professors can share fascinating information with their students. Psychologists work as professors in a variety of academic departments of psychology and schools of education. Some who are trained in industrial/organizational psychology, human factors psychology, or social psychology work in business schools and even within departments of engineering. Psychologists trained in clinical or health psychology sometimes work as professors in medical schools. As you can see, psychologists working in academia are found in a variety of departments and schools—and sometimes in places you might never have imagined.

In addition to differences among departments and schools, academic careers also vary by institution. There are several types of colleges and universities. For example, community colleges and liberal arts colleges tend to focus heavily on teaching. In these settings, faculty often teach four or five courses per semester, leaving little time to conduct research or engage in scholarly writing. Faculty at community colleges and liberal arts colleges sometimes are asked to do little or no research and publishing, because performance evaluations are based on teaching and service to the community. At the other extreme are research universities. At these large schools with prestigious graduate programs, faculty teach only one or two courses per semester. They focus heavily on research rather than teaching, because they are judged on their reputations as scholars, and teaching contributes less to their professional advancement (Vesilind, 2000). Many four-year universities fall somewhere between the two extremes and encourage faculty to engage in both research and teaching. As you can see, even within academia psychologists can follow any of several career tracks.

Despite the different types of institutions, all academic careers share certain features. As you consider a career as a professor, recognize that there is more to the professorate than lecturing. Before a professor steps into the classroom, a great deal of time and effort has gone into preparation. Each lecture requires background reading of chapters and journal articles in addition to the text, note taking, and preparation of overheads, activities, and discussion questions. This work is never complete, because even experienced professors must update their notes to remain current with the ever-changing field. Professors who teach three, four, or even five courses per semester may find that preparation takes all of their time, especially in the early years of a career (Roediger, 1997). A professor's teaching activities extend beyond the classroom to include grading, writing student recommendation letters, meeting with students to answer questions and discuss course content and professional issues, and advising students on career choices.

In addition to teaching, professorial careers entail many roles, usually including research and service to the campus and community (such as advising, committee work, and administrative work). During a typical week, professors often divide their time among multiple research tasks, including writing an article or book, conducting statistical analyses, planning research, writing grant proposals, searching the literature, reading research articles, meeting with student research assistants, advising students on their research, and preparing or giving talks at professional meetings. Professors also must spend time on service to the university and community. They participate in faculty meetings as well as some of the many committees that administer and run the university. Some faculty engage in consulting work, serving as consultants and advisors for community agencies, for example.

Many students seek a graduate degree in order to teach in a college or university setting. With a master's degree, one can become a community college professor. However, faculty positions at two-year and community colleges have become more competitive in recent years; many are held by psychologists with doctoral degrees (Lloyd, 2000; Peters, 1992). Similarly, although master's degree holders may be hired to teach part-time at four-year colleges, they tend not to receive full-time positions (Peters, 1992). If your goal is to teach at the college level, pursuing a doctoral degree will provide you with the most opportunities for employment, mobility, and advancement as a faculty member (Lloyd, 2000). Graduates with doctoral degrees may teach undergraduate, master's, and doctoral students in a variety of educational settings, including universities, professional schools, and medical schools.

An additional aspect of training that might not be covered in graduate school, but is necessary for success as a professor, and often for winning a faculty position in the first place, is training in pedagogy (Kuther, 2002). *Pedagogy* refers to the art of teaching. Successful professors learn the techniques of their trade: how to compose lectures; lead discussions; create syllabi; enhance student learning through effective use of the blackboard, overheads, or PowerPoint presentations; and model best practices for interacting with students and handling disagreements. We hope you have experienced a professor who made the course material "come to life" and whose class you looked forward to attending. Such skill comes with work and effort; good teachers are made, not born.

If you're interested in becoming a professor, seek a graduate program that helps prepare students for the teaching aspects of the professorate. Many graduate programs present seminars or courses in how to teach. The Preparing Future Faculty program is designed to prepare aspiring academics for the variety of teaching, research, and service roles entailed in the professorate; this program has also created a wealth of resources, including a website at http://www.preparing-faculty.org (American Psychological Association, 2001; Preparing Future Faculty, n.d.). Further, seek practical experience as a teaching assistant or adjunct professor at your university or a nearby college. You can also volunteer to teach a class or two for your primary instructors or for instructors teaching courses in your area of interest. Most important, find a mentor in graduate school who can help you with these essential aspects of training.

The professorate offers many advantages, but perhaps the greatest are academic freedom and the autonomy and flexibility of academic life. Academic freedom means that professors are intellectually free; they may conduct whatever research interests them and may "teach the truth as they see it" (Vesilind, 2000, p. 10). In other words, professors decide on the best methods to teach their courses. Texts, reading assignments, grading, and evaluation procedures often remain up to the professor. Aside from class time, professors' schedules tend to be flexible. Most develop work habits that fit their lives, allowing time to pick up children from school, spend time with their families, and complete preparation and writing in the late evenings or early mornings. Another advantage is tenure. Tenure provides complete academic freedom because it prevents professors from being fired for airing unpopular views or pursuing

TABLE 2.1 Mean Salaries for Professors	
Institution and Position	**Average Salary**
Doctoral Institutions	
Professor	$104,411
Associate Professor	$71,077
Assistant Professor	$60,567
Comprehensive Institutions (master's level)	
Professor	$77,900
Associate Professor	$61,528
Assistant Professor	$51,339
Baccalaureate Institutions	
Professor	$74,408
Associate Professor	$57,468
Assistant Professor	$47,864

Source: Adapted from *Chronicle of Higher Education*, 2005.

controversial research. Professors with documented teaching histories, excellent student evaluations, publications, campus committee work, and outreach to the community earn tenure and its associated job security. The professorate also offers intangible benefits such as the excitement of discovery and innovation as well as the rewards of imparting knowledge and introducing students to a life of the mind (Roediger, 1997; Vesilind, 2000).

The disadvantages of the academic life stem mainly from the scarcity of academic positions. The academic job market is very competitive. Some applicants spend several years on the job market, working in postdoctoral research, in one-year instructor appointments, or in adjunct positions (teaching part-time, often at several colleges at once). Applicants must be prepared to seek faculty positions in a variety of geographic locations; applicants cannot limit themselves to searching in only one place. Applicants also cannot afford to limit themselves to positions in psychology departments but must consider positions in other departments, medical schools, and business schools. Once a position is obtained, new professors juggle many demands. In addition to teaching loads and service responsibilities, most new faculty are expected to begin a research program, because in recent years research has increased in importance as well— even for those in "teaching" colleges (Salzinger, 1995). Faculty in research universities experience pressure to win large competitive research grants and publish in the best journals. Finally, as shown in Table 2.1, professors' salaries allow them to live comfortably, but certainly do not make them rich!

RESEARCH IN AND OUT OF THE IVORY TOWER

A graduate degree in psychology opens many doors to a career in research. Research psychologists conduct basic and applied studies of human and animal behavior. They conduct their research in universities, government agencies, private organizations, and businesses and corporations. Some psychologists conduct their research in military settings, whereas others work in research and development departments at pharmaceutical companies and businesses (Lloyd, 2000). Let's look at the variety of settings in which psychologists conduct research.

Academia

Many psychologists work in university settings as research scientists, conducting basic and applied research. For example, a research scientist might study how neurotransmitters affect learning in rats. Another research psychologist might design a research program to examine smoking cessation. Her basic research might explore the environmental factors that help or hinder quitting smoking. She might conduct applied research as well, developing and evaluating school-based programs to prevent smoking in children. Medical schools are emerging as an important employment setting for research psychologists, who work on multidisciplinary teams addressing health problems in people of all ages. Interdisciplinary study and the merging of scientific fields such as anatomy, biochemistry, physiology, pharmacology, and microbiology are leading to more research opportunities for psychologists outside psychology departments (Balster, 1995).

A research career in academia offers a flexible schedule and is prestigious. Research scientists gain independence and autonomy as they progress in their careers. By writing and winning research grants, research scientists can fund and study problems of their choosing. With advancement, research scientists take on supervisory roles, run their own labs, and train graduate and postdoctoral students. They also enjoy opportunities for travel and contact with the public through speaking at conferences, consulting, and writing for the popular press (Bartholomew, 2001a). A disadvantage of a research career in academia is the competition. Generally, academic positions that don't require teaching can be difficult to obtain. Applicants may need to be geographically mobile and able to relocate for available positions.

Research and professorial careers in academia entail long hours, especially in institutions that maintain the "publish or perish" mantra. Publish or perish is just that: Publish many articles in prestigious journals, or lose your job! As you might imagine, psychologists in research and professorial positions experience a great deal of stress. Because publishing is a tenuous and lengthy process, professors may spend many evenings in the lab or at the computer completing or writing research results for publication. Once completed, however, a published work provides the satisfaction of a sense of accomplishment, contribution to the field, and seeing one's name in print—primary benefits of this research track.

Industry

Some psychologists conduct research in business and industry. Psychologists in business might conduct surveys of consumer opinion, for example. Others who work for pharmaceutical companies might test the effectiveness of drugs or work as statisticians, analyzing the data from a variety of research projects. Psychologists in industry design and test products for human use. For example, a psychologist might design a car's dashboard to allow drivers to see and reach the displays and knobs easily while viewing the road. Or a psychologist might design a computer monitor to reduce glare and eyestrain.

A career in industry differs from one in academia mainly because industry focuses on promoting the success of the company. Research aims at creating products that benefit the company, employees, and shareholders (Bartholomew, 2001b). Research takes place at a faster pace in industry than in academia because information must be gathered quickly to help create and sell products. Teams conduct the research, enabling greater productivity. In addition, psychologists in business and industry settings tend to have access to more funding than do those in academia, meaning that they tend to work with newer and more sophisticated equipment. The primary drawback of conducting research in business and industry is that your research questions are assigned based on the needs of the company, not necessarily on your interests. An important benefit of working in industry is contact with people of diverse fields and educational backgrounds. Other benefits include high salaries and regular work schedules; in business and industry, your weekends generally are your own.

Government

Although research psychologists engage in similar activities regardless of work setting—whether universities, industry, or government—these three settings differ in terms of the autonomy afforded researchers. As with researchers in industry, those employed by the government and military usually examine research questions not conceived by them

(Herrman, 1997). Instead, researchers in government examine questions created by politicians and policy makers, designed to promote the security and well-being of the American people. As Copper (1997) points out,

> The critical aspect of working in a public-policy environment is that many people can be directly affected by decisions over a very long period of time. Therefore, the research questions and hypotheses are often more complex, sensitive, and require much broader data collection efforts and greater coordination with staff from federal branch agencies and the private sector.

An advantage of a research career in government is that it exposes you to many different projects. Unlike academia, where researchers spend a career focused on a particular research problem or area, research psychologists in government work on a diverse range of projects and become generalists. Most research projects initiated by the government are short (taking about one year to complete), because the research is intended to help resolve practical problems. Also, shifts in public opinion and interest lead political leaders to eliminate some projects and initiate new ones; whether this is an advantage or disadvantage perhaps depends on your interest in the project. If you're interested in a research career in government, be prepared to engage in lots of supervisory work, because contractors conduct much of the hands-on work under supervision by government researchers. This enables government researchers to work on multiple projects at once and not become overly involved in any one project. Like industry, government research involves working on a team, because the government focuses mainly on applied research. This requires creativity and planning by an interdisciplinary team of researchers consisting of psychologists, sociologists, statisticians, computer scientists, economists, and more.

Social Service Agencies and Nonprofits

Research psychologists employed at social service or nonprofit agencies conduct research to assess and improve the agency's programs and often write grants to help fund the agency. Social service and nonprofit agencies often are contracted by the government to conduct policy analyses, literature reviews, and research to improve decision making by political leaders and consumers. A psychologist at such an agency might examine the effectiveness of new drug-control interventions such as mandatory minimum sanctions, residential and group home treatments for youthful offenders identified as drug users, and school-based prevention programs.

The primary benefit of working in a nonprofit or social service agency is that you spend your time on research that may lead to social change

TABLE 2.2 Median Salaries for Doctoral-Level Careers in Research	
	Median Salary
University Research Center	$52,000
Private Research Organization	$65,000
Government Research Organization	$70,000
Consulting/Industry	$76,500

Source: Adapted from Pate, Frincke, & Kohout, 2005.

rather than spending it on teaching or academic curriculum meetings. Such agencies tend to conduct interdisciplinary research, enabling research psychologists to work with a diverse range of specialists from other fields. Though the salaries in nonprofit and social service agencies tend to be lower than in other research settings, the research often directly benefits consumers and families.

Preparation and Salary

Although bachelor's degree holders often can become research assistants, graduate degrees offer more opportunities for advancement. Many research positions are available to master's degree holders, especially in industry, government, and nonprofit and social service agencies. In academic settings, the doctoral degree offers the most flexibility, access to advancement, and opportunities to serve as the primary investigator of federal grants (Lloyd, 2000). Research psychologists in academia often obtain two or three years of postdoctoral training after obtaining the doctoral degree. To be competitive for research positions within academic and nonacademic settings, hone your skills in research methods and statistics (Copper, 1997). As shown in Table 2.2, salaries for research positions vary by setting.

THE MILITARY

The military offers a range of opportunities for psychologists in all disciplines. Psychologists in the military work in a variety of areas, including personnel selection and classification, training, human factors, leadership and team effectiveness, as well as clinical settings (American Psychological Association, n.d.b; Wiskoff, 1997).

Psychologists in the Military

Some military psychologists engage in personnel selection and classification. They screen, select, and place recruits, and they select personnel for jobs requiring special skills such as piloting aircraft, air traffic control, and special operations. They create procedures for evaluating the performance of enlisted and officer personnel and conduct research on how to use simulators to evaluate special abilities. Military psychologists also train personnel. They conduct research examining the most effective techniques for training personnel in basic skills, military skills, and technical skills, as well as increasing operational readiness. They conduct research on how to design effective instructional systems, how to measure training performance, and how best to use computer-simulated scenarios and technology such as virtual reality.

Other psychologists in the military work in human factors and engineering to design the human–machine interfaces that improve the functioning of military systems and equipment. For example, how can artificial intelligence and the use of sophisticated computer systems enhance human decision making? Psychologists study how to help military personnel operate most efficiently, maintain health, enhance performance, and reduce human error under adverse circumstances such as sleep deprivation or hazardous or extreme environmental conditions.

Some psychologists study team effectiveness and ways to improve communication in multinational forces. Psychologists study how to promote effective leadership, as well as how to select, train, and evaluate leaders. Some psychologists might get involved in political-psychological issues such as the study of the behavior of world leaders. Others examine team processes such as structure, communication, subordinate–supervisor relations, team cohesion, the functioning of small groups, and tactical decision making.

Clinical and counseling psychologists in the military often work in counseling or mental health clinics providing mental health services and counseling to military personnel and their families. They focus on how to help personnel adjust to military life, deal with stress, and cope with serious psychological reactions in the aftermath of combat. Counseling and clinical psychologists serve in a wide variety of settings such as military hospitals, outpatient clinics, mental health centers, day-care centers, military prisons, and naval vessels.

Advantages, Disadvantages, and Salary

Psychologists in the military often spend significant amounts of time overseas. Depending on your inclination and family situation, this may represent an advantage or a disadvantage. Clinical and counseling psychologists go wherever there are concentrations of troops, in peacetime and war, and to hostile environments. A uniformed psychologist can count on a change of geographic location every two to three years (Wiskoff, 1997). Thus, in spite of potential familial conflicts, military psychologists' opportunities to see the world remain unmatched by nonmilitary psychology positions.

A significant limitation for practicing psychologists is the absence of the traditional confidential therapeutic relationship. Members of the military who seek or are referred for mental health services do not have the same rights and privileges to confidentiality that nonmilitary clients enjoy. Rather, higher-ranking personnel may and do request information regarding the functioning of a military client, and psychologists must become comfortable with the military process and the limits and professional dilemmas this presents. Furthermore, research psychologists experience many of the same limitations as their colleagues in government and industry, because their research is directed by practical problems and questions rather than by their own intellectual curiosity.

A final potential limitation for psychologists in the military is the issue of enlistment. Unlike other psychology positions, working for the military is not optional once you "join the ranks"; rather, you become an officer and must serve for the duration of your commitment. Psychologists in academia, business and industry, or other branches of the government can leave their job if they decide they no longer want to do it, but military psychologists cannot. Thus, it is important to consider your own level of satisfaction and comfort with the military lifestyle, because once you are sworn in as an officer, you cannot change your mind and simply do something else.

Important benefits of military service include job security, opportunities for additional education, and an excellent benefits and retirement system. Few professional positions offer the opportunity to retire after as few as 20 years of service, and to do so with a pension. The salary scale for military psychologists is aligned with government pay scales (Wiskoff, 1997). In 2001, the government starting salary for master's-level psychologists was $33,300; the starting salary for doctoral-level psychologists was $40,200 (Bureau of Labor Statistics, 2002). In addition to base pay, all military receive subsistence and housing allowances, which are not taxable and which substantially increase income.

PUBLISHING AND WRITING

Publishing and the media offer new career opportunities for students of psychology. Some psychologists pursue careers in publishing as acquisitions editors and developmental editors. Others become science writers for print, Internet, radio, and television.

Book Publishing

Publishing generally is an apprenticeship field, so most successful editors begin in entry-level positions and work their way up. Many begin as assistants to acquisitions editors or as sales representatives who ensure that every customer (such as a professor or bookstore) knows of the publisher's book offerings. Sales representatives are often on the road, traveling to their customers, sales conferences, and professional conferences, where they market books. With time, some sales representatives gain the experience and contacts to become acquisitions editors.

An *acquisitions editor* is responsible for acquiring books for a publishing company. The job entails a variety of tasks, including reading book proposals, making decisions about the financial viability of proposals and whether to offer book contracts to authors, ensuring the quality of proposals and completed manuscripts by getting reviews from specialists in the field, interpreting reviews, approaching potential authors with book ideas, attending conferences to meet potential authors and reviewers, and discussing works-in-progress with authors. The acquisitions editor often oversees all stages of the publication process, including contract negotiation, promotional planning, manuscript delivery, and financial planning. The position is appropriate for individuals who like the messiness of problem solving in the real world and have broad interests, because acquisitions editors often oversee manuscripts in multiple subfields, not just the ones in which they have extensive training (Amsel, 1996).

With a graduate degree in psychology and writing experience, you might consider a position as a developmental editor. A *developmental editor* handles the day-to-day work of coordinating and editing manuscripts for large publishing projects such as psychology textbooks. The developmental editor is involved in all aspects of developing a textbook, beginning with the early stages of conceptual and structural planning before the author writes. Developmental editors often nurture authors through the writing process and coordinate the artwork, writing style, and preparation of supplements or ancillaries (that is, instructor's manuals, student study guides, test banks, websites, and more; Hart, 1996).

Positions in publishing offer opportunities for psychology degree holders at all levels who have interests in writing and the ability to think critically and solve problems effectively. Bachelor's degree holders usually begin in entry-level positions such as editorial assistants or sales representatives, whereas applicants with graduate degrees and editorial skill may be hired to midlevel editorial positions. Advanced positions in publishing come with extensive experience. Individuals who seek careers in publishing must be able to juggle multiple tasks, meet budgets, and cope with the pressure of deadlines.

Writing

Scientific writing careers come in many shapes and forms. Some science writers engage in technical writing. Others work in public relations and traditional or new media venues. A technical writer translates large amounts of information into useful and easily digested forms for specialized readers. Technical writers create user guides, repair manuals, online help files, and reference manuals for new products, computer software, hardware, and toys (Randall, 1998). Technical writers must be able to explain complex phenomena for general readers. Other science writing positions are found in public relations or public information fields. Universities, medical centers, hospitals, and other institutions where research is conducted have staffs of reporters that keep track of research findings and events at the institution (Goetnick, 1998). Public information officers write press releases to distribute to the media. They also contribute to institutional publications and alumni magazines, monitor news and media trends to determine which institutional staff might have something notable to contribute, and act as liaisons between journalists and the institution's staff (Goetnick, 1998). Some writers work in research or human service settings as grant writers, who assemble the pieces of a grant proposal prepared by a group of researchers and check for style, accuracy, formatting, grammar, and spelling (Turner, 1998).

Science writers and journalists also write as staff members and freelancers for newspapers, magazines, the Internet, radio, and television. They learn about scientific findings and translate them accurately into a form that will interest the general reader. By teasing out details and anecdotes, they write to draw casual readers, listeners, or viewers into topics that they ordinarily might not care much about. Science writing requires omnivorous reading of newspapers, books, reports, journals, and Internet news groups to look for story ideas. Writers attend scientific conventions, interview scientists, and regularly check in with laboratories, factories, hospitals, universities, and government agencies for breaking news and interesting stories (National Association of Science Writers, n.d.).

Science writing offers an opportunity to write about science without becoming immersed in the lab, focusing on one minute area of research, or being confined to the stilted and formal academic style of writing (C. Carpenter, 2002). It offers a chance to be in the real world, explore a variety of topics, interview great thinkers, share psychological findings with the rest of the world, and see your writing in print quickly (Augenbraun & Vergoth, 1998). Individuals who love learning, have broad scientific interests, are fluent writers, and like challenges are well suited to careers in science writing. However, science writing is a highly competitive field. Writers must be able to juggle multiple stories at once, meet deadlines,

TABLE 2.3   Median Salaries for Careers in Writing and Publishing

	Median Salary
Grants/Proposal Writer	$41,485
Technical Writer	$50,285
Public Relations Writer	$49,950
Web Writer	$52,640
Acquisitions Editor	$58,750
Newspaper Writer	$26,873
Sales Representative	$44,025

Sources: Adapted from Abbott, Langer, and Associates, 2005b; Salary.com, 2005.

and deal well with criticism (no thin skins allowed!). Freelancers must be prepared to pay for their own benefits, save for retirement, and weather ups and downs in work.

If you're interested in a science-writing career, seek opportunities to publish in nonscientific publications. Write for the university newspaper, local organizations, or any other sources to earn writing clips. *Clips,* or clippings of your published articles, are your ticket to a writing career. Understand that science writing differs greatly from the academic writing that you learned in college or graduate school. Aspiring science writers should seek training opportunities such as media fellowships, internships (often unpaid), and science journalism programs to gain excellent training, sources of networking contacts, and clips (Randall, 1998). Table 2.3 illustrates salaries for careers in writing and publishing.

A graduate degree in psychology opens doors to a variety of careers for individuals with diverse interests ranging from therapy to research, teaching to publishing, and more. Remember that the advice in this chapter is offered as a first step. Seek assistance from your advisor and the career center at your university to help you learn more so that you can choose career goals that match your interests and aspirations.

SUGGESTED READINGS

Amsel, J. (1996). An interesting career in psychology: Acquisitions editor. *Psychological Science Agenda.* Retrieved January 18, 2002, from http://www.apa.org/science/ic-amsel.html

Balster, R. L. (1995). An interesting career in psychology: A research psychologist in a medical school. *Psychological Science Agenda.* Retrieved February 1, 2002, from http://www.apa.org/science/ic-balster.html

Bly, R. W. (2003). *Careers for writers and others who have a way with words.* New York: McGraw-Hill.

Carpenter, C. (2002). An interesting career in psychology: Becoming a science writer. *Psychological Science Agenda.* Retrieved November 4, 2005, from http://www.apa.org/science/ic-carpenter.html

Carter, R. A., Pattis, W., & Camenson, B. (2000). *Opportunities in publishing careers.* New York: McGraw-Hill.

Czerwinski, M. (2002). An interesting career in psychology: Research psychology at Microsoft. *Psychological Science Agenda.* Retrieved November 4, 2005, from http://www.apa.org/science/ic-czerwinski.html

Goldberg, J. (1996). *Opportunities in research and development careers.* New York: McGraw-Hill.

Hancock, E. (2003). *Ideas into words: Mastering the craft of science writing.* Baltimore: The John Hopkins University Press.

Hayes, W. (2003). *So you want to be a college professor?* Lanham, MD: Scarecrow Education.

Keller, P. A. (1994). *Academic paths: Career decisions and experiences of psychologists.* Mahwah, NJ: Erlbaum.

Sternberg, R. J. (1997). *Career paths in psychology: Where your degree can take you.* Washington, DC: American Psychological Association.

U.S. Department of Defense. (2003). *America's top military careers: Official guide to occupations in the armed forces.* Indianapolis, IN: Jist.

Vesilind, P. A. (2000). *So you want to be a professor? A handbook for graduate students.* Thousand Oaks, CA: Sage.

Yager, F., & Yager, J. (2005). *Career opportunities in the publishing industry.* New York: Facts on File.

Zeleznik, J. M., & Burnett, R. E. (1999). *Technical writing: What it is and how to do it.* Albany, NY: Delmar Learning.

WEB RESOURCES

Career Path Less Traveled
  http://www.apa.org/monitor/feb01/careerpath.html

Council of Teachers of Undergraduate Psychology
  http://www.psych.txstate.edu/ctup

Society for the Teaching of Psychology
  http://teachpsych.lemoyne.edu

Office of Teaching Resources in Psychology
  http://www.lemoyne.edu/OTRP/index.html

Preparing Future Faculty
  http://www.preparing-faculty.org

Military Career Guide Online
  http://www.todaysmilitary.com/app/tm/careers

About the U.S. Military
  http://usmilitary.about.com

All About Publishing
    http://www.publishers.org/careers/faq.cfm
A Guide to Careers in Science Writing
    http://www.casw.org/booklet.htm
Career Development Center for Postdocs and Junior Faculty
    http://sciencecareers.sciencemag.org
Science, Math, and Engineering Career Resources
    http://www.phds.org
So You Want to Be a Science Writer?
    http://www.absw.org.uk/So_you_want_to_be_a_science_writer.htm
Advice for Beginning Science Writers
    http://nasw.org/advice.htm
How Do I Become a Science Journalist?
    http://www.scidev.net/ms/howdoi/index.cfm?pageid=55

CHECKLIST: IS AN ADVANCED CAREER IN PSYCHOLOGY FOR YOU?

Do you:

☐ Want to teach college?

☐ Think you would enjoy a career interacting with students?

☐ Like to challenge others to think?

☐ Think broadly and have a unique ability to apply psychology to many different fields?

☐ Have an interest in applying psychology to a nonpsychology type of career?

☐ Like to write?

☐ Think quickly on your feet?

☐ Enjoy giving presentations and speeches?

☐ Enjoy research?

☐ Think analytically?

☐ Want to work for an agency or the government?

☐ Want to have a career with flexible hours?

☐ Want to attend graduate school?

Scoring: The more boxes you checked, the more likely it is a graduate-level career in psychology is for you.

CLINICAL AND COUNSELING PSYCHOLOGY

CHAPTER

3

CHAPTER GUIDE

Did you know that about 61 percent of psychology doctoral graduate are from the subfields of clinical, counseling, or school psychology (American Psychological Association Research Office, 2003)? Clearly, mental health service providers comprise the largest subfields in psychology. Why are these subfields so popular? Many students explain their career choice by stating simply, "I want to help people." Being a mental health service provider offers students opportunities to gain specialized skills and knowledge that can assist people suffering from mental illness, emotional or behavioral problems, or other psychological distress. Because the mental health service field is so large, we'll discuss it within the next two chapters. In this chapter we examine clinical and counseling psychology, and in Chapter 4 we explore the subfield of school psychology. Do clinical and counseling psychologists have the same jobs? If not, how do they differ? These are important questions for students considering careers as mental health service providers.

CLINICAL PSYCHOLOGY

Clinical psychology is the integration of science, theory, and practice to explain and understand, predict, and alleviate psychological problems and distress as well as promote healthy human development (American Psychological Association Society of Clinical Psychology, 2002). Assessment and diagnosis, intervention or treatment, consultation, research, and application of ethical and professional principles are the skills clinical psychologists need in their profession (Resnick, 1991). In other words, clinical psychologists work to help people alleviate distress or to improve their functioning via (1) psychological practice, or the provision of services such as assessment, diagnosis, and treatment; (2) consultation; or (3) conducting research aimed at understanding human phenomena, with the goal of helping people. But where are clinical psychologists found and how do they spend their time?

As Table 3.1 shows, primary employment settings of clinical psychologists include private practice, university settings, hospital settings, outpatient clinics and community mental health centers, medical schools, Veteran's Administrative (VA) Medical Centers, and "other" settings such as correctional facilities, child and family services, rehabilitation centers, and so on (Norcross, Karg, & Prochaska, 1997).Table 3.2 presents how clinical psychologists spend their time. Most of it goes to direct client intervention (such as psychotherapy) and assessment and diagnostic-related activities. Somewhat less frequent activities of clinical psychologists

TABLE 3.1 Primary Employment Settings of Clinical Psychologists	
Setting	**Percentage of Psychologists**
Private Practice	40
University Settings	19
Hospital Settings	9
Outpatient Clinics/Mental Health Centers	8
Medical Schools	9
VA Medical Centers	3
Other	11

Source: Norcross, Karg, & Prochaska, 1997.

include administrative responsibilities, research/writing activities, teaching, supervision of other mental health service providers, and professional consultation (Norcross, Karg, & Prochaska, 1997).

COUNSELING PSYCHOLOGY

Like their clinical psychologist colleagues, *counseling psychologists* work to alleviate distress and emotional or behavioral difficulties associated with psychological problems. However, counseling psychology maintains an equal focus on helping people improve their well-being across the lifespan, including emotional, social, vocational, health-related, developmental, and organizational concerns (Counseling Psychology Division 17, 1999). Additionally, counseling psychologists have been instrumental in

TABLE 3.2 Activities of Clinical Psychologists	
Activity	**Percentage of Psychologists**
Direct Client Intervention	37
Assessment and Diagnosis	15
Administration	11
Research/Writing	10
Teaching	9
Supervision	7
Professional Consultation	7

Source: Norcross, Karg, & Prochaska, 1997.

TABLE 3.3 How Counseling Psychologists Identify Themselves	
Role	Percentage of Psychologists
Clinical Practitioner	48
Academician	28
Administrator	11
Consultant	6
Researcher	3

Source: Watkins, Lopez, Campbell, & Himmel, 1986.

sensitizing psychologists to an understanding and appreciation of human diversity, particularly in terms of how multicultural issues relate to human functioning. Defined more simply, counseling psychology is a field of study that works to improve human functioning, either by enhancing current functioning or by alleviating distress.

The roots of counseling psychology lie in five unifying themes: (1) focus on intact or normative functioning rather than profoundly disturbed functioning; (2) focus on clients' assets and strengths and positive mental health; (3) emphasis on brief interventions (for example, counseling of less than 15 sessions); (4) emphasis on person–environment interactions, rather than focus on the person or environment as separate entities; and (5) emphasis on educational and career development and vocational environments (Gelso & Fretz, 2001). Not surprisingly, then, counseling psychologists are more likely to identify themselves primarily as clinical practitioners than other professional roles such as academicians, administrators, consultants, and researchers (Watkins, Lopez, Campbell, & Himmel, 1986; see Table 3.3). Like their clinical psychology colleagues, counseling psychologists are employed in a variety of settings: colleges and universities, including university counseling centers; private practices; community mental health centers; psychiatric hospitals; medical facilities; correctional facilities; Veterans Administration (VA) medical centers; health maintenance organizations; family services; business and consulting firms; and rehabilitation agencies.

Other Mental Health Professions

Some mental health professions are not based in the discipline of psychology. That is, some mental health training does not have psychology as its disciplinary root. Many students may find marriage and family therapy (MFT) programs, rehabilitation or rehabilitation counseling programs, social work programs, or addictions counseling programs a better fit for their career interests (for more information see American Association of Marriage and Family Therapy, 2002; American Counseling Association, 2002; National Association of Social Workers, 2005; National Rehabilitation Counseling Association, 2001). Students in these programs may earn a doctoral-level degree (such as a PhD or EdD), but a terminal master's degree is more common. These students will typically seek registration or licensure as a mental health professional, as in Licensed Professional Counseling (LPC) certification, to provide counseling or related clinical services.

The professions of marriage and family therapist, rehabilitation counselor, social worker, and clinical and counseling psychologist overlap in terms of professional services provided and employment settings. The primary distinction, with regard to clinical services, is that psychologists are trained to administer and interpret psychological tests. Additionally, psychology-based programs at the master's and doctoral levels typically place greater emphasis on conducting research. Of course, students in other mental health programs are often trained in research, particularly at the doctoral level; however, research appears to be more heavily emphasized in the training of clinical and counseling psychologists. Regarding employment settings, these mental health professionals overlap with clinical and counseling psychologists and will be found in community mental health centers, psychiatric hospitals, private practice, medical facilities, family services, and rehabilitation agencies.

OPPORTUNITIES WITH A BACHELOR'S DEGREE

A graduate degree is required for an entry-level position in professional psychology. Nonetheless, undergraduate psychology majors choosing not to pursue graduate education will find many opportunities for helping people. Let's take a look at service opportunities for bachelor's degree holders in psychology.

Human Services Worker

Human services workers occupy a range of positions, including social service worker, case management aide, social work assistant, community support worker, mental health aide, community outreach worker, life skills counselor, and gerontology aide (Bureau of Labor Statistics, 2004). These positions are paraprofessional positions with "a support role that overlaps with job duties and responsibilities of a psychologist; however, the paraprofessional does not have the education, responsibility, nor salary of the psychologist"(Landrum, Davis, & Landrum, 2000, p. 17). Human services workers provide services, both direct and indirect, to clients that typically include assessing clients' needs and eligibility for services; helping clients obtain services such as food stamps, Medicaid, or transportation; and providing emotional support (Bureau of Labor Statistics, 2004). In community settings (such as group homes or government-supported housing programs), human services workers offer counseling, assist with daily living skills, and organize group activities. In clinical settings (such as psychiatric hospitals or outpatient clinics), human service workers support clients' participation in treatment plans, assist with daily living skills, help clients communicate more effectively, and promote social functioning (Bureau of Labor Statistics, 2004).

A position in human services offers the opportunity to help others in need. It also offers a steady job market, because human services positions are expected to increase much faster than the average for all occupations through 2012 (Bureau of Labor Statistics, 2004). Unfortunately, long hours, difficult cases, and low income often lead to burnout. In 2000, the median salary of human service workers was $23,700, with a range of $18,670 to $29,520 for the middle 50 percent, and a peak salary of approximately $37,550 for human service workers (Bureau of Labor Statistics, 2004).

Social Worker

Although a degree in social work is sometimes a prerequisite, entry-level social work positions often can be obtained with a bachelor's degree in psychology. Through counseling and identifying needed resources (such as housing and food stamps), social workers aim at helping people improve their lives. Frequent duties include individual and group counseling sessions, as well as identifying the need for federal and state program assistance (such as housing assistance, disability benefits, food stamps, and so forth) (Bureau of Labor Statistics, 2004). Social workers are employed in a variety of settings: hospitals, schools, community mental health centers, social service agencies, and courts and correctional institutions. Thus, social workers can seek a setting that best suits their needs and abilities.

Salaries for social workers tend to be moderate, with a median yearly salary of $33,150 (Bureau of Labor Statistics, 2004). Other benefits of this career choice include an increasing job market and the satisfaction of helping people at the grassroots level. A primary limitation of this career is the stress resulting from difficulty identifying or securing appropriate resources for clients.

Although you can obtain many social work positions with a bachelor's degree, continuing education in the form of a part-time master's program will increase your job security, opportunities for advancement, and ability to start a private practice (Bureau of Labor Statistics, 2004). Salary will also increase with more education. All states have licensing or certification requirements for private practice and the use of the title "social worker." Standards for licensing vary by state, so it's a good idea to check with your school's career development office and the Association of Social Work Boards (http://www.aswb.org) to ensure that you are not disappointed.

Substance Abuse Counselor

Although most counseling professions require graduate degrees for employment, substance abuse counselors are a common exception. Substance abuse counselors provide counseling or rehabilitation services in residential treatment programs or as part of comprehensive substance abuse programs. The substance abuse counselor often is the primary therapist working with clients on their alcohol or drug dependence or abuse. Substance abuse counselors may spend their days facilitating therapy groups (particularly focusing on teaching clients about addiction and its related problems), as well as meeting individually with clients. Individual sessions allow therapists one-on-one time to focus on a client's specific problems.

The demand for drug and alcohol abuse counselors is strong, which is reflected in the median income: $30,180 per year (Bureau of Labor Statistics, 2004). As with other mental health positions, one of the primary benefits of this career lies in the opportunity to help disturbed people who desperately need that help. In addition, the opportunity to enter the helping field at the baccalaureate level is attractive for students who want to enter the mental health profession but don't want to go to graduate school. Limitations of this career choice include the difficulty of professional advancement at the bachelor's degree level and the challenges of working with substance abusers, who often are resistant clients and can be difficult to work with.

Substance abuse counselors often are employed at the associate or bachelor's level, with certification. The requirements for certification as a drug and alcohol abuse counselor vary by state. Most states require the completion of four courses in drug and alcohol abuse counseling and 300–600 hours of supervised training. For more information about certification as a drug and alcohol abuse counselor, contact the National Association of Alcoholism and Drug Abuse Counselors (NAADAC) at http://www.naadac.org.

OPPORTUNITIES WITH A GRADUATE DEGREE

As you may have realized, your career options in clinical and counseling psychology careers expand dramatically with a graduate degree. Before we discuss graduate-level careers for students with interests in clinical and counseling psychology, let's take a look at graduate training and related issues.

Graduate Education and Training Considerations

"Do your homework" before entering graduate programs in clinical or counseling psychology. The most successful students are those who enter programs that are right for them, that is, there is a good fit between the type of graduate program and their professional interests. If you haven't realized it yet, many different types of programs are available to you; critically evaluate them in light of your interests and career goals. Ask yourself the following: Do I understand the differences between the various programs (for instance, how clinical and counseling psychology are different, what a combined program is)? What type of degree program is right for me (PhD, PsyD, or EdD)? How do I get licensed after graduation? Are there other practice-related issues that I should be aware of?

Differentiating Clinical and Counseling Psychology   Although the fields of counseling and clinical psychology overlap significantly (Cobb et al., 2004), you may have gleaned subtle differences from the definitions provided earlier in this chapter. It has commonly been suggested that clinical psychology is based on the medical model (in which psychologists assess, diagnose, and treat an ailment), whereas counseling psychology is less focused on pathology, favoring a holistic perspective emphasizing all aspects of a client's life. Not surprisingly, counseling psychologists tend to work with healthier individuals who are experiencing less psychopathology or distress than their clinical psychology colleagues work with (Norcross, Sayette, Mayne, Karg, & Turkson, 1998).

Furthermore, as is consistent with a holistic perspective across the lifespan, counseling psychologists are more likely to conduct career and vocational assessments. Clinical psychologists, with their focus on assessment and diagnosing pathology for treatment purposes, are more likely to receive training in projective personality assessments, such as the Rorschach or Thematic Apperception Test (TAT) (Norcross et al., 1998). Counseling psychologists tend to be employed in university counseling centers more often than clinical psychologists, whereas clinical psychologists are more likely to work in hospital settings (Gaddy, Charlot-Swilley, Nelson, & Reich, 1995; Watkins et al., 1986).

Another difference between the disciplines of clinical and counseling psychology is found in therapists' theoretical orientations. Clinical psychologists are more likely to endorse a behavioral or psychodynamic theoretical orientation, whereas their counseling psychology colleagues are more likely to endorse a person-centered (or Rogerian) theoretical orientation (Norcross, Prochaska, & Gallagher, 1989a, 1989b; Watkins et al., 1986).

With regard to training, counseling psychologists are more likely to receive training in group psychotherapy than are clinical psychologists (Weinstein & Rossini, 1999). Counseling psychology programs tend to rely on external practicum sites for their graduate students, whereas clinical psychology programs are more likely to have in-house training clinics (that is, psychology clinics operated by the department, offering graduate-student therapists opportunities to provide psychological services under close supervision of the faculty) (Romans, Boswell, Carlozzi, & Ferguson, 1995).

Opportunities for Graduate Education   If you're planning to seek graduate training in clinical or counseling psychology, understand that there is a large discrepancy in the number of graduate programs for each discipline. There are 227 doctoral programs in clinical psychology that are accredited by the American Psychological Association (APA), compared with 74 APA-accredited doctoral programs in counseling psychology, and 2 combined (clinical, counseling, and school psychology) APA-accredited doctoral programs (American Psychological Association, 2004). Not surprisingly, clinical psychology students accounted for 49 percent of all psychology doctorate degrees granted in 2003 (American Psychological Association Research Office, 2003). Both clinical and counseling psychology programs remain very competitive for admission, with an average admission rate of 6 percent for clinical psychology programs and 8 percent for counseling psychology programs (Norcross et al., 1998).

Admission criteria for clinical and counseling psychology programs are quite similar, with some differences noted. Clinical psychology programs tend to require slightly higher verbal and quantitative GRE (Graduate Record Examination) scores than do counseling programs. Another significant difference is in the percentage of students admitted with a master's degree versus a bachelor's degree. Counseling psychology programs are much more likely to admit a student who has already obtained a master's degree than are clinical psychology PhD programs, which tend to admit students who have a bachelor's degree (Norcross et al., 1998).

Somewhat less common than clinical and counseling programs are combined programs that integrate training from two or three of the subfields—counseling, school, and clinical psychology programs—without distinguishing among the disciplines. In other words, students in combined programs are trained in the principles of each of the specified subfields. Combined programs are not all alike; some integrate all three of the applied psychology disciplines, whereas other programs incorporate either clinical or counseling psychology with school psychology. Although few combined programs exist, compared with traditional counseling and clinical psychology programs, combined programs may offer increased diversity and a broader-based training experience for students; however, this has not been empirically examined.

PhD versus PsyD Degrees   There are two types of doctoral degrees that a psychology student may obtain: PhD and PsyD, that is, Doctor of Philosophy and Doctor of Psychology. Although students may earn a Doctor of Education (EdD) degree, it is less common in psychology; therefore, we are limiting our discussion to distinctions between the more common PhD and PsyD. How can we distinguish between these degrees? The first level of distinction centers on their history. The PsyD has traditionally involved the training of practitioners; thus, graduate training has focused more heavily on service provision than on research. The PhD, on the other hand, has historically been based equally on science and practice (as in the Boulder model), and so PhD programs to this day provide a greater focus on research skills than do PsyD programs. Students earning a PhD complete a doctoral dissertation based in empirical research, whereas often only a written project is sufficient to complete requirements for the PsyD. Alternatively, students in PsyD programs often accrue many more hours of clinical experience than do students in PhD programs. So, how do you know which degree is for you?

Consider two key issues. First, what do you hope to be doing in 10 years? Programs offering both the PhD and PsyD train students to be clinicians, whereas PhD programs are more likely to train students to be scientists. If you're interested in becoming a practitioner and seek a program that emphasizes practice, the PsyD may fit your needs. However, if you're interested in developing your skills as a scientific researcher as well as your clinical skills, then the PhD is in order. Which degree you choose is your decision, but recognize that applicants to PsyD and PhD programs share similar qualifications (Norcross et al., 1998). In other words, both options are highly competitive.

The second issue to consider is whether you prefer to attend a professional school or a more traditional university. The majority of PsyD programs are housed in professional schools, whereas programs offering the PhD are primarily housed in major state or private universities. What's the difference? We've already discussed the educational differences between the PhD and PsyD, but there's one more difference to consider: finances. PhD programs based in universities and private schools generally are less expensive and offer more funding to students (Norcross, Castle, Sayette, & Mayne, 2004). Professional schools, on the other hand, are not only more expensive, but they also tend to offer less financial assistance in the form of research and teaching assistantships (Norcross et al., 1998; 2004). Although you should not base your decision solely on finances, understanding the economic realities of graduate education is important. For more information about graduate education, see Chapter 13.

Licensure   The title of psychologist is protected; in order to provide psychological services (such as therapy, assessment, consultation) as a psychologist, you must be licensed in the state in which you wish to practice. Each state has a slightly different path to licensure; however, the basic process is roughly equivalent for all states.

First, a potential licensee must complete a doctoral program in clinical or counseling psychology (in a small minority of states, master's-level psychologists can seek licensure). Most states require that the doctoral degree be obtained in a program accredited by the APA, thereby certifying its rigor and training emphases. However, in some states you can seek licensure with a degree from a program that is not APA accredited.

In addition to a doctoral degree, at least two years of supervised practice are required. Most students complete the first year as part of their degree requirements, that is, the one-year full-time internship (or a two-year part-time internship) in which they receive supervision for providing psychological services such as therapy, assessment, and crisis intervention. After completion of the doctoral degree (including the one-year internship), the licensee must acquire an additional year of supervised experience. This experience can take the form of a formal postdoctoral program, but it can also be less structured as long as it includes providing psychological services under the supervision of a doctoral-level licensed psychologist.

After all degree and supervision requirements are met, the next step is to apply for licensure, which entails a national written examination and a jurisprudence examination. The national examination is multiple choice, covering a broad range of issues and topics relevant to the practice of psychology. Because this is a national examination, the test is written for licensure applicants in all states and is thus fairly general. Most states require a 70 percent accuracy rate in order to pass, with some variations. The jurisprudence examination is also a written test; however, it is specific to the ethical code and licensure laws of each state. Thus, if you're applying for licensure in California, you'll be asked questions regarding California law and its ethical code, but if you're applying for licensure in New York, you'll answer questions about the New York statutes and ethics code.

After completion of the written examinations, many states require an additional oral examination in which licensees are presented with a case vignette and asked questions regarding diagnosis, treatment planning, and ethical concerns, as well as what multicultural issues might impact the case. As you can see, the process of obtaining licensure is time consuming. It's also costly. For example, for one of the authors, pursuing licensure from start to finish cost approximately $1,300 after the examination and application fees. Furthermore, the expense and time commitment increase if a licensee fails a particular examination and therefore must repeat it. Despite the challenges involved, licensure enables you to earn your stripes, so to speak. With licensure, you are eligible to practice psychology without supervision.

Innovative Training Opportunities   Technological advances (such as telemedicine), marketplace demands (such as managed care, prescription privileges for psychologists), and informational gains (such as evidence-supported practice, formerly referred to as empirically based practice) continue to alter the face of psychology with the potential to profoundly impact the future of psychological practice. Two current issues that are gaining increased attention in psychology are prescription privileges and telemedicine or telehealth.

Prescriptive authority for mental health professionals has historically been limited to physicians and psychiatric nurses; however, psychologists in the United States military, New Mexico, Louisiana, and Guam recently gained the ability to prescribe psychotropic medications to clients, independent of psychiatrists or physicians. This new privilege meets a mental health service need in these agencies, states, or territories. For example, legislation was initiated in New Mexico because of a drought of psychiatrists in rural areas. Further, it creates many new practice and research opportunities for psychologists.

Similarly, the delivery of psychological services via computer networks, referred to as behavioral medicine or *telehealth,* is significantly expanding professional practice opportunities. In telehealth, a psychologist remains in one location and provides a psychological service, such as therapy, to a client in a hospital, prison, or community agency in another location. This practice significantly alters the service delivery area of psychologists and may afford clients care from a specialist that they would otherwise be unable to visit.

Relatively new practice strategies such as these generate many issues, including ethical and legal ones, that affect training and competency.

Nonetheless, the doors are wide open to the innovative student. If you have interests in these or other groundbreaking opportunities, seek specialized experiences during graduate school that will best facilitate your future options. For example, you may elect to complete coursework in psychopharmacology and seek practicum placements that require collaboration with psychiatrists. You might seek practicum opportunities in hospitals that rely on telehealth, or complete elective coursework in computer science to become as familiar as possible with computer technology. These are just a couple of examples of the myriad professional opportunities currently evolving in psychology. Students planning on pursuing a graduate degree in psychology are strongly encouraged to maintain an open mind and to seek innovative opportunities that may enhance future career possibilities.

Although applied career opportunities exist for students who earn a bachelor's degree in psychology, many more opportunities exist for those earning a graduate degree. For example, students completing their master's (MA, MS), PhD, or PsyD may pursue applied careers as practitioners, program developers or evaluators, or consultants.

Practice

Undoubtedly, the greatest number of applied psychologists use their knowledge and skills as practitioners. Practitioners work in a variety of settings, including private practices, hospitals, community mental health centers, schools, university or college counseling centers, criminal justice settings, and specialty clinics, to name just a few. In addition to selecting the setting where they will practice, psychologists also decide if they want to specialize with a particular kind of client or problem. For example, some practitioners prefer to specialize in forensic psychology or sport psychology, whereas others prefer to specialize in a particular type of presenting problem, such as depression, anxiety, or relationship problems.

One of the primary benefits of a graduate degree in clinical or counseling psychology is the flexibility to pursue career opportunities that match one's own interests and abilities. Advanced degrees also afford practitioners a salary that is competitive with other psychology-related positions. In 2003, the median salary of all clinical psychologists (regardless of experience) was $75,000, and counseling psychologists earned a median salary of $65,000 (Pate, Frincke, & Kohout, 2005), varying by geographic location, setting, and clientele.

Another benefit for those interested in the practice of psychology is the expansion of the field. Psychology continues to break new ground.

As we just discussed, recent advances include delivering mental health services via telehealth and legislated prescription privileges. Although the days of seeing individual clients in one's private office are not extinct, neither does this type of service delivery remain the all-encompassing method of mental health services it has been. The future is exciting for current students; innovative opportunities abound for those of you with imagination and foresight.

Program Development and Evaluation

In addition to direct service delivery, clinical and counseling psychologists often pursue career opportunities in program development and evaluation. Psychologists may choose to develop the programs that, say, schools or community placements offer, rather than being the practitioner who provides the service. One of the authors of this book, for example, is involved in the development of a psychotherapy program for adult offenders. Although he may never actually provide this program as an aspect of his academic job, he is nevertheless evaluating such developments in the hope that other practitioners can implement the therapeutic approach to help adult offenders transition back into the community.

Careers in program development and evaluation offer several benefits that practitioners don't always have. First is the opportunity to identify and develop the types of programs that best serve a particular agency or type of client. Working at the grassroots level such as this can be extremely rewarding, especially when a program succeeds in helping the intended audience. Second, program developers avoid the stress of daily service provision to clients. On the other hand, psychologists involved in program development may miss the intimate contact and satisfaction from client progress that practitioners experience regularly. Typically, psychologists who take positions in program evaluation work as research associates at nonprofit organizations or as consultants. In 1999, the median salary for such positions for new doctoral-level psychologists was $55,000 (Williams, Wicherski, & Kohout, 2000).

Administration

In addition to careers in practice or as researchers, many clinical and counseling psychologists choose careers in administration. Administrators may be specialists who manage clinical services, or generalists who manage an entire agency or organization (Bureau of Labor Statistics, 2002). Administrators are responsible for overseeing the operation of an agency, including staffing and budget issues, health care delivery systems, and technological advances, as well as daily operations (for example, mental health service delivery). If you're interested in a career in administration, take additional coursework in business administration, finance, and management.

Psychologists work in administrative roles within hospitals and clinics, community mental health centers and community organizations, correctional and rehabilitation centers, and nursing homes, to name just a few examples. Administrative positions offer an attractive salary, with a median of $61,370, with slightly more for those in general medical settings and slightly less for those in outpatient service centers. Another benefit of an administrative career is the direct influence administrators have on the services an organization delivers and the care clients or patients receive. On the other hand, administrative work typically requires long hours and job-related stress, particularly when dealing with personnel and budgetary issues (Bureau of Labor Statistics, 2004).

In this chapter, we've covered just a few of the myriad possibilities available for people with a graduate degree in clinical or counseling psychology. Opportunities also exist for careers in writing and publishing (Chapter 2), research and academia (Chapter 2), corrections (Chapter 5), public health (Chapter 6), industry consulting (Chapter 8), marketing (Chapter 10), and social policy (Chapter 11).

SUGGESTED READINGS

Brown, S. D., & Lent, R. W. (Eds.). (2000). *Handbook of counseling psychology.* 3rd ed. New York: Wiley.

Collison, B. B., & Garfield, N. J. (1996). *Careers in counseling and human services.* New York: Taylor & Francis.

Gelso, C., & Fretz, B. (2001). *Counseling psychology* (2nd ed.). Orlando, FL: Harcourt.

Ginsberg, L. H. (2000). *Careers in social work.* Boston: Allyn and Bacon.

Kuther, T. L., Habben, C. J., & Morgan, R. D. (2005). Today's new psychologist: Traditional and emerging career paths. In R. D. Morgan, T. L. Kuther, & C. Habben (Eds.), *Life after graduate school in psychology: Insider's advice from new psychologists* (pp. 1–11). New York: Psychology Press.

Landrum, R. E. (2001). I'm getting my bachelor's degree in psychology—what can I do with it? *Eye on Psi Chi, 6,* 22–24.

Morgan, B. L., & Korschgen, A. (2001). *Majoring in psych? Career options for psychology undergraduates* (2nd ed.). Boston: Allyn and Bacon.

Srebalus, D. J., & Brown, D. (2000). *Guide to the helping professions.* Boston: Allyn and Bacon.

Woody, R. H., & Robertson, M. H. (1997). *A career in clinical psychology: From training to employment.* Madison, CT: International Universities Press.

WEB RESOURCES

Division 12 of the American Psychological Association (Society of Clinical Psychology)
   http://www.apa.org/divisions/div12

Division 17 of the American Psychological Association (Counseling Psychology)
   http://www.div17.org

So You're Considering Graduate Study in Clinical Psychology
   http://www.cas.northwestern.edu/psych/undergraduate/clinical.html

Social Work Career
   http://www.collegeview.com/career/careersearch/job_profiles/human/sw.html

Appreciating the PsyD: The Facts
   http://psichi.org/pubs/article.asp?article_id=171

Clinical Versus Counseling Psychology: *What's the Diff?*
   http://psichi.org/pubs/article.asp?article_id=73

Counseling Psychology: Making Lives Better
   http://psichi.org/pubs/article.asp?article_id=97

CHECKLIST: IS CLINICAL OR COUNSELING PSYCHOLOGY FOR YOU?

Do you:

☐   Like working with people?

☐   Have an interest in helping people with problems?

☐   Want to work with healthy people to improve their current functioning?

☐   Have an interest in why people do the things they do?

☐   Have an interest in identifying people's abilities or personality functioning?

☐   Think you would enjoy working in a hospital, clinic, university counseling center, or other health care setting?

☐   Find that you're a person others feel comfortable talking to about their problems?

☐   Find yourself interested in other people's problems?

☐   Have good listening skills and avoid tuning out when people talk about their lives?

☐   Have an interest in mental illness?

☐   Enjoy reading about abnormal psychology?

☐   Enjoy reading research about mental illness?

☐   Think you would enjoy a career providing psychotherapy and assessment?

☐   Have an interest in applied research that can be used to better people's lives?

☐   Keep secrets and protect information that others feel is personal?

☐   Find that people consider you trustworthy?

☐   Have compassion and feel for other people when they suffer?

Scoring: The more boxes you checked, the more likely it is that you're a good match for clinical or counseling psychology.

SCHOOL PSYCHOLOGY

CHAPTER GUIDE

As you know, the majority of psychology graduate students specialize in the mental health service provider subfields (American Psychological Association Research Office, 2001). We've discussed the fields of clinical and counseling psychology; however, school psychology also is considered a mental health service provider subfield. School psychology offers unique training and professional opportunities that diverge from those of counseling and clinical psychology.

School psychology overlaps with clinical and counseling psychology with regard to job activities, but school psychologists work with a more specific population. Trained in both psychology and education (National Association of School Psychologists, 2003), school psychologists work with children, families, and school systems (American Psychological Association Division 16, 2005). Consistent with their job title, the majority of school psychologists are found in school districts or school systems. School psychologists are also employed in clinics (such as community mental health centers), medical centers, correctional facilities, colleges and universities, and private practices.

School psychologists provide assessment and treatment services for children and families, consult with teachers and school officials, develop and evaluate programs, conduct research, and promote health in children and adolescents (American Psychological Association Division 16, 2005; Trull & Phares, 2001). School psychologists work with children and adolescents who present a broad array of psychological needs that are of a developmental or school-related nature. An estimated one in five children and adolescents experience significant mental health problems during their school years (National Association of School Psychologists, 2003). Typical presenting problems school psychologists work with include fears about starting school, deficits in time management and study skills, family and relationship problems, psychopathology (such as depression or anxiety), drug and alcohol problems, developmental and life stage problems (such as sexual, college, and work issues), and concerns regarding academic aptitude and intellectual abilities. The school psychologist's task is to help families, teachers, and the educational system understand and resolve these problems while promoting the child's overall health and development.

OPPORTUNITIES WITH A BACHELOR'S DEGREE

Many psychology students are interested in working with and helping children and adolescents. If these are your interests, consider a career in teaching, school counseling, or child care.

Teacher

Few career paths enable you to be as intimately involved with children as teachers are. Teachers clearly need an understanding of behavior, learning, and development. If you're interested in a position where you can make a difference in the lives of others, consider teaching.

Given your school experiences, you're probably aware of the instructional duties required of teachers, but a teacher's day involves many other obligations as well. Teachers are responsible for supervising study halls, homerooms, and extracurricular activities, all of which provide extended contact with students and therefore afford teachers the opportunity to identify physical or mental health problems and refer the child for the appropriate services. Thus, a background in psychology may assist teachers, not only in their work in the classroom but also in identifying and helping students who are experiencing problems.

Salaries for public educators are respectable, with an average income between $39,810 and $44,340 (Bureau of Labor Statistics, 2004), which is based on a nine-month salary ($53,080 to $59,120 extrapolated to 12 months). A career as a teacher can afford financial stability. In addition to a respectable salary, the benefits of the teaching career parallel those of the college professor, especially regarding time off. Schools routinely allow for traditional holidays such as Thanksgiving, with extended holiday leave around Christmas (approximately two weeks) as well as spring and, increasingly, fall breaks. So, during the academic year of nine months, an educator may reasonably expect to receive anywhere from two to four weeks of time off. In addition, as the educator is tied to a nine-month salary, summers remain open. This allows for extra vacation time, pursuit of additional occupational interests, family time, and so forth. Another benefit to a teaching career is the opportunity for advancement with additional education. School administrators often come from the teaching ranks and advance.

As we've indicated, the primary benefit of a career as a schoolteacher may be the opportunity to be involved in and influence the lives of the children or adolescents who will lead our country into the future. As a schoolteacher, you'll have the opportunity to make a difference in a young person's life. The primary drawback to a career as a schoolteacher is the limited availability for professional advancement. Although some opportunities exist for advancement (as an administrator or a teaching mentor, for instance), these positions are relatively rare. Thus, schoolteachers most often remain in the classroom, which may lead to burnout for some.

If you're considering a career as a schoolteacher, understand that all teaching positions require the completion of a bachelor's degree and an approved teacher education program, plus certification, which is obtained after completing a specified number of courses in education and passing a standardized exam. The exact requirements vary by state, so consult your advisor and the education department at your college or university.

Child-Care Worker

Students who are interested in school psychology often seek positions as child-care workers in child-care centers, nursery schools, preschools, public schools, private homes, and after school programs. Child-care workers care for children and engage them in activities that promote their development while their parents are at work. They teach children and stimulate physical, emotional, intellectual, and social development (Bureau of Labor Statistics, 2004). They keep records on children's progress and maintain contact with parents to discuss children's needs and progress. In other words, child-care workers provide children with care and opportunities to learn through play and more formal activities. As a child-care worker, you'll prepare day-to-day and long-term schedules of activities that include quiet and active time, as well as individual and group play.

Child care is strenuous work that can be physically and emotionally taxing. Although child-care workers interact with parents or guardians, they work mostly with children. Thus, the work requires high energy with frequent bending and stooping as well as lifting of children in times of need (as in children who are sad when their parents drop them off). The work may become routine, and hours may be long because child-care centers are open year round and typically have extended hours to allow time for child drop-off and pickup that accommodates parents' schedules (Bureau of Labor Statistics, 2004).

An important disadvantage to a career in child care is the high degree of burnout and employee turnover. In a large child-care center or preschool, you might advance to a supervisory or administrative position; however, other opportunities for advancement are limited. Other disadvantages of a career in child care include dealing with children who have behavioral problems and working with difficult parents.

Nevertheless, few careers offer as many intrinsic rewards, which stem from an intimate view of and important role in the learning, growth, and development of children. The working conditions vary by employment setting (such as one's own home versus an agency). The high turnover discussed earlier as a drawback also creates excellent job opportunities for those recently graduating from college and may provide a professional stepping-stone to other opportunities or career paths (Bureau of Labor Statistics, 2004).

Unfortunately, child-care workers often earn income that is low relative to their education (Whitebrook & Phillips, 1999). The median salary for a child-care worker in 2002 was $7.86 per hour (an increase of only 0.43 cents from 2000) and, unfortunately, benefits are also relatively poor (Bureau of Labor Statistics, 2004). In 2002, a typical child-care worker earned a median salary of $19,205 (Salary.com, 2002). For many, the disadvantages of a career in child care are outweighed by the joy they experience in helping young children grow and flourish.

If child care interests you, take additional courses in child development and early childhood education. You must develop an understanding of normative childhood development, because child-care providers often help identify children with disabilities or special needs. A career in child care can be demanding, because you must be enthusiastic, alert, and have lots of physical energy and endurance (for lifting, holding, carrying, and playing with all of those kids!). Good communication skills with children and parents are important, and child-care workers must be able to anticipate problems and act to promote children's welfare.

OPPORTUNITIES WITH A GRADUATE DEGREE

If you're interested in school psychology and desire a wide range of professional opportunities, consider earning a graduate degree in school psychology or school counseling (often available through departments of education). Training in school psychology emphasizes mental health services (assessment, counseling), child development, school organization, and learning/behavior and motivation theory (National Association of School Psychologists, 2003). Like their counseling and clinical psychology counterparts, many school psychologists earn a PhD; however, some school psychologists practice with a master's degree and/or receive national certification (from the National Association of School Psychologists) as a school psychologist, which requires a more advanced degree called a specialist's degree. A *specialist's degree* falls between the master's and doctoral degrees and typically adds an extra semester to a year of study beyond the master's degree. Because a specialist's degree is required for certification, if you're interested in school psychology at the master's degree level, plan on taking the time to earn the specialist's degree. Now let's take a look at graduate-level careers in school psychology.

School Psychologist

Although school psychologists are known for their work in schools, they are found in a variety of settings.

School Settings   The primary responsibilities of the school psychologist in a public or private school setting are to provide consultation, assessment, intervention and prevention, educational or training services, and research and program development (National Association of School Psychologists, 2003).

Consultation and educational services are a primary task of the school psychologist in a school setting (Bardon,1989). School psychologists consult with administrators, teachers, and parents to help them better understand how child development affects learning and behavior (National Association of School Psychologists, 2003). For example, a school psychologist in a school setting may facilitate coordination between parents and the school system to ensure that all parties are promoting the best interest of the child. Similarly, the psychologist offers educational services to administrators, teachers, and parents to facilitate effective learning environments and address problem behaviors. Educational services may take the form of classroom management techniques, instruction in learning strategies, and ways of identifying at-risk learners.

Assessment also falls to the school psychologist in school settings (Bardon,1989). School psychologists use a myriad of instruments and techniques to evaluate the nature of a student's problem and identify the most appropriate intervention. School psychologists may be asked to evaluate students' academic skills and learning aptitudes, personality and emotional development, social skills, learning environment and school climate, and eligibility for special education, as well as the effectiveness of intervention strategies (National Association of School Psychologists, 2003). In other words, although school psychologists provide direct services such as counseling, they more typically assess a problem and then teach parents, teachers, and other people directly involved with the student how to be helpful to the child.

School psychologists also provide direct services via prevention and intervention strategies. Prevention strategies are designed to identify at-risk children and provide services to prevent the onset of learning or behavioral problems. Prevention services that school psychologists may provide include the following:

- Program development and teacher education for identifying children at risk for learning disorders or mental health problems
- Skills training for parents and teachers to cope with disruptive behavior
- Developing school initiatives to facilitate school safety (for example, preventing bullying and aggression)
- Facilitating tolerance of individual differences and diversity (National Association of School Psychologists, 2003).

Intervention services, on the other hand, are designed to help children who already have learning or behavioral problems. Examples of intervention services a school psychologist may provide include individual or group counseling, skills training (such as social skills, time management, study skills, problem-solving skills, and coping strategies), crisis management, grief counseling, family therapy, and substance abuse counseling (National Association of School Psychologists, 2003).

Finally, school psychologists may be involved in research and program development within school settings. School psychologists evaluate the effectiveness of their services, academic programs, and behavior management systems, as well as develop new programs (or "best practices") to facilitate student learning and development or for educational reform or restructuring (National Association of School Psychologists, 2003).

Salaries for school psychologists in elementary and secondary school settings compare with counseling and clinical psychologists. In 2002, school psychologists earned a median salary of approximately $54,480 annually (Bureau of Labor Statistics, 2004). See Chapter 3 for more information on salaries in the applied areas of psychology, including clinical and counseling psychology. A primary benefit for the psychologist in a school setting is flexibility. Because school psychologists engage in a range of activities, they have diverse daily schedules and routines. An additional advantage is that psychologists in school settings adhere to the academic schedule, which affords extended leaves for winter holidays, fall and spring breaks, and summer breaks. Some school districts may employ their psychologists throughout the summer, although this usually includes increased pay.

A disadvantage for psychologists working in the school system is lack of access to colleagues. Although large school districts often employ more than one school psychologist, most employ only one; this can lead to a sense of professional isolation. Further, one school psychologist may be responsible for all of the children in the district and across all grade levels, which can easily amount to overseeing the needs of hundreds and perhaps over a thousand students spread across several schools, requiring frequent travel between settings. Traveling among schools can leave some school psychologists feeling that they lack a "home base"; however, this diversity and travel between schools may be refreshing for some, preventing feelings of boredom or staleness.

Private Practice   School psychologists in private practice engage in activities similar to those of their colleagues in school settings. Although some have questioned the appropriateness of school psychologists in private practice, a child's behaviors at school are not always directly related to the school or educational system. Thus, private practitioners are as capable as psychologists employed in school settings of providing consultation, assessment, and prevention and intervention services for learning and behavioral problems. Therefore, school psychologists in both private practice and school settings can provide similar services and perform similar tasks.

School psychologists in private practice enjoy benefits their counterparts in the schools do not have. First, private practitioners have greater flexibility in the scheduling of their appointments, with the exception that many students will not be seen until after 4:00 P.M., which often requires evening work. Nevertheless, this schedule may prove desirable for individuals who aren't "morning people." Second, school psychologists in private practice spend less time traveling from school to school and are more likely to see clients in their office. Thus, they have a central office from which to work and are less distracted by shuffling about. Finally, school psychologists in private practice are not limited in their clientele by an agency. Thus they have opportunities to branch out and provide other services (such as relationship counseling, individual counseling to nonstudents) if they receive the appropriate training and supervision. Salaries for school psychologists in private offices may also be slightly higher than for those working in elementary and secondary school settings, with a median 2002 salary of $59,600 (Bureau of Labor Statistics, 2004).

A limitation for the private practitioner is the lack of availability and access to a child's learning environment. Whereas a school psychologist employed in a school setting has immediate access to a child and the classroom, the private practitioner must seek permission and approval from the school to observe a classroom and must wait for the student to be transported to his or her office. An additional disadvantage for the private practitioner is the overhead cost of maintaining a private practice. Psychologists in school settings have little to no overhead costs, because the school district provides office space, computer access or computing services for report writing, and testing materials. The private practitioner must cover these expenses as business costs.

Other Settings   In addition to school settings and private practice, school psychologists are found in many other settings, including clinics and hospitals, criminal justice settings, universities and medical schools, businesses, and residential settings (see D'Amato & Dean, 1989, for a review of school psychologists in these settings). Similar to graduate degrees in counseling and clinical psychology, a graduate degree in school psychology affords great flexibility with regard to professional settings and responsibilities. Regardless of where a school psychologist works, however, he or she focuses on providing services that help students (children, adolescents, or adults) succeed academically, emotionally, and socially (National Association of School Psychologists, 2003). They do this by engaging in consulting and educational services, providing assessments, developing prevention and intervention programs, and conducting research.

School Counselor

Remember the school counselor in your high school—a trusted professional who would help you or your friends when you needed information about colleges and college admissions, or who offered assistance in times of need, or who simply offered a friendly smile and a comfortable place to talk about "stuff" that was occurring in your life? This, in essence, is the career of the school counselor.

As described in the *Occupational Outlook Handbook* (Bureau of Labor Statistics, 2004), school counselors help students understand and cope with social, behavioral, and personal problems. School counselors use counseling skills to emphasize prevention as well as skill development to enhance personal, social, and academic growth. School counselors may provide special services such as substance abuse prevention programs, conflict management, and parenting education training, as well as supervising peer counseling programs.

School counselors may work with individuals, small groups, or entire classes. Although this job description may appear to overlap with that of the school psychologist, the school counselor's role is vastly different. Whereas school psychologists work with children with special needs, school counselors are available for all children and maintain regular school hours to help students as they navigate the educational process. Furthermore, unlike school psychologists, school counselors typically have less formal training in psychopathology, assessment, and counseling skills. When students are encountering severe problems or distress (academic, personal, behavior, social), the student is referred to the school psychologist, who has specialized training to deal with such issues.

Career opportunities for the school counselor are very good. The job outlook for school counselors is expected to grow faster than the average for all occupations through 2012 (Bureau of Labor Statistics, 2004). Other advantages of a career as a school counselor include the salary and work schedule. In 2002, school counselors earned a median income of $49,530 annually (Bureau of Labor Statistics, 2004). Keep in mind, however, that this annual salary is typically based only on a nine- or ten-month contract. An additional benefit is the work schedule. School counselors, like teachers, have two or three months off every year to pursue other interests or employment. In addition, they receive the same generous vacation packages that teachers enjoy.

Although a small handful of states allow bachelor's degree holders to work as school counselors, all states require school counselors to hold state school counseling certification (Bureau of Labor Statistics, 2004). This usually requires additional training and credentials beyond the bachelor's degree. Some states require public school counselors to have both counseling and teaching certificates (Bureau of Labor Statistics, 2004). A growing number of states require school counselors to hold master's degrees in school counseling (usually available within departments of education). If you're considering a career as a school counselor, look into the education and certification requirements in your state. The American School Counselor Association is a great place to start your research: http://www. schoolcounselor.org.

SUGGESTED READINGS

Burden, K. (2000). Psychology in education and instruction. In K. Pawlik & M. R. Rosenzweig (Eds.), *International handbook of psychology* (pp. 466–478). Thousand Oaks, CA: Sage.

Fagan, T. K., & Warden, P. G. (Eds.). (1996). *Historical encyclopedia of school psychology.* Westport, CT: Greenwood.

Gilman, R., & Teague, T. L. (2005). School psychologists in nontraditional settings: Alternative roles and functions in psychological service delivery. In R. D. Morgan, T. L. Kuther, & C. Habben (Eds.), *Life after graduate school in psychology: Insider's advice from new psychologists* (pp. 167–180). New York: Psychology Press.

Moffatt, C. V., & Moffatt, T. L. (1999). *How to get a teaching job.* Boston: Allyn and Bacon.

Renolds, C. B., Gutkin, T. B. (1999). *The handbook of school psychology* (3rd ed.). New York: Wiley.

Saklofske, D., II., & Janzen, H. L. (1993). Contemporary issues in school psychology. In K. S. Dobson & D. J. C. Dobson (Eds.), *Professional psychology in Canada* (pp. 313–350). Seattle, WA: Hogrefe & Huber.

Talley, R. C., Kubiszyn, T., Brassard, M., & Short, R. J. (Eds.). (1996). *Making psychologists in schools indispensable: Critical questions and emerging perspectives.* Washington, DC: American Psychological Association.

WEB RESOURCES

American Academy of Child & Adolescent Psychiatry (AACAP)
    http://www.aacap.org

Canadian Association of School Psychologists (CASP)
    http://www.stemnet.nf.ca/casp

Division 16 of the American Psychological Association (School Psychology)
    http://www.indiana.edu/~div16/index.html

Educational Psychology: Division of Educational and Child Psychology of the British Psychological Society
    http://www.bps.org.uk/careers/areas/educational.cfm

European Agency for Development in Special Needs Education
    http://www.european-agency.org

International School Psychology Association (ISPA)
    http://www.ispaweb.org

National Association of School Psychologists (NASP)
    http://www.nasponline.org/index2.html

American School Counselor Association
    http://www.schoolcounselor.org

Selections from *A Complete Guide to the Advanced Study in and the Profession of School Psychology*
    http://www-gse.berkeley.edu/program/sp/html/spguide.html

Becoming a School Psychologist
    http://www.nasponline.org/certification/becoming.html

CHECKLIST: IS SCHOOL PSYCHOLOGY FOR YOU?

Do you:

☐   Want to work with healthy people to improve their current functioning?

☐   Find that you are a person others feel comfortable talking to about their problems?

☐   Have good listening skills and avoid tuning out when people talk about their lives?

☐   Think you would enjoy a career providing assessment?

☐   Have an interest in applied research that can be used to better people's lives?

☐   Keep secrets and protect information that others feel is personal?

☐   Find that people consider you trustworthy?

☐   Have compassion and feel for other people when they suffer?

☐   Prefer working with children rather than adults?

☐   Have an interest in working in a school system?

☐   Prefer identifying the source of peoples' problems rather than working with them directly to resolve their problems?

☐   Enjoy working with children?

☐   Have the courage to report people who abuse children?

☐   Like to see children succeed?

☐   Enjoy developmental psychology?

☐   Enjoy watching children play?

☐   Consider children and their problems to be as important as adult problems?

Scoring: The more boxes you checked, the more likely it is that you're a good match for a career in school psychology.

LEGAL AND FORENSIC PSYCHOLOGY

CHAPTER GUIDE

PSYCHOLOGY AND LAW: WHAT IS IT?

Arriving at a crime scene with badge in hand, analyzing the scene, exploring the intimacies of the alleged offender's life, and ultimately assisting in the offender's apprehension—certainly this must be the interface of psychology and the law, right? Not surprisingly, when we think about careers in psychology and law, we think of forensic psychology, especially criminal profiling. As an increasing number of psychology majors express the desire to become forensic psychologists (R. Maki, personal communication, February 6, 2002), more courses are being offered in psychology and law (Liss, 1992). But what exactly is a forensic psychologist? Popular films like *Silence of the Lambs* and television shows like *Profiler* depict forensic psychology as an action-packed career of apprehending dangerous criminals. Understandably, these exciting dramas pique the interest of many psychology students. Although the media portrays forensic psychology and careers in psychology and law this way, rarely do they see such action. So then, what is the field of psychology and law? This chapter explores opportunities for students at all educational levels who are interested in this type of career.

Psychologists study human behavior, whereas judges and attorneys study the legal system. Clearly, each field is distinct. Yet both disciplines aim at improving the quality of human life. Psychology, for example, studies human behavior to help people understand their own behavior and to maximize human functioning. The law provides a recognized set of rules to ensure that we all coexist equally. Psychology and law, then, is the interface or merging of these two disciplines.

Before we discuss career options in psychology and law, let's consider forensic psychology again. Forensic psychology is a narrow application of psychology to the legal system. Though many undergraduate students express interest in becoming forensic psychologists with the explicit intent to engage in criminal profiling, understand that criminal profiling is a rare professional activity that very few forensic psychologists do. Forensic psychology is a mental health discipline, whereas profiling is a criminal investigative technique (American Psychology-Law Society, 2004). Students specifically interested in the rare opportunity to be involved in profiling are encouraged to pursue a career in law enforcement.

Although forensic psychology does not typically include profiling activities, it remains a dynamic and challenging field. A *forensic psychologist* is any psychologist (although usually trained in clinical or counseling psychology) who works within the legal system (Brigham, 1999). Settings for this work include secure forensic units, jails, prisons, court-related services and/or community mental health centers, other specialized agencies, and private practices (providing forensic assessment and treatment services). Forensic psychologists are probably best known as practitioners; however, researchers and educators can also be engaged in forensic psychology-related activities. For example, the former might engage in attorney consultation or jury selection; the latter might work in colleges, medical schools, and law enforcement agencies. *Forensic psychology*, then, refers to any application to the legal system by a doctoral-level psychologist, whereas psychology and law also includes broader applications such as social/public policy, trial consultation, and law enforcement, to name just a few.

OPPORTUNITIES WITH A BACHELOR'S DEGREE

You don't need a doctorate in psychology to be involved in the legal or the criminal justice system. Bachelor's-level positions that incorporate aspects of psychology and law include law enforcement positions such as police or correctional officers, probation and parole officers, and juvenile detention workers. Few professions are as noble or vital to societal functioning as law enforcement and support. Police and correctional officers work within the legal system to enforce the law, and psychology is an important component of their job. This is particularly true today because the mentally ill are increasingly present within the criminal justice system (Condelli, Bradigan, & Holanchock, 1997; Ditton, 1999; Hodgins, 1995; Steadman, Morris, & Dennis, 1995; Torrey, 1995). Police, correctional, probation, and parole officers, along with juvenile detention workers, are responsible for controlling human behavior and frequently must de-escalate volatile situations. Clearly psychology, with its understanding of human behavior, plays an essential role in their success and safety.

Police Officer

Policing is one of the most demanding and taxing of all service positions, because officers hold the ultimate responsibility of protecting our lives and property. Depending on seniority and promotional opportunities, typical activities of police officers include maintaining regular patrols, responding to calls for service, directing traffic as needed (as at the scene of a fire), investigating a crime scene, or providing first aid to an accident victim (Bureau of Labor Statistics, 2004). As an officer matures through the police ranks, other opportunities develop. For example, a police officer may be promoted to detective, the primary responsibility of which is investigating crime scenes. Also, with experience, police officers might take an administrative position such as Sergeant, Captain, or Chief of Police. Such positions allow an officer to influence or administer policing more directly within a given community. In large police departments, officers usually are assigned to a specific type of duty. Many urban police agencies are becoming more involved in *community policing*—a practice in which an officer builds relationships with the citizens of local neighborhoods and mobilizes the public to help fight crime. Given the diversity of activities and the direct nature of public service, the law enforcement officer greatly benefits from an understanding of the principles that govern human behavior (that is, psychology).

Unfortunately, salaries in law enforcement do not fully compensate for the level of professional responsibility or job-related stress; nonetheless, law enforcement officers earn respectable salaries. For example, the median salary for police officers in 2002 was $42,270 (Bureau of Labor Statistics, 2004). If you're interested in criminal profiling, remember that, with advancement, a police officer may become a detective, and detectives occasionally use profiling as an investigative technique. In addition to increased professional opportunities, promotions carry financial incentives. The median income of police and detective supervisors in 2002 was $61,010 (Bureau of Labor Statistics, 2004). As you might imagine, the primary disadvantage to policing is job-related stress (Anson & Bloom, 1988; Birmingham & Morgan, 2001). Other disadvantages include security and safety concerns, as well as the public's occasional negative stereotypes about police officers. Perhaps the primary advantage of law enforcement is that few professions offer such a direct opportunity for public service; rarely does anyone have as great an opportunity to influence others as does the police officer.

Correctional Officer

Correctional officers are similar to police officers in that they protect public safety as well as are responsible for the safety and well-being of others; in this case, however, "others" refers to offenders. Once arrested, offenders are housed in jail and prison facilities. These facilities are stressful and dangerous for inmates as well as staff (Morgan, Van Haveren, & Pearson, 2002). Correctional officers maintain peace in a violent world by monitoring the activities and work assignments of inmates, searching inmates and their living quarters for contraband (such as drugs, weapons), enforcing discipline, settling disputes between conflicting inmates, and maintaining security by routinely inspecting locks, window bars, doors, and gates for signs of malfunction or tampering (Bureau of Labor Statistics, 2004).

Because correctional officers work in the offenders' living environment, an understanding and healthy appreciation of psychology is clearly beneficial. In a typical day, for example, a correctional officer might resolve a dispute between inmates, console an inmate who has lost a family member and cannot attend the funeral, and work with inmates on correcting their behavior to increase the likelihood that they will be successful upon release. Correctional officers rely on interpersonal skills and knowledge of human functioning to navigate these difficult situations.

An advantage of this career is the opportunity to serve those typically forgotten by the rest of society and to protect society from those too dangerous to live in our world. Another advantage is relative job security, given the increasing prison population. However, few occupational environments present as many challenges as a penitentiary. Correctional officers work in a potentially volatile environment, and although this may add a level of excitement and novelty to the job, stress and burnout remain occupational hazards (Anson & Bloom, 1988; Cheek & Miller, 1983; Harris, 1983; Lindquist & Whitehead, 1986; Morgan et al., 2002). Salaries for correctional officers are slightly less than those of police officers, with a median salary of $32,670 in 2002 and a range of $22,010 to $52,370 (Bureau of Labor Statistics, 2004).

Probation and Parole Officer

Probation and parole officers also work with offenders within the criminal justice system. However, they do not work within correctional settings, like correctional officers, nor do they work with the public, like police officers. Rather, probation and parole officers supervise offenders while they are in the community to ensure that they are in compliance with the stipulations of their parole or probation.

At times, probation and parole officers must enforce the law, as when offenders fail to comply with the conditions of their parole or probation and must be returned to prison or the court. They also help offenders get the resources they need in order to remain in the free world. These job activities necessitate an understanding of human behavior, particularly an appreciation of the mental health and psychological needs of offenders. The primary advantage of this career is that, whereas it is a law enforcement position, it typically affords greater safety than does policing; however, like all law enforcement positions, it generates much stress. Probation and parole officers earn salaries comparable to other law enforcement officers, with a median salary of $38,360 in 2002 and a range of $25,810 to $62,520 (Bureau of Labor Statistics, 2004).

Juvenile Detention Worker

Like correctional officers, juvenile detention workers work within a setting of confinement, but they focus on *juveniles*—offenders typically younger than 18 years—rather than adults. Juvenile detention workers have many of the same responsibilities as correctional officers and probation or parole officers, but they may have a more desirable work setting because many hold the hope that juveniles can change. It is commonly believed in the adult criminal justice system that "nothing works" and that offenders don't change—that prisons are merely warehouses (Martinson, 1974). This belief is inaccurate, because rehabilitation programs do increase the postrelease functioning of inmates (D. A. Andrews & Bonta,1994; D. A. Andrews et al., 1990; Garrett, 1985; Gendreau & Andrews, 1990; Gendreau & Ross, 1979, 1981; Lipsey, 1992). Nonetheless, working with juvenile offenders who are stereotypically seen as less hardened offers the perceived potential for effective change. A primary disadvantage of juvenile detention work is coping with juvenile attitudes and impulsiveness, which often results in frustration and feelings of futility. Salaries and benefits for juvenile detention workers are consistent with those of correctional officers (Bureau of Labor Statistics, 2004).

If you're interested in any of these careers in law enforcement, a psychology major will suit you well. Seek additional coursework in criminal justice and political science. Sociology classes in criminology, deviance, the criminal justice system, policing, and corrections can provide background knowledge that will be useful in deciding whether law enforcement is for you. Political science classes on the legal and criminal justice system will provide you with a broader understanding of how the legal and criminal justice systems operate. Also, seek practicum experiences with local police or sheriff's departments or in the local jail, in order to get some experience and determine whether this really is the career for you.

OPPORTUNITIES WITH A GRADUATE DEGREE

A graduate degree opens the door to a variety of career opportunities in psychology and law. Practitioners may conduct forensic assessments, provide treatment services for offenders, or assist law enforcement officers. Research psychologists may seek opportunities to be directly involved in the legal system through trial consultation, or may conduct research that impacts the legal system (for example, research about children's developmental level and their ability to participate in court proceedings).

Psychologists of any discipline—counseling/clinical, developmental, social, cognitive—may pursue political careers. Psychologists have been elected to both federal and state legislative bodies (Sullivan, 2005), and opportunities for psychologists to affect public policy have never been greater. The doctoral degree provides the most flexibility for those seeking careers in psychology and the law. More specifically, the PhD in psychology (typically in counseling or clinical psychology) affords much greater flexibility in forensic psychology than does the master's degree.

Correctional Psychology

As the prison population continues to rise (Boothby & Clements, 2001; Irwin, 1996), correctional psychology is becoming an increasingly frequent career option for many psychologists with forensic interests. In fact, psychologists have been encouraged to seek employment in correctional facilities (Hawk, 1997). Further, prison and jail settings may become leading employers of psychologists, especially if the current incarceration rate continues to climb. Correctional psychologists report enjoying their jobs (Boothby & Clements, 2001; Ferrell, Morgan, & Winterowd, 2000); however, working in correctional environments is stressful for both inmates (Hassine, 1996; Toch, 1992) and staff (Morgan et al., 2002), including health professionals (Brodsky, 1982; Inwald, 1982). Nevertheless, correctional mental health can be enjoyable and rewarding because it gives professionals the chance to make a difference with an underrepresented population.

Options for Master's Degree Holders   Although the doctorate in psychology is the entry-level degree for many psychology- and law-related activities, several options exist for graduates with master's degrees, particularly in forensic psychology. Master's degree holders in clinical and counseling psychology frequently work as treatment providers for offenders in institutional or correctional settings, such as prisons (for examples, see Boothby & Clements, 2001; Morgan, Winterowd, & Ferrell, 1999). Such correctional settings provide basic mental health services to all inmates and include both assessment and treatment services that focus on symptom reduction and coping within the correctional environment (Morgan, 2002). The hiring of master's-level clinicians is debated (see, for instance, Morgan et al., 1999), but it remains a common practice, particularly for state correctional systems, and affords mental health professionals with job security.

An important benefit of correctional mental health is that the salaries are slightly higher than similar entry-level positions in noncorrectional settings. Whereas the median salary for a master's-level clinician in 2002 was approximately $32,618 annually (Singleton, Tate, & Kohout, 2003), in corrections this salary jumps to $40,000 or more (Boothby & Clements, 2001).

No specific training beyond psychotherapy and assessment skills is usually required for employment in a correctional facility; however, applicants benefit from any practicum experience working with offenders or other difficult clients such as clients mandated to attend treatment or psychiatric inpatients.

Options for Doctoral Degree Holders   Like master's-level clinicians, doctoral-level psychologists in correctional facilities typically are involved in direct service (Boothby & Clements, 2001). However, doctoral-level providers have more opportunities to become involved in rehabilitative efforts through program development (Morgan et al., 1999). In other words, master's-level correctional mental health professionals frequently engage in service delivery, whereas doctoral-level providers may become more involved in developing specialized programs for offenders and evaluating the effectiveness of these programs. Doctoral-level psychologists in correctional settings receive good compensation for their time, with a substantial benefits package and a 40-hour workweek. Job security is another advantage, especially given the current rise in the prison population. The primary disadvantages of correctional mental health are job-related stress and a potential feeling of dissociation from correctional administrators who have a goal of incarceration (by necessity), as opposed to the rehabilitative preference of most mental health professionals (Morgan et al., 1999).

A scan of specialized classified ads, such as the *Monitor on Psychology*, indicates that correctional psychology positions are readily available and have been for several years. Whereas master's-level clinicians earn on average $40,000 in correctional settings, their doctoral-level counterparts earn significantly more. In the Federal Bureau of Prisons, for which the doctorate is the entry-level degree, the starting salary is approximately $42,000, with an average salary of $61,800 (Boothby & Clements, 2000). Employment in state correctional facilities provides a slightly lower average income for doctoral-level providers ($53,400). No specialized experience beyond doctoral training is required for employment as a correctional psychologist. Nevertheless, field experience is always a plus. If you're interested in this career, consider pursuing internship or postdoctoral experiences in secure forensic institutions or in correctional settings such as the Federal Bureau of Prisons, which currently have nine accredited doctoral-level internship sites.

Forensic Examiner

Many forensic psychologists seek work as forensic examiners. In fact, many doctoral-level interns apply to forensic sites to conduct criminal evaluations such as sanity evaluations (Ax & Morgan, 2002). Master's- and doctoral-level psychologists also conduct examinations for other types of court cases, including divorce and child custody, family and children's court, civil commitment, personal injury, and anti-discrimination and enti-tlement cases (Ackerman,1999; Melton, Petrila, Poythress, & Slobogin, 1997).

Because of such high-profile offenders as John Hinkley or the Unabomber, most students are familiar with psychologists' involvement in criminal cases. In criminal cases, psychologists may be asked to assess a defendant's competency to stand trial or mental state at the time of the alleged offense (evaluating the insanity plea). Other issues also may be raised regarding a defendant's competency during the criminal justice process. For example, a defendant's competency to consent to search or seizure, to confess, to plead guilty, to waive the right to counsel, to refuse an insanity defense, to testify, and to be sentenced and executed may be questioned. (Several sources provide much greater detail on the nature and purpose of these evaluations, including Huss, 2001; Melton et al., 1997.)

Forensic psychologists are also heavily involved in noncriminal cases. These cases differ from criminal cases in that a person's liberty is not in jeopardy; instead, a plaintiff seeks to obtain something that is in dispute, such as custody of children or financial compensation for damages. Divorce proceedings often produce requests for child custody evaluations, which the court usually hires psychologists to conduct. Such evaluations are requested in approximately 10 percent of custody hear-ings, with the aim of assisting the court by investigating the facts that would be relevant to a judge or jury making a custody decision (Melton et al., 1997).

Psychologists are becoming increasingly involved in personal injury lit-igation cases (Butcher & Miller, 1999). Personal injury cases include those in which a person is injured either physically or psychologically and seeks compensation for damages (Ackerman, 1999). Worker's compensation cases, medical malpractice suits, and sexual harassment cases are just a few of the examples of personal injury cases in which a psychological eval-uation may be requested as part of the legal process. The role of the psy-chologist in personal injury cases, in general, is to assist the court in determining if a mental injury occurred as a result of some specific inci-dent. This evaluation is similar to the insanity evaluation, because the examiner conducts a retrospective study (Melton et al., 1997); that is, the examiner determines the plaintiff's mental functioning before and after the given incident.

Where do forensic examiners work? Many are in private practice. Some criminal forensic psychologists work in state institutions such as secure units, community mental health centers, and hospitals. Entry-level psychologists providing forensic services in hospitals and community settings may begin at approximately $40,000 annually, but salaries tend to vary by state and jurisdiction (American Psychology-Law Society, 2004). Forensic psychologists in private practice typically bill between $100 and $300 per hour (American Psychology-Law Society, 2004), but do not enjoy the benefit of a steady income. The primary advantages of forensic evaluation are job satisfaction and the potential for a relatively lucrative income. One disadvantage of this career path is the need for advanced training beyond academic coursework, such as internship and/or postdoctoral training that specializes in forensic assessments. Another disadvantage is the potential for lawsuits and ethics complaints filed against forensic examiners (see examples in Kirkland & Kirkland, 2001). Even frivolous lawsuits or ethics complaints can be costly in terms of money, time, stress, and professional image.

In order to conduct forensic evaluations, you must receive training in psychological assessment (for example, personality assessment, intellectual assessment, mental status examinations), as well as specialized training in forensic issues. Most forensic psychologists receive their training during the predoctoral internship (a field experience obtained while pursuing the doctoral degree) or in specialized postdoctoral training programs that focus on forensic psychology. Because very few training programs provide specialized training in forensic psychology practice, field experience in the form of predoctoral and postdoctoral internships is essential. Some master's-level practitioners receive on-the-job training in assessment; however, most states do not allow independent practice without a doctoral degree and license.

Police Psychology

Police psychology has become increasingly necessary in law enforcement (Birmingham & Morgan, 2001), despite law enforcement officers' sometimes negative perceptions toward such services (Max, 2000). Police psychologists provide a variety of services, including the following (Weiner & Hess, 2006):

- **Management consultation.** This involves consulting on administrative decision making that has agencywide implications.
- **Preemployment psychological assessments and fitness-for-duty evaluations.** These evaluations help determine if a person is suitable for law enforcement work or fit for continued duty.
- **Special unit evaluations.** These assessments are conducted to assist with promotional decisions for specialized police assignments such as

Special Weapons and Tactics (SWAT), Tactical Response Teams (TRT), and Hostage Negotiation Teams (HNT).

- **Hostage negotiation team consultations.** Here, psychologists provide consulting for and assistance with hostage negotiations.
- **Deadly force incident investigations.** These involve assisting with investigations regarding the appropriateness of an officer's use of deadly force.
- **Field consultations.** These include assisting an officer in the apprehension or security of a mentally ill person.

Less frequently, police psychologists perform investigative activities as well (Bartol, 1996).

Stress is a prevalent problem in law enforcement (Anson & Bloom,1988; Birmingham & Morgan, 2001). Police psychologists provide counseling services to help officers cope with their stress. The most common activity of police psychologists is to provide preemployment evaluations (Weiner & Hess, 2006). Preemployment evaluations are requested to determine if would-be officers have the disposition and personality style to cope with stress and serve in the capacity of law enforcer. Typically, police psychologists hold doctoral degrees and may be consultants to a law enforcement agency or may be employed (often actually sworn in as a law enforcement officer) by an agency (Bartol, 1996). Entry-level salaries appear commensurate with other entry-level doctoral psychology positions, with an annual salary of approximately $40,000. As with other forensic psychology positions, if you're interested in police psychology, seek specialized training through predoctoral internships or postdoctoral training, because there are few formal opportunities for training in police psychology during graduate school.

Trial Consultant

Yet another potential occupational opportunity exists in trial consultation, and is of equal interest for psychological practitioners and other psychologists. In fact, social and cognitive psychologists have particular skills and expertise that translate well to courtroom consultations (American Psychology-Law Society, 2005). *Trial consultation* refers to any service provided to assist in the process of a trial, including focus group research; exploratory focus groups; experimental, quasi-experimental, and comparative studies; mock trials; or pretrial case analysis (C. K. Andrews, 2005). Trial consultations usually are provided to help a client attain a favorable outcome during the course of a civil or criminal legal action (S. Roberson, personal communication, February 2002) by better understanding how the judge or jury will understand and process information (C. K. Andrews, 2005).

A trial consultant may conduct research that influences the trial process, such as research regarding decision making by the trier-of-fact (that is, judge or jury), the impact of evidentiary psycholegal research, and eyewitness identification and recall (American Psychology-Law Society, 2004; C. K. Andrews, 2005; Huss, 2001). In addition to research, psychologists may advise attorneys regarding jury selection and the effects of courtroom trial procedures on jury decision making. For example, trial consultants often use jury simulations or mock jurors to assist attorneys in developing strategies for jury selection and the trial itself (C. K. Andrews, 2005; Huss, 2001). Trial consultation occurs in both criminal and civil trials. Although high-profile cases such as the tobacco settlement bring notoriety to this profession, such notoriety appears to remain a relatively infrequent occupational consideration for psychologists in training.

The largest advantage of a career as a trial consultant is the potential income. Because establishing oneself in the private industry is difficult, the early years of a career as a trial consultant provide a limited income (S. Roberson, personal communication, February 2002). However, psychologists with appropriate experience and legal connections who are fortunate enough to be hired for high-profile cases have earned incomes in excess of $1 million annually. Remember that this is the high end of the salary spectrum; entry-level positions appear comparable to other entry-level psychology positions. As in most careers, doctoral degrees afford additional opportunities and autonomy over master's degrees.

Politics

A bachelor's degree in psychology may enable you somewhat to become involved in the political process. Master's degrees provide similar opportunities; not surprisingly, the PhD provides many more. Psychologists have become increasingly politically aware and active. In fact, by 2004, 17 psychologists were serving as legislators—12 in state legislatures and 5 in the U.S. Congress (Sullivan, 2005). Although this represents a significant improvement over psychologists' political contributions of the past, much work is yet to be done—or, stated more provocatively, *must* be done. Considering the social and public policy implications of psychological work, we feel that political involvement is not simply an opportunity for psychologists; rather, it is their duty. Psychologists should seek to apply the techniques of their trade to meet larger public needs (DeLeon, 1988). Just as clinical, counseling, and school psychologists seek to achieve the betterment of the client, so can the political psychologist use psychological principals to help society.

What do psychologists do in politics? They may assist in developing briefs, conduct psycholegal research, or become involved in planning strategies and drafting laws. To prepare psychologists for politics, the American Psychological Association developed a congressional fellowship program in 1974. The purpose of this program is to provide "psychologists with an invaluable public policy learning experience, to contribute to the more effective use of psychological knowledge in government, and to broaden awareness about the value of psychology-government interaction among psychologists and within the federal government" (American Psychology-Law Society, 2005). Psychologists who enroll in this training program spend one year assigned to a member of Congress or a congressional committee and may perform such tasks as assisting in congressional hearings and debates or preparing briefs (American Psychology Association, 2005). Initially, this program was geared exclusively to entry-level psychologists; however, it now targets senior-level psychologists as well (Fowler, 1996).

Salaries of psychologists holding political positions are governed by the United States or the state they represent and vary accordingly. On the high end, a United States senator earns $154,700 (Bureau of Labor Statistics, 2004). Salaries of political employees vary according to level of government and jurisdiction. Entry-level psychologist fellows in the American Psychological Association fellowship program earn approximately $55,000, with the range increasing to $70,000 depending on level of experience (American Psychological Association, 2005). In addition, fellows receive the cost of relocation and/or travel expenses during the fellowship year. Although any United States citizen has the opportunity for political involvement, specialized training such as that provided by the American Psychological Association fellowship program affords psychologists specialized knowledge and experience that is directly applicable to their political interests.

Throughout this chapter we've examined many opportunities for those who are interested in the interface of psychology and law at either the baccalaureate-degree or graduate-degree levels. Crime and social problems remain. Psychologists' specialized training as scientists, and in many cases practitioners, offers opportunities for combating these problems. In many cases, no additional training beyond an academic degree is necessary. Furthermore, many of the career options described here offer job security and salaries competitive with comparable positions. Although the field of psychology and law rarely includes activities such as analyzing a crime scene or conducting profile analyses, it does afford exciting and rewarding career options.

SUGGESTED READINGS

American Psychology-Law Society. (2004). *Careers in psychology and law: A guide for prospective students.* Retrieved October 15, 2005, from http://www.ap-ls.org/students/careers%20in%20psychology.pdf

American Psychology-Law Society. (2005). *Careers in psychology and law: Subspecialties in psychology and law: A closer look.* Retrieved October 15, 2005, from http://www.unl.edu/ap-ls/student/careers_closerlook.html

Andrews, C. K. (2005). Trial consulting: Moving psychology into the courtroom. In R. D. Morgan, T. L. Kuther, & C. J. Habben (Eds.), *Life after graduate school in psychology: Insider's advice from new psychologists* (pp. 257–274). New York: Psychology Press.

Fagan, T., & Ax, R. K. (2003). *Correctional mental health handbook.* Thousand Oaks, CA: Sage.

Huss, M. T. (2001). Psychology and law, now and in the next century: The promise of an emerging area of psychology. In J. S. Halonen & S. F. Davis (Eds.), *The many faces of psychological research in the 21st century.* Society for the Teaching of Psychology. Retrieved February 13, 2006, from http://teachpsych.lemoyne.edu/teachpsych/faces/text/Chll.htm

Kuther, T. L. (2004). *Your career in psychology: Psychology and the law.* Belmont, CA: Wadsworth.

Melton, G. B., Petrila, J., Poythress, N. G., & Slobogin, C. (1997). *Psychological evaluations for the courts: A handbook for mental health professionals and lawyers* (2nd ed.). New York: Guilford Press.

Stern, R. (1988). *Law enforcement careers: A complete guide from application to employment.* Tarzana, CA: Lawman Press.

Weiner, I. B., & Hess, A. K. (2006). *The handbook of forensic psychology* (3rd ed.). New York: Wiley.

WEB RESOURCES

American Psychology-Law Society
    http://www.ap-ls.org
American Society of Trial Consultants
    http://www.astcweb.org
Federal Bureau of Prisons
    http://www.bop.gov
Corrections Connection
    http://www.corrections.com
Law and Society Association
    http://www.lawandsociety.org
Mental Health in Corrections Consortium
    http://www.forest.edu/mhcca/index-main.html

National Criminal Justice Reference Service
   http://www.ncjrs.org
National Institute of Corrections
   http://www.nicic.org
National Institute of Justice
   http://www.ojp.usdoj.gov/nij
Police Stress
   http://www.policefamilies.com
Police Psychology Online
   http://www.policepsych.com

CHECKLIST: IS LEGAL OR FORENSIC PSYCHOLOGY FOR YOU?

Do you:

- ☐ Enjoy shows like *Law and Order, CSI, or COPS?*
- ☐ Have an interest in politics?
- ☐ Think offenders have rights and should be treated justly and fairly?
- ☐ Think some people are so mentally ill that they shouldn't be punished for the bad things they do?
- ☐ Think you could try to help someone who murdered or raped someone?
- ☐ Think you could try to help someone who abused a child?
- ☐ Like solving puzzles?
- ☐ Like reading about criminal activity in your local newspaper?
- ☐ Like reading biographies about high-profile criminals?
- ☐ Think you would like to work in a prison?
- ☐ Like studying about mental illness?
- ☐ Like a good debate?
- ☐ Like people to challenge your thoughts and opinions?
- ☐ Like to write?

Scoring: The more boxes you checked, the more likely it is that legal or forensic psychology is for you.

HEALTH AND SPORT PSYCHOLOGY

CHAPTER GUIDE

The events of September 11, 2001, created chaos in New York City and Washington, D.C., as well as fear, anxiety, anger, and myriad other feelings for all citizens of the United States. In 2005, Hurricane Katrina resulted in similar emotions in New Orleans and Mississippi. These traumatic events raised health concerns for U.S. citizens, not only those directly traumatized by these events, but also those exposed to toxins and disease in relief efforts. How do people cope with such life-altering medical situations?

Further, in the days that followed the September 11 attacks on New York and Washington, all major sporting events were cancelled. This raised a debate about the role of professional athletics, such as major league baseball, in maintaining the morale and patriotism of U.S. citizens. How did professional athletes remain focused on their sports while the remainder of the world reeled from the devastation?

Questions such as these are at the heart of two of the most recent disciplines in psychology: health psychology and sport psychology. Although health and sport psychology are distinct disciplines with differing training requirements and professional activities, they share an emphasis on increasing functioning, whether it be physiological functioning, in health psychology, or athletic performance, in sport psychology.

HEALTH PSYCHOLOGY

Health psychology is the study of psychological influences on health, why people become ill and how people respond when they become ill, as well as the application of preventive strategies and interventions aimed at helping people maintain or improve their health (Taylor, 1999). Health psychologists study the interactive influences of biological, behavioral, and social factors on health and illness (American Psychological Association Division 38, n.d.). In other words, health psychologists examine how our emotions, thoughts, behaviors, and social interactions influence our physical well-being (that is, health and wellness) and response to illness. Health psychologists study ways to promote healthy behavior, as in helping people stop smoking, urging the use of sunblock, and sharing information on healthy eating. They also study how to prevent and treat illnesses through the use of behavioral management, stress management, and coping techniques. What are the effects of stress? Can stress lead to illness? Health psychologists study the role of psychological and social factors, such as stress and social support, in the development of disease.

Health psychologists may engage in applied activities, such as providing psychological services for the prevention or treatment of health-related problems and behaviors, or they may do research and academic activities, such as conducting research to investigate health-related issues and behaviors or teaching at a university. Health psychologists are also found in medical settings, such as primary care programs, inpatient medical units, medical schools, and specialized health care programs (pain management centers, long-term care facilities, rehabilitation centers, and so forth).

SPORT PSYCHOLOGY

Sport psychology is related to health psychology in that it emphasizes the improvement of physical functioning. The difference is that sport psychology focuses on athletic function rather than overall health. *Sport psychology* can be defined as the "study of the psychological aspects of sport" (Anderson, 2000; p. xiii); however, sport psychology isn't limited to sports and may include any type of physical activity or exercise (American Psychological Association Division 47, 2004). Thus, sport psychology services may address any aspect of athletes' or performers' lives, competitive or otherwise, to assist them in their performance and life endeavors (Anderson, 2000).

Sport psychologists examine topics such as the ways an athlete can use visualization techniques to improve performance, ways to manage performance anxiety, and ways sports teams can cooperate to work more effectively together. Like other psychologists, some sport psychologists conduct research in academic, clinical, government, and business settings. Others engage in clinical or consulting practice, helping individuals and teams improve their athletic performance and training coaches to help them become more efficient and productive in leading athletic teams. It's easy to see why students are intrigued by sport psychology as the philosophy and principles of improving performance work for more than just athletes—they are effective beyond the field as well.

OPPORTUNITIES WITH A BACHELOR'S DEGREE

If you're interested in health or sport psychology, you'll be glad to know that these fields offer many opportunities for bachelor's degree holders to work in rewarding careers that challenge them to use their general training in psychology as well as any specialized knowledge in health and sport psychology. Examples of such careers include fitness instructor and recreational worker, physical education teacher, recreational therapist, and occupational therapy assistant.

Fitness Instructor and Recreational Worker

Fitness instructors and recreational workers develop, plan, organize, and direct recreational activities—such as aerobics, arts and crafts, performing arts, camping, and recreational sports—for both healthy and physically or psychologically disabled people. In other words, fitness instructors and recreational workers are not limited to a specific clientele or people with particular health-related issues. Fitness instructors and recreational workers are employed in educational and university settings, nursing homes, parks-and-recreation centers, community activity centers, health clubs and fitness centers, and medical and rehabilitation centers. Fitness instructors and recreational workers often major in recreational studies, such as parks-and-recreation or leisure studies, or in other related fields, such as health science (Bureau of Labor Statistics, 2004). However, psychology majors, particularly when accompanied by a dual major or minor in recreational studies or related fields, are highly competitive for this career, because psychology provides broad-based training in human functioning and development.

Typical activities of fitness and recreational workers vary depending on agency type and clientele. For example, directors of parks-and-recreation programs spend the majority of their time developing and managing recreational programs in parks, playgrounds, and other child-oriented settings (Bureau of Labor Statistics, 2004). Although they may be responsible for parks-and-recreation budgets, they may also work directly with program participants. Camp counselors, on the other hand, are recreational workers who "lead and instruct" children and adolescents in outdoor activities such as swimming and boating, horseback riding, camping, hiking, sports, music, drama, art, and computers. Recreational workers may also assume more of a therapeutic role in residential camps, where they provide assistance in skill building to individuals lacking daily-living skills, social skills, and problem-solving skills. Fitness workers, on the other hand, coach groups or individuals in sports or exercise activities with the goal of developing skills or promoting physical fitness and healthy living (Bureau of Labor Statistics, 2004).

Median salaries for recreational workers ($18,075) and fitness instructors ($23,940) are modest for entry-level positions. However, one of the benefits of these careers is the opportunity to advance to supervisory positions or to pursue self-employment as a personal trainer, both of which offer salary increases. The job market for fitness instructors is very favorable; however, positions for recreational workers tend to be more competitive (Bureau of Labor Statistics, 2004). Advantages of these jobs include the employment setting: The work requires much time spent outdoors in parks, the wilderness, or near water, as well as other unique employment settings including vacation getaway spots. Imagine the enjoyment of working as a recreational worker on a cruise ship, on an island resort in the Bahamas, or at a secluded mountain spa. Although such positions remain highly coveted, and therefore competitive, such opportunities do exist. Another benefit is health—a fitness career will require you to maintain your fitness. As mentioned, the primary limitation of this career choice is the modest salary, along with the competition for entry-level positions for recreational workers. Recognize, however, that those with a bachelor's degree will most likely fare more favorably, because many applicants for recreational positions will be applying with an associate degree or a high school diploma.

Physical Education Teacher

Physical education (PE) teachers rarely major in psychology. Even so, training in psychology, such as a double major or minor in it, may prove to be a great asset to PE teachers. Recall that Chapters 2 and 4 provided a review of the role of psychology in academic and school settings. Here, we focus on the ways that specialized information in health and sports psychology can benefit PE teachers. Undergraduate course work in health and sport psychology can particularly help PE teachers in their roles as educators, trainers, and coaches. A foundation in psychology provides the necessary tools and principals to motivate students as well as to access the best learning strategies, such as principles of reinforcement and over-learning for skill development. In addition, PE teachers are rarely restricted to the gym; thus a degree in psychology, especially with a focus on health and sport psychology, may make you more competitive as you market yourself dually as a teacher of physical education as well as health and psychology-related classes. The advantages and disadvantages, as well as the salary, for a PE teacher are similar to those of other educators; we refer you to Chapters 2 and 4 for a review of this information.

Recreational Therapist

Recreational therapists provide treatment and recreational activities to individuals with physical or emotional disabilities in a variety of settings, including medical settings, prisons, and community-based programs such as parks and recreation, special education programs for students, adult-living programs, and community mental health centers (Bureau of Labor Statistics, 2004). Recreational therapists differ from recreational workers in that the therapists provide treatment services to assist individuals with disabilities or problems and deficits, whereas recreational workers generally work with healthy and/or disabled individuals and emphasize developing their clients' interests rather than treating problems.

Recreational therapists assess and treat individuals with physical or psychological problems. They use standardized assessments and observations, medical records, and collateral information to assess clients' problems and develop treatment strategies targeting the physical, mental, or emotional well-being of clients. Typical treatment activities include arts and crafts, pet therapy, gardening, sports, games, dance and movement, drama, music, and community outings, as well as specific strategies such as stress management and relaxation techniques. Recreational therapists frequently are employed in hospitals, nursing homes, community-based programs such as assisted living and outpatient physical and psychiatric rehabilitation, residential and correctional centers, adult day-care facilities, and social service agencies (Bureau of Labor Statistics, 2004).

The median salary for recreational therapists in 2002 was $30,540. Although the job outlook for this profession has slowed in recent years (Bureau of Labor Statistics, 2004), the rapidly growing number of aging adults ensures that this will remain a viable profession for many. Another benefit of this profession is the opportunity for advancement. Therapists may grow weary of the therapeutic contact and physical energy required to provide recreational therapy on a daily basis, particularly as they themselves age; however, this profession offers the chance to advance to supervisory positions or to pursue teaching interests in the field (Bureau of Labor Statistics, 2004). Recreational therapists typically have a bachelor's degree. Psychology's emphasis on understanding behavior, coupled with training in therapeutic recreation, would suit you well in this career.

Occupational Therapy Assistant

Occupational therapy assistants help occupational therapists provide rehabilitative services to patients with physical, developmental, or psychological impairments (Bureau of Labor Statistics, 2004). Occupational therapy assistants are not limited to working with patients who are attempting to reenter the labor force; rather, this work is much broader and focuses on any aspect of a patient's life, for example, developing the skills necessary for independent living such as cooking, cleaning, and accessing transportation. Aides to occupational therapists are intimately involved with all aspects of a patient's rehabilitation from disabilities caused by injuries (as in an automobile accident); they also help individuals with developmental disabilities such as mental retardation to acquire skills for independent living.

Occupational therapy assistants may work with occupational therapists in hospitals, outpatient clinics, and offices. In a private medical office, the hours may vary or include evenings or weekends in order to accommodate client schedules. In clinics and hospital settings, the hours tend to be more traditional (8:00 to 5:00). The job outlook for occupational therapy assistants is outstanding, because the job market is expected to grow much faster than the average occupation over the next 10 years. Salaries of occupational therapy assistants are competitive, with a median salary of $36,660 (Bureau of Labor Statistics, 2004). One disadvantage of this career choice is the physical demand. Occupational therapy assistants must be strong enough to help lift patients (including overweight ones) as well as to stand, kneel, bend, stoop, and move from station to station for long periods of the day.

Note that a bachelor's degree is not sufficient for this occupation; a certificate in occupational therapy is also required (Bureau of Labor Statistics, 2004). It may be advisable to complete two years of college in a field such as psychology and then work toward the completion of the certificate program. Most states regulate this career option, and occupational therapy assistants must pass a national certification examination before being appropriately credentialed to practice. For more information, consult the American Occupational Therapy Association at http://www.aota.org.

OPPORTUNITIES WITH A GRADUATE DEGREE

The specialized nature of a career in health and sport psychology generally requires a PhD or PsyD degree that includes specialized training during the year-long internship and/or postdoctoral experience. In other words, the majority of health and sport psychologists receive general training as counseling or clinical psychologists, then gain specialized training in the health or sport psychology fields. The various occupational opportunities that follow such training include academia and program development, medical support, private practice and consultation, and public health.

Health Psychologist

Before proceeding with our discussion of careers in health psychology, let's first clear up some potentially confusing terminology. *Health psychology* is a subfield of psychology and has frequently been referred to as behavioral medicine, medical psychology, and psychosomatic medicine; however, these terms are neither accurate nor appropriate. *Behavioral medicine* is the most commonly used alternative term, but it is an interdisciplinary term (including behavioral and biomedical science), and psychologists practice psychology, not behavioral medicine (Belar & Deardorff, 1995). Thus, *health psychology* is the most appropriate term for this specialized field, and so we use it in this chapter.

Health psychologists earn a doctoral degree in psychology (Belar, 1997), with the health psychology specialization occurring during internship and postdoctoral training. Because scientific knowledge in health psychology has experienced considerable growth in the past two decades, there are many career opportunities for health psychologists, and the potential to expand clinical practice in this area is dramatic (Belar et al., 2001). In fact, the management of health and disease is one of the fastest-growing research and practice specialties in professional psychology (Levant et al., 2001). Health psychologists are employed in myriad settings, which often determine the professional activities that are performed. Let's take a closer look at the settings and activities in which health psychologists engage.

Academic and Research Settings   In academia and research settings, health psychologists teach, conduct research to understand and treat illnesses, and develop preventive and treatment programs to avoid or reduce health-related problems and concerns. Like other professors, health psychologists in academia teach undergraduate and graduate students about the field and conduct research to expand the field.

Although health psychologists engaged in research are not directly involved in client care, their work often profoundly affects the care that clients receive. Research conducted by health psychologists provides practitioners with information about lifestyle and personality factors as well as the psychosocial factors that influence health (Sarafino, 2002). Researchers develop and evaluate therapeutic programs aimed at improving healthy functioning or reducing the likelihood of illness (such as smoking cessation programs), as well as programs aimed at treating existing conditions (such as stress-reduction programs for people with coronary heart disease). As the goals of these programs are to increase the well-being and health of individuals in high-risk groups (such as patients with high blood pressure) or those actively engaged in risky behaviors (such as smokers), researchers greatly influence the health and care of today's medical patient.

We have already discussed the benefits and pitfalls, as well as the credentials and job responsibilities, of an academic career (see Chapter 2). Note here, however, that health psychologists tend to have specialized training that frequently includes postdoctoral experience, which can lead to slightly higher salaries than most other assistant professors.

Service Delivery Settings   Health psychology service providers are employed in hospitals, long-term care facilities, rehabilitation centers, medical schools, or private practice. In each of these settings, health psychologists provide assessment and intervention services and usually collaborate with other health care professionals such as physicians, dentists, nurses, physician's assistants, dietitians, social workers, pharmacists, physical and occupational therapists, and chaplains in an effort to provide comprehensive and holistic health care (American Psychological Association Division 38, n.d.). The clinical activities of health psychologists generally include assessment activities or prevention/intervention services.

Health psychologists often conduct assessments in conjunction with other medical professionals to determine the etiology (cause of) and correlates of healthful living and health-related problems (S. E. Taylor, 1999). Assessments conducted by health psychologists may include cognitive and/or behavioral assessments, psychophysical assessments, personality assessments, demographic surveys and clinical interviews, and other clinical protocols (American Psychological Association Division 38, n.d.).

Further, health psychologists may provide treatment services, which aim at either prevention or intervention. The goal of prevention is to help people improve their lifestyle and avoid major illnesses or health complications, whereas interventions target existing health-related problems with a focus on helping people cope with or adjust to those problems (Kaplan, Sallis, & Patterson, 1993). Examples of preventive care include programs aimed at educating at-risk populations or the general population about the importance of lifestyle improvements. For instance, the Just Say No to Drugs program addresses a problem area, whereas programs advocating the health benefits of exercise and a proper nutritional diet work toward wellness for all people. Examples of interventions include stress management for medical patients with high blood pressure and pain management for people who have been injured in an accident. Health psychologists not only design and implement treatment strategies but also conduct research to assess the effectiveness of prevention and intervention programs, as research and assessment activities often occur simultaneously.

The benefits of a career in health psychology service delivery, especially in medical settings, include a slightly elevated salary compared with that of other psychologists. Benefits also include the opportunity to influence directly the quality of life and wellness of clients in a relatively short time; treatment gains in health psychology may be slightly more rapid than treatment gains by psychologists treating other problems or concerns such as severe mental illness. An advantage of becoming a health psychologist in private practice or developing a consulting career is flexibility in scheduling clients. One limitation of a career choice in health psychology service delivery is the occasional experience of not being well received by the medical community, where the MD is the preferred degree (compared with the PhD or PsyD). However, psychologists' contribution to wellness and healthy living is becoming increasingly recognized, particularly as the biopsychosocial model of health and illness becomes more widely accepted within the medical community (Sarafino, 2002).

Public Health Settings   Health psychologists also pursue careers in public health. Psychologists in public health settings are usually involved in researching health issues, teaching and training future professionals, providing public health practice and service, or consulting with health organizations, professionals, and political leaders (Baskin, 2005). For example, psychologists in public health may develop or evaluate programs for public health organizations, or they may pursue involvement in social policy. Program developers, as we've discussed, are responsible for developing and implementing health-related programs in communities to promote wellness and healthy living or to treat health-related problems or concerns. For example, program developers may implement community-based AIDS education and support programs. Health psychologists in social policy positions, on the other hand, spend their time developing and drafting legal statutes and proposals in an effort to create federal or state legislation that promotes wellness and health. An example of such legislation is the requirement that tobacco products carry warning labels on their packaging to warn customers of the health risks associated with using these products.

A primary benefit of seeking employment as a health psychologist in public health is the opportunity to influence directly the services available to communities and individuals in need. Unfortunately, the time to develop and implement services can be extensive, which can frustrate professionals when faced with people in need or other urgent problems. Salaries in public health are comparable to those of other psychology-related positions discussed in this text. For more information on policy-related careers, see Chapter 11.

Sport Psychologist

Sport psychology is a stimulating field offering a variety of career opportunities (Carter, 2005). Educational requirements for sport psychology generally are more flexible than for other psychology careers. Academic degrees may be earned from departments of physical education, psychology, counseling, or sports science. In fact, sport psychology is a multidisciplinary field: Course work usually includes psychology and counseling, as well as exercise physiology, sport sociology, and biomechanics (American Psychological Association Division 47, 2003). Although many employment opportunities for sport psychologists require the completion of a doctoral degree, some opportunities exist for individuals with a master's degree. Note, however, that master's-level professionals encounter a more limited and competitive job market. Regardless of the educational track being pursued, students should seek specialized training, such as internships, that provide experience in the field of sport psychology. Unfortunately, such opportunities are limited.

Sport psychologists have three primary roles: practice, research, and teaching (American Psychological Association Division 47, 2003). However, sport psychology is a highly specialized field that has lent itself to less career diversity than have other areas of psychology. The vast majority of sport psychologists are employed in academic settings (47 percent) and private practice (37 percent) (Meyers, Coleman, Whelan, & Mehlenbeck, 2001).

Academic and Research Settings   Within academia, sport psychologists may be affiliated with departments of psychology, sports exercise programs, and PE programs. Not surprisingly, within academia they spend the majority of their time in teaching and research activities, with some time available for consulting or service delivery activities (Meyers et al., 2001). The aim of sport psychology research is to identify the effects of athletic participation (including exercise and other physical activities) on development, health, and overall well-being throughout the lifespan (American Psychological Association Division 47, 2003). Much of this research focuses on strategies for improving athletic performance; however, sport psychologists also are interested in the overall life functioning of athletes and performers. Therefore, issues of life satisfaction, vocational plans for retired athletes, and relationship issues are a few examples of the varied research interests of sport psychologists.

As is true with other psychological specialties, academic careers in sport psychology afford the opportunity to collaborate with other professionals. Another benefit is the potential for access to an athletic population via college sports teams, as well as a flexible schedule that allows the pursuit of practice or consultation interests. The primary pitfall for academically inclined sport psychologists is the job demand, as competition is at a premium because of the limited number of available positions at any given time. Academic salaries of sport psychologists are consistent with those of other academic psychologists (Meyers et al., 2001).

Practice Settings   The goal of the practicing sport psychologist is to use psychological principles to help athletes and performers achieve optimal physical performance (American Psychological Association Division 47, 2004).

For example, techniques such as relaxation, imagery, self-talk, and goal setting help athletes improve their performance (Anderson, 2000). Relaxation strategies are taught to athletes and performers to reduce anxiety and stress in order to maximize performance (Sherman & Poczwardowski, 2000). Sport psychologists direct athletes to use imagery (Simmons, 2000) and self-talk (Perry & Marsh, 2000) before, during, and after an event to improve their focus and mental clarity with the expectation of improved performance. Goal setting is used with athletes and performers to increase their sense of self-control and to enhance performance over the long term (Marchant, 2000).

Sport psychologists tend to enjoy a flexible work environment. A sport psychologist may see an athlete in the office but also may travel to the relevant athletic arena for service delivery. For example, a sport psychologist may work with a golfer at the driving range or putting green to implement focusing strategies previously discussed in the office. A sport psychologist working with a basketball player may meet the client at the arena to implement relaxation strategies while shooting free throws. Thus, careers in sport psychology require flexibility and often creativity for service delivery. Sport psychologists who provide services are employed in university counseling centers, sports medicine clinics, consulting agencies, and private practice.

Sport psychologists who work in private practice provide clients with performance enhancement, life skills training, organizational consulting, psychotherapy and counseling interventions, and rehabilitation (Danish, Petitpas, & Hale, 1993). Private practice, however, tends to be less financially successful and stable for sport psychologists than is academia; practitioners often must supplement their income by providing non-sports-related psychological services (Meyers et al., 2001). Once supplemented, the income of sport psychologists in private practice appears equivalent to that of other psychologists in private practice. Furthermore, sport psychologists who are fortunate enough to be affiliated with collegiate or professional teams and athletes tend to have higher incomes than do sport psychologists who are not.

Throughout this chapter, we've seen that the fields of health psychology and sport psychology offer knowledge and training that is relevant to many careers at the bachelor's and graduate levels. At the bachelor's level, careers tend to be multidisciplinary. If you're interested in pursuing a health or sports-related position with your baccalaureate degree, supplement your academic training in psychology with courses in other health- and recreation-related areas such as health education, nutrition, and safety. Careers at the doctoral level are more specialized. If you're considering a graduate-level career in health or sport psychology, pursue generalist training during graduate school (that is, clinical or counseling psychology programs), followed by specialized training in health or sport psychology during internship or postdoctoral work.

Suggested Readings

Anderson, M. B. (Ed.). (2000). *Doing sport psychology.* Champaign, IL: Human Kinetics.

Baskin, M. L. (2005). Public health: Career opportunities for psychologists in public health. In R. D. Morgan, T. L. Kuther, & C. J. Habben (Eds.), *Life after graduate school in psychology: Insider's advice from new psychologists.* New York: Psychology Press.

Belar, C. D., & Deardorff, W. W. (1995). *Clinical health psychology in medical settings: A practitioner's guidebook.* Washington, DC: American Psychological Association.

Boll, T. J., Johnson, S. B., Perry, N., & Rozensky, R. H. (2002). *Handbook of clinical health psychology: Volume 1. Medical disorders and behavioral applications.* Washington, DC: American Psychological Association.

Carter, J. E. (2005). Sport psychology: Locker room confessions. In R. D. Morgan, T. L. Kuther, & C. J. Habben (Eds.), *Life after graduate school in psychology: Insider's advice from new psychologists* (pp. 275–287). New York: Psychology Press.

Cohen, L., McChargue, D., & Collins, E (2003). *The health psychology handbook: Practical issues for the behavioral medicine specialist.* Thousand Oaks, CA: Sage.

Van Raalte, J. L., & Brewer, B. W. (2002). *Exploring sport and exercise psychology* (2nd ed.). Washington, DC: American Psychological Association.

Web Resources

American Psychological Association, Division of Health Psychology (Division 38)
   http://www.health-psych.org

Society of Behavioral Medicine
   http://www.sbm.org

Association for the Advancement of Applied Sport Psychology
   http://www.aaasponline.org/index.php

European Federation of Sport Psychology
   http://www.psychology.lu.se/FEPSAC

Sport Psychology OverSite
   http://www-personal.umich.edu/~bing/oversite/sportpsych.html

Athletic Insight: The Online Journal of Sports Psychology
   http://www.athleticinsight.com

Sports and Performance Psychology
   http://www.selfhelpmagazine.com/articles/sports/index.shtml

Health Psychology and Rehabilitation
   http://www.healthpsych.com

The Health Psychology Network
   http://www.healthpsychology.net

CHECKLIST: IS HEALTH OR SPORT PSYCHOLOGY FOR YOU?

Do you:

☐   Want to work in a medical setting?

☐   Want to understand medical problems better ?

☐   Want to conduct research with the aim of helping people with health problems?

☐   Enjoy reading about health problems or concerns?

☐   Find satisfaction in the recent tobacco settlements?

☐   Want to help people live healthier lives?

☐   Want to understand the effects of stress and lifestyle choices on health?

☐   Have interest in the growing health concerns across the globe?

☐   Enjoy sports?

☐   Want to work with athletes?

☐   Like conducting research?

☐   Want to learn more about athletic performance?

☐   Often wonder why some people succeed whereas others fail?

☐   Want to understand how the mind influences the body?

Scoring: The more boxes you checked, the more likely it is that health or sport psychology is a good match for you.

BIOPSYCHOLOGY, COGNITIVE NEUROPSYCHOLOGY, AND CLINICAL NEUROPSYCHOLOGY

CHAPTER GUIDE

Do children act aggressively because they inherited an aggressive gene, or do they learn aggressive behavior early in life? Are quiet people born shy, or do they develop shyness in response to their early environment? You've undoubtedly been asked to think about such nature-versus-nurture issues in your college education, and you've probably found it difficult to develop satisfactory answers. Don't worry, you're not alone! In fact, an entire field of psychology is devoted to one aspect of these questions—the study of the biological bases of behavior.

Technological breakthroughs—such as DNA research, cloning, and stem cell research—are rapidly advancing scientific knowledge in the biological sciences. What do these advances mean for psychology? With increased technology and refined research methods, we can identify more accurately the biological processes and neurological functioning that impacts human behavior. Thus, biopsychology, cognitive neuropsychology, and clinical neuropsychology have enormous potential for altering our understanding of human behavior. This will not only increase our knowledge base but will also influence how psychology is applied in the real world. Before discussing applications of biopsychology, cognitive neuropsychology, and clinical neuropsychology, let's spend some time defining the fields.

BIOPSYCHOLOGY

Biopsychology, or physiological psychology, is the branch of psychology that studies the relationship between biology and behavior (Myers, 2001). Biopsychology integrates various areas of neuroscience to explain the biological bases of behavior. These areas include neuroanatomy, the study of the structure of the nervous system; neurochemistry, the study of the chemical composition of neural activity; neuroendocrinology, the study of the interplay between the nervous system and endocrine system; neuropathology, the study of disorders that affect the nervous system; and neuropharmacology, the study of how drugs affect neural activity. A biopsychologist might, for example, study how genetics and experience interact to influence behavior. Others might study the influence of hormones and other chemicals on behavior, addressing such questions as: Is there a "love hormone?" or Do gambling and other risky behaviors release endorphins into the bloodstream? Biopsychologists predominantly work as researchers and academicians, employed by universities, government, research institutes, and pharmaceutical companies.

COGNITIVE NEUROPSYCHOLOGY

Cognitive neuropsychology is a branch of cognitive psychology that aims to understand cognition from the perspective of the brain, thereby merging cognitive psychology and biopsychology. Cognitive neuropsychologists study the brain to understand the neural bases of mental processes such as thinking, memory, attention, and language (S. Carpenter, 2001). A cognitive neuropsychologist may use brain-imaging techniques to study what happens in people's brains when they tackle math problems (Murray, 2000). How does the brain of someone with dyslexia function differently from a typical brain? What areas of the brain are responsible for language, short-term memory, or decision making? Cognitive neuropsychologists conduct research to examine how neural activity translates into mental activity: How do collections of neurons communicate and how do we interpret that communication as thought? As you might guess, cognitive neuropsychology is primarily a research-oriented field, and cognitive neuropsychologists are found in a variety of research and academic settings.

CLINICAL NEUROPSYCHOLOGY

Whereas cognitive neuropsychology represents the joining of cognitive psychology and biopsychology, clinical neuropsychology applies findings from biopsychology within clinical and counseling contexts. *Clinical neuropsychology* is the application of psychological assessments and interventions based on the study of the central nervous system (American Psychological Association Division of Clinical Neuropsychology, 1989). In other words, clinical neuropsychology integrates biopsychology and clinical/counseling psychology to assist clients suffering from brain dysfunction, such as a patient suffering memory loss following a traumatic brain injury.

Clinical neuropsychologists conduct neuropsychological assessments to identify the extent of brain damage or severity of impairment in clients. They also develop interventions to help clients adapt or regain function in order to maximize the potential for independent living and a good quality of life. Like other psychologists, clinical neuropsychologists work in applied settings such as medical hospitals, clinics, and private practice, as well as in university settings as academics or in academia, government, or industry as researchers.

OPPORTUNITIES WITH A BACHELOR'S DEGREE

Although much training in biopsychology or neuropsychology occurs at the graduate level, students with interests at the baccalaureate level have many career options, including science technician, psychiatric aide, psychiatric technician, clinical laboratory technician, and pharmacy technician. These positions provide students an opportunity to apply their knowledge of psychology along with their knowledge and interest in biopsychology.

Science Technician

Science technicians are involved in laboratory research and "use the principals and theories of science and mathematics to solve problems in research and development" (Bureau of Labor Statistics, 2004). They are a scientist's "hands," so to speak. They maintain scientific laboratories, operate and maintain laboratory instruments and equipment, monitor experiments, make observations and record data, and work with scientists who are forming conclusions based on experiments and lab work. Because many fields require technical assistance, there are many different kinds of technicians. Thus, professional titles are designated according to the specific field, such as agricultural technician, forensic science technician, or nuclear technician (Bureau of Labor Statistics, 2004). Bachelor's degree holders in psychology with interests in biopsychology may choose positions as biological technicians or research technicians.

In collaboration with biologists, biological technicians study living organisms and may be involved in medical or pharmaceutical research in microbiological or biotechnological laboratories (Bureau of Labor Statistics, 2004). Examples of such research include studying cures for physiological diseases, such as Alzheimer's and AIDS, or analyzing organic substances and the effects of chemicals on the treatment of mental illness. Other research technicians may assist biopsychologists with their research. Science technicians typically work in research laboratories. Sometimes, though, they work in other settings; for example, a crime scene may be the "laboratory" of a forensic science technician (Bureau of Labor Statistics, 2004).

The job outlook for science technicians is expected to remain steady through 2012. Competitive salaries are one of the advantages of a career as a science technician. For example, in 2003, biological technicians working in government settings earned an average salary of $30,440, and physical science technicians earned $44,068 (Bureau of Labor Statistics, 2004). As in other fields, the salaries of science technicians fluctuate by employer (private employers tend to pay more than the government) and type of science work (forensic science technicians earn slightly more than do biological technicians). In addition to salary, the perks of this job include a comfortable working environment (laboratories are typically comfortable), casual dress codes (the laboratory can get messy, so most science technicians wear jeans and casual clothing to work), and a 40-hour workweek with normal business hours. The primary disadvantage of this career is the limited opportunity to develop and design research projects of your own interest. Although science technicians may have input into the research they are working on, typically the employer or agency being served determines the focus of research studies. If you're interested in this career choice, supplement your biopsychology training with additional research and laboratory-related coursework, such as biology, chemistry, and physics. The more laboratory experience you have, the greater your marketability.

Psychiatric Technician

A career as a psychiatric technician involves assisting psychiatrists or other mental health professionals in their care of mentally ill or emotionally disturbed patients (Bureau of Labor Statistics, 2004). A psychiatric technician follows both a physician's instructions and hospital procedures, monitors patients' physical and emotional well-being, reports to medical staff, and may also provide therapeutic services and administer medications. Psychiatric technicians may also develop specialized skills, such as providing biofeedback in a clinic or for a private practitioner or providing EEG services in a sleep disorder clinic.

Rewards of a career as a psychiatric technician include direct work with clients, the chance to make a difference in someone's life, and the opportunity to work with an interdisciplinary team (Health—psychiatric technician, 2002). Unfortunately, this career can be stressful, with limited job opportunities and few chances for advancement. Compared with other health care professionals, salaries in this field are marginal; as a psychiatric technician, you can expect to earn an entry salary of $26,000 (Salary.com, 2005). If you're interested in becoming a psychiatric technician, supplement your psychology coursework with courses in nursing and seek certification as a psychiatric technician (available through many colleges and universities).

Clinical Laboratory Technologist or Technician

Graduates with biopsychology interests sometimes obtain positions within clinical laboratories, as clinical laboratory technicians or clinical laboratory technologists, where they play a vital role in detecting, diagnosing, and treating diseases through their work analyzing a patient's physical samples (such as body fluids, tissues, and cells). Clinical laboratory technicians conduct work similar to that of science technicians. Under the supervision of laboratory technologists or managers, they maintain the laboratory, prepare specimens, and conduct basic tests either manually or with automated analyzers (Bureau of Labor Statistics, 2004).

Clinical laboratory technologists supervise technicians and perform sophisticated medical testing including "chemical, biological, hematological, immunological, microscopic, and bacteriological tests" (Bureau of Labor Statistics, 2004). In other words, clinical laboratory technologists conduct the sophisticated medical tests that your physician orders when you visit for a routine exam or suspect that you are ill; these include testing for blood glucose and cholesterol levels or searching for microscopic signs of pathology in blood and tissue samples. Clinical laboratory technologists "make cultures of body fluid and tissue samples to determine the presence of bacteria, fungi, parasites, or other microorganisms" (Bureau of Labor Statistics, 2004).

The job outlook for clinical laboratory workers over the next 10 years is excellent, with more job openings than qualified professionals to fill them. As a clinical laboratory technologist, you can expect to earn approximately $42,910 per year. Disadvantages to a clinical laboratory career include physical hazards, which include handling infectious agents. In addition, clinical laboratory personnel often are exposed to fumes for significant periods and spend a significant portion of their work day on their feet (Bureau of Labor Statistics, 2004).

If you're considering a position within a clinical laboratory setting, understand that your psychology degree will enable you to pursue a position as a technician. For a technologist position, take additional courses in biology, chemistry, and medical technology to be competitive. Understand that some states require laboratory personnel to be certified, registered, or licensed, so contact your state department of health for more information (Bureau of Labor Statistics, 2004).

Pharmacy Technician

Pharmacy technicians often work in retail pharmacies, where they help pharmacists distribute medication and information to customers. Pharmacy technicians verify customer and prescription information, perform the many clerical duties that arise within a pharmacy, and prepare medications for patients, including counting medications and preparing bottle labels (Bureau of Labor Statistics, 2004).

Benefits of a career as a pharmacy technician include a very good job market for both full-time and part-time work. Benefits also include an opportunity to work directly with the public, making public relations an important aspect of this career. A career as a pharmacy technician typically offers a very comfortable work environment plus business hours. Salaries for pharmacy technicians are modest, with a median salary in 2002 of approximately $22,256. Additionally, opportunities for job advancement are limited. Higher salaries are available for those employed in hospital and grocery store pharmacies (Bureau of Labor Statistics, 2004).

Although formal pharmacy technician programs and certification are available and preferred by many employers, many pharmacy technicians are trained on the job (Bureau of Labor Statistics, 2004). As such, psychology graduates with emphasis in biopsychology should find themselves quite marketable for this career. Nevertheless, supplemental course work in chemistry is likely to enhance your application. Once employed, or prior to employment if you're trying to maximize your credentials, you may want to pursue certification via the Pharmacy Technician Certification Board, which administers a national exam for certification (Bureau of Labor Statistics, 2004; visit http://www.ptcb.org). Although this examination and certification are voluntary in most states, some states require certification, and a particular pharmacy or pharmacist may prefer or require it.

Opportunities with a Graduate Degree

A graduate degree in biopsychology, cognitive neuropsychology, or clinical neuropsychology is versatile, provides training for a career in teaching or research, and enables the pursuit of applied interests. Although some opportunities are available to master's degree holders, a doctoral degree is preferred for applied work. You may obtain a doctoral degree in biopsychology, cognitive neuropsychology, or cognitive psychology within a program that specializes in cognitive neuropsychology, or you may earn a doctorate in clinical/counseling psychology followed by specialized training in clinical neuropsychology during the year-long internship and/or postdoctoral training. Let's take a closer look at the academic and applied work of biopsychologists, cognitive neuropsychologists, and clinical neuropsychologists.

Academia

By now you probably understand what academic careers are all about: teaching undergraduate and graduate students and conducting research to further the discipline. Like all other subfields in psychology, biopsychologists, clinical neuropsychologists, and cognitive neuropsychologists may pursue careers in academia, typically within departments of psychology. We described the salaries, benefits, and pitfalls of an academic career in Chapter 2. Here, a brief discussion of a challenge unique to an academic career within these subfields is warranted.

Biopsychologists, clinical neuropsychologists, and cognitive neuropsychologists in academia often require expensive laboratory equipment to conduct their research. Thus, getting a laboratory up and running can be problematic, because it requires significant space and money. Although the university provides start-up funds to help new faculty develop a psychophysiological or neuroanatomy lab, additional funds are often needed. Thus, psychologists must spend time on grant writing, which is time consuming and detracts from the research and publication that new professors are expected to do. Once received, though, grants offer new faculty many perks, including increased salary via summer pay, course release time, paid research assistants, and status within the department.

Research

In addition to academia, biopsychologists, clinical neuropsychologists, and cognitive neuropsychologists may pursue research careers in pharmaceutical or biotechnology companies (as well as within government settings, as described in Chapter 2). Researchers with pharmaceutical companies work to develop medications and evaluate the effectiveness of existing medicines. Researchers in biotechnology manipulate biological organisms to make products such as medicine and food products to benefit the human race (Levine, 2002). Psychologists employed in biotechnology agencies or companies may evaluate the effectiveness of a product or help develop new products.

A research career with a pharmaceutical or biotechnology company can be quite rewarding, because you'll have the opportunity to develop and evaluate products designed to benefit people, whether food or medicine. Starting salaries for researchers with established pharmaceutical companies stand typically well above other entry-level positions. You may expect to begin your first job earning more than $80,000 per year, with a rise to six figures expected in a short time (L. Cohen, personal communication, October 27, 2005). On the other hand, research positions with pharmaceutical and biotechnology companies can be stressful because fluctuations in the stock market and product development continually push developers and evaluators to produce new and better products. In this career your work is never done, as you will always be looking for ways to improve current products or produce new, more effective ones.

Applied Settings

Of the subfields discussed in this chapter, clinical neuropsychology most lends itself to an applied career. The most common practice of clinical neuropsychologists is neuropsychological diagnostic assessment to identify the extent of brain damage or severity of impairment. They may, for example, be asked to conduct an evaluation to discriminate between neurological and psychiatric symptoms, to identify a neurological disorder or help distinguish between different neurological conditions, or to help localize a lesion site. Other reasons for neuropsychological assessments include patient care and planning (including cognitive capacities), rehabilitation and treatment evaluations, and research purposes (Lezak, 1995).

The goals of clinical neuropsychological assessment differ from those of the general psychological evaluation. In the former, four primary goals exist: (1) to localize and diagnose cortical damage or dysfunction, (2) to facilitate patient treatment and rehabilitation, (3) to identify the presence of mild disturbance that is unrecognized in other examination procedures, and (4) to examine brain dysfunction in clients with a preexisting condition (Kolb & Whishaw, 1995). Aside from these goals, the neuropsychological assessment serves four primary functions in the treatment of mental health patients: diagnosis, treatment planning, rehabilitational evaluations, and research (Lezak, 1995).

As psychologists, clinical neuropsychologists are interested in behavior; behavior in this career refers to cognition, emotionality, and executive functioning. Lezak (1995, p. 22) defines *cognition* as including receptive functions (including the ability to "select, acquire, classify, and integrate information") and includes expressive functions (such as speaking), memory, constructional abilities (as with building blocks), attention and concentration, consciousness, and mentation (speed of mental activities). *Emotionality* refers to personality or emotional changes that occur following a brain injury. Finally, Lezak (1995, p. 42) refers to *executive functioning* as the abilities that contribute to the expression of behavior, specifically, "those capacities that enable a person to engage successfully in independent, purposive, self-serving behavior." Referral questions may include one or any combination of these behaviors, and these questions determine the type of neuropsychological evaluation to be conducted.

Examination procedures may include any or all of the following: clinical interview, detailed case history, mental status examination, or standardized neuropsychological assessments (Hallstead-Reitan Battery,

Luria-Nebraska Neuropsychological Battery), standardized psychological instruments such as intelligence tests (Wechsler Adult Intelligence Scale III, Wechsler Intelligence Scale for Children–IV, Stanford-Binet Intelligence Scale–Fifth Edition) and memory tests (Wechsler Memory Scale–III), other brief examination instruments to assess specific deficits (Rey Auditory-Verbal Learning Test, Rey-Osterrieth Complex Figure Test, Finger Tapping Test), personality assessment (Minnesota Multiphasic Personality Inventory–2), and vocational/occupational assessments. A thorough clinical neuropsychological assessment can be completed in 4 to 6 hours but may require 8 to 12 hours of testing. Thus, neuropsychologists in full-time practice may spend the majority of their time conducting and reporting the results of assessments.

Clinical neuropsychologists may also be involved in providing treatment and rehabilitation services. For example, they may provide therapeutic services to help patients adapt to their injuries or develop new skills to compensate for lost abilities. Although neuropsychologists occasionally use psychotherapy or counseling to assist patients and their families struggling to cope with the life-altering effects of a brain injury, they typically offer cognitive therapeutic services instead. In other words, the behaviors previously discussed as the targets of neuropsychological evaluations are the same behaviors that will be treated following a brain injury. For example, a patient suffering from short-term memory loss due to a stroke may by presented with memory strategies such as developing strategies which allow clients to remember information in "chunks" rather than individual units. In addition, the patient may be encouraged to participate in a game—such as "concentration" or the card game "memory"—that requires remembering information during the course of play.

Interventions, particularly rehabilitation, are becoming a primary task for clinical neuropsychologists (Golden, Zillmer, & Spiers, 1992). *Rehabilitation psychology* is the application of psychosocial principals to people with physical, sensory, cognitive, developmental, or emotional difficulties (American Psychological Association Division 22, n.d.) with a goal of helping clients "relearn" lost functions, develop new functions, or alter the environment to maximize quality of life (Golden et al., 1992).

An applied career as a clinical neuropsychologist offers many benefits. First, clinical neuropsychology is a very specialized field that typically allows for hourly billing at a rate greater than general psychological billing; thus, salaries of clinical neuropsychologists often exceed those of nonspecialized psychologists (see Chapter 3 for a review of applied psychology salaries). In addition, clinical neuropsychologists often receive special status in medical settings, because they work in conjunction with physicians and are the psychological professionals most closely aligned with the medical field. They may even be required to be present during brain surgery, for example, to map cognitive functions or to localize a lesion or a particular cognitive function. Lastly, clinical neuropsychology training affords a psychologist flexibility with regard to employment settings, and clinical neuropsychologists are employed in medical settings (such as hospitals, rehabilitation centers, specialty medical clinics, medical schools), private practice, private and public agencies, and other settings typical of the counseling and clinical psychologist without clinical neuropsychological training.

A primary drawback to an applied career as a clinical neuropsychologist is the amount of time spent writing reports. For every evaluation conducted, the clinical neuropsychologist must write a report, and these reports can be quite lengthy and time consuming. For example, you may expect to spend anywhere from one to six hours for a single report (D. Johnson, personal communication, October 27, 2005). Another disadvantage is the stress of continued work with severely injured people, including children. Automobile accidents, violent crime, and terrorism are a few of the types of incidents that lead to neurological damage, and clinical neuropsychologists must continually deal with these issues and their effects. On a positive note, clinical neuropsychology is one of the fastest-growing fields in professional psychology, and it will continue to be as our society continues to age. In fact, many consider clinical neuropsychology to be one of the leading careers for psychologists in the twenty-first century.

SUGGESTED READINGS

Adams, R. L., Parsons, O. A., & Culbertson, J. L. (Eds.). (1996). *Neuropsychology for clinical practice: Etiology, assessment, and treatment.* Washington DC: American Psychological Association.

Frank, R. G., & Elliott, T. R. (Eds.). (2000). *Handbook of rehabilitation psychology.* Washington, DC: American Psychological Association.

Kolb, B., & Whisaw, I. Q. (1995). *Fundamentals of human neuropsychology.* New York: Freeman.

Lezak, M. D. (1995). *Neuropsychological assessment* (3rd ed.). New York: Oxford University Press.

Myers, D. G. (2001). *Psychology* (6th ed). New York: Worth.

Snyder, P. J., & Nassbaum P. D. (Eds.). (1998). *Clinical neuropsychology: A pocket handbook for assessment.* Washington, DC: American Psychological Association.

WEB RESOURCES

Biopsychology.org
    http://www.biopsychology.org
American Board of Clinical Neuropsychology
    http://www.theabcn.org
American Academy of Clinical Neuropsychology
    http://www.theaacn.org
American Board of Professional Neuropsychology
    http://abpn.net/index.php
International Neuropsychological Society
    http://www.the-ins.org
National Academy of Neuropsychology
    http://nanonline.org
Behavioral Neuroscience and Comparative Psychology
    http://www.apa.org/divisions/div6
Rehabilitation Psychology
    http://www.apa.org/divisions/div22
Clinical Neuropsychology
    http://www.div40.org
Neuropsychology Central
    http://www.neuropsychologycentral.com
Neuropsychology Homepage
    http://www.tbidoc.com

CHECKLIST: IS BIOPSYCHOLOGY, CLINICAL NEUROPSYCHOLOGY, OR COGNITIVE NEUROPSYCHOLOGY FOR YOU?

Do you

☐   Enjoy biology classes?

☐   Remember dissecting frogs in biology class as a pleasant or nonaversive experience?

☐   Enjoy reading about the functions of the human brain?

☐   Get excited about human anatomy and biological functioning?

☐   Think you would enjoy conducting research aimed at identifying specific brain functioning?

☐   Want to work in a medical setting with brain-injured patients?

☐   Enjoy solving complex puzzles?

☐   Want to work in a hospital?

☐   Have an interest in technology?

☐   Believe that much of human behavior has a biological cause or component?

☐   Want to conduct neurological assessments?

☐   Want to help people overcome brain injuries and neurological problems?

☐   Like science?

☐   Want to go to graduate school?

☐   Want to conduct research (such as psychosurgery) with animals?

Scoring: The more boxes you checked, the more likely it is that a career in biopsychology, neuropsychology, or cognitive neuropsychology is for you.

INDUSTRIAL, ORGANIZATIONAL, AND HUMAN FACTORS PSYCHOLOGY

CHAPTER GUIDE

As we've seen, psychologists have a variety of career opportunities open to them. In this chapter, we explore the intersection of psychology and business. Several subdisciplines of psychology address the needs of business and industry: industrial psychology, organizational psychology, and human factors psychology. Collectively, these areas are referred to as "work psychology" (Patterson, 2001).

Psychologists work with owners, managers, and employees of business and industry to select, train, and manage employees; design and market products; and organize work environments. Industrial and organizational psychologists apply psychological principles to the workplace, and human factors psychologists apply psychological principles to the design of equipment, work spaces, and computer software. In this chapter, you'll learn about each of these areas of psychology and explore careers that combine psychology with business and industry.

INDUSTRIAL PSYCHOLOGY

Industrial psychology, sometimes called personnel psychology, is the study of individual behavior in work settings. A career as an industrial psychologist entails one or more of the following activities.

Selection and Placement

Careful selection and appropriate placement of employees promotes their job satisfaction and productivity. Industrial psychologists employ a scientific approach toward selecting and placing employees. They conduct job analyses to determine the specific tasks a job entails and the individual abilities and characteristics needed to be successful. They create, validate, and choose tests and interviews that are administered to job applicants to determine whether they should be hired and where they should be placed (Kasserman, 2005; Kuther, 2005). Placing employees involves identifying what jobs are most compatible with an employee's skills and interests, as assessed through questionnaires and interviews (Muchinsky, 2006). Industrial psychologists also follow up on employees to determine how well the assessment tests have predicted later job performance.

Training and Development

Industrial psychologists conduct needs analyses to determine the skills and technical needs of employees, and they develop training programs to impart those skills. They create assessment centers, collections of questionnaires, vignettes to assess problem-solving skills, and simulated work situations to determine an employee's skills and abilities (Aamodt, 2004; Tenopyr, 1997). Training needs may include assisting new employees during their transition to the workplace, updating current employees' technical skills, preparing employees for new responsibilities, and providing diversity training to address employees' attitudes, prejudices, and stereotypes (Muchinsky, 2006; Kasserman, 2005; Scrader, 2001). Industrial psychologists also devise methods for evaluating the effectiveness of training programs.

Performance Evaluation

Industrial psychologists determine the criteria or standards by which employees will be evaluated. In other words, they determine the ways to define employee success. Industrial psychologists choose, create, and validate methods for measuring the criteria for employee success. They assess employees' abilities and performance, providing feedback and documentation about the quality and quantity of an employee's work, which in turn is used to determine pay increases and promotions (Aamodt, 2004; Muchinsky, 2006). Industrial psychologists train supervisors to evaluate employee performance and to communicate the results to employees.

Laws and Litigation

Industrial psychologists understand legal issues related to the workplace, such as selecting, hiring, and promoting employees. They create policies and conduct regular training workshops to promote a positive work environment and to prevent harassment and other issues that harm it. Drawing on their knowledge of laws regulating personnel procedures, these psychologists prepare for litigation in response to complaints from employees and former employees under the various federal, state, and local civil rights acts (Tenopyr, 1997). They may advise the company's attorneys and explain the science behind a company's hiring and promotion policies (that is, the validity of the assessment tests and interviews). As expert court witnesses, industrial psychologists persuade judges and juries that work was done correctly. As you might imagine, industrial psychologists who design employee selection and placement procedures must learn a great deal about civil rights laws and build compliance with the laws into their research and development efforts (Aamodt, 2004; Tenopyr, 1997). They must understand the legal context for personnel decisions and help their employers make personnel decisions that are legal. Companies faced with layoffs seek advice from industrial psychologists on sensitive behaviors that will avoid litigation from disgruntled former employees (Murray, 2002).

ORGANIZATIONAL PSYCHOLOGY

The distinction between industrial and organizational psychology is fuzzy because practicing industrial and organizational psychologists often share job descriptions and duties. The two areas are therefore often referred to as industrial/organizational psychology. As we've discussed, industrial psychologists traditionally focus on the individual worker: selection, placement, training, and evaluation. The *organizational psychologist,* however, works at the organizational level to understand how workers function in the organization and how the organization functions as a whole. The following activities are typically ascribed to organizational psychologists.

Job Satisfaction and Quality of Work Life

Organizational psychologists determine what factors contribute to a healthy and productive work force. They examine job satisfaction and study the factors associated with it, such as employee turnover, absenteeism, age, pay, motivation, and attitudes toward the organization. Organizational psychologists develop and evaluate systems that promote job satisfaction by rewarding good performance and redesigning jobs to make them more challenging, meaningful, and satisfying to employees (Muchinsky, 2006). Promoting job satisfaction entails understanding workers' needs and creating incentives that build job commitment and loyalty. For example, organizational psychologists attempt to understand how Generation X workers differ from earlier generations and how companies can tailor employee incentives to maximize their satisfaction (Cohen, 2002). They also study how employee services such as office-based child care and gym facilities influence morale, job satisfaction, and productivity.

Leadership

Organizational psychologists study leadership: What makes a good leader? They identify the characteristics of effective leaders and determine the types of leaders that are most effective in particular positions. They also create individual and group training programs to improve the leadership and communication skills of supervisors and managers (Williams, 2005).

In this way, organizational psychologists may act as executive coaches (Kilburg, 1996; Witherspoon & White, 1996).

Organizational Development

Organizational psychologists help companies determine when changes are needed. They help organizations make changes, transition to new ways of managing things, and accept change. As Muchinsky (2006, p. 6) explains, "Organizations grow and mature just as people do; thus, the field of organizational development is directed toward facilitating the organizational growth process."

The organizational psychologist is an agent of change who identifies problems, studies potential solutions, and makes recommendations (Aamodt, 2004; Kasserman, 2005; Tenopyr, 1997). Organizational psychologists might examine and refine business procedures, such as developing a paperwork processing plan that is concise, consistent, and efficient. They also help organizations manage and resolve interpersonal problems (Williams, 2005). For example, organizational psychologists might use conflict-resolution skills to work out a solution for feuding departments or team members. Finally, they examine the lines of authority or communication and redesign them when necessary.

Industrial/organizational psychologists work in a variety of settings, including businesses, consulting firms, and government departments. Some industrial psychologists conduct research in universities, the government, and industry, as discussed in Chapter 2.

HUMAN FACTORS

Human factors psychologists, sometimes called engineering psychologists, are concerned with the interaction between humans and their environments, and especially humans and machines. They design work environments to optimize productivity, employee satisfaction, and safety, as well as to limit stress, fatigue, and error. In order to improve computer applications and hardware designs, some human factors psychologists specialize in the study of how people interact with computers (Chapman, 2005; Day, 1996). A human factors psychologist might study how to make websites more user friendly (Clay, 2000a) or engage in device testing, new product design, and the development of warnings and labels for products (Callan, 2004). Others may conduct research and develop programs in military command, aircraft and ship control systems, or Internet systems (Callan, 2004).

Still other human factors psychologists focus on error prevention and management in order to predict and prevent human error through excellent design. For example, they might help design products that consumers will use safely and accurately. Similarly, human factors psychologists might work to reduce human error in medicine by improving the accessibility of software for recording patient information, streamlining reporting procedures, or adding cross-checks before surgeries or other medical procedures are conducted (Woods, 2002). Psychologists in this field conduct research to find ways to reduce accidents and injury, death, and property losses on highways (Ferguson, 1997). Some conduct research on pilot error and avaiation safety (Lauber, 1997; Tyler, 2000). Human factors psychologists can play a role in improving national security by deterring future terrorist threats directed toward air travel; they would do this by evaluating proposed changes in equipment, procedures, and regulations and by studying how they impact the efficiency of people operating them and the system as a whole (Callan, 2004; Hart, 2002).

Human factors psychologists also work in ergonomics, studying work environments and how to modify them to enhance productivity. They adapt work environments, including computer interfaces and other equipment, to compensate for the limitations and qualities of people, in order to increase safety and reduce accidents. They study the effects of environmental factors such as light, noise, temperature, and work schedules (such as night shifts or compressed work weeks) on worker safety, productivity, and satisfaction (Muchinsky, 2006). Others work to improve the safety and comfort of spaces. For example, a human factors psychologist might investigate the capacity and comfort of aircraft seating and study the user interface of anything with which an airline customer will interact (Landwehr, 2001).

OPPORTUNITIES WITH A BACHELOR'S DEGREE

A bachelor's degree prepares graduates for a variety of entry-level positions within business and industry. Because of their solid liberal arts background, psychology majors with interests in business are good matches for positions in human resources departments.

Human Resources

Human resources departments, also known as personnel departments, help employers manage their employees by serving a variety of functions, including employment and placement, wage and salary administration, training and development, benefits administration, and research. Human resources personnel work to attract the most qualified employees, match them to the jobs for which they are best suited, help them succeed in their jobs, and ensure that the organization complies with labor laws (Society for Human Resource Management, n.d.). Depending on your interests and experience, you could choose from a variety of positions at all levels of education within human resource departments located in businesses, government, and private and nonprofit agencies. We discuss some of these positions as follows.

Human Resource Generalist   Human resource generalists handle all aspects of personnel work and engage in many activities, including the recruitment, placement, training, and development of employees. They may also administer salary and benefits and develop personnel policies that conform to labor laws (Society for Human Resource Management, n.d.). Entry-level generalist positions typically fall under the following titles: human resource assistant, human resource specialist, personnel assistant, personnel specialist, or employee relations specialist.

Employment, Recruitment, and Placement Specialist   Employment, recruitment, and placement specialists recruit personnel, collect applications and resumes for jobs, assemble applicant files, perform background checks, interview applicants, administer preemployment assessments and tests, and place employees (Bureau of Labor Statistics, 2004; Society for Human Resource Management, n.d.). They also orient new employees, educate employees about salary and benefits, and assess departmental needs for staffing. Common entry-level positions include interviewer, recruiter, employment representative, or EEO (equal employment and opportunity) specialist.

Training and Development Specialist   Training and development specialists conduct training sessions, provide on-the-job training, and maintain records of employee participation in training and development programs (Bureau of Labor Statistics, 2004). They help employees improve their knowledge and skills—by reviewing sales techniques or safety guidelines, for example—and help supervisors and managers improve their interpersonal skills in dealing with employees (Society for Human Resource Management, n.d.). More-advanced training and development positions involve human resource planning and organizational development. For example, a training specialist might create a leadership development program to develop employees' leadership potential and prepare them for

TABLE 8.1 Salaries in Human Resources	
Title	**Median 2005 Salary**
Benefits Analyst	$41,417
Employee Relations Specialist	$41,817
Employment Representative	$40,453
Human Resources Assistant	$34,179
Human Resources Generalist	$41,156
Recruiter	$40,453
Training Specialist	$41,677

Source: Adapted from Salary.com, 2005.

promotion and advancement. Entry-level positions in this area include training specialist and orientation specialist.

Compensation and Benefits Specialist   Compensation and benefits specialists engage in job analysis, write job descriptions, collect and organize information about an organization's benefits programs, administer benefits plans, and monitor costs. Typical titles include benefits analyst, compensation specialist, and salary administrator (Society for Human Resource Management, n.d.).

Evaluating Careers in Human Resources   A career in human resources offers many advantages, including an office environment, a 40-hour workweek, and opportunities for advancement. As a human resources employee, you'll have the opportunity to help people directly, solve practical problems, and use your knowledge of psychology. You'll interact with a wide range of people, which requires flexibility, patience, and excellent communication skills (Society for Human Resource Management, n.d.). Sometimes the "people" part of the job can be stressful and challenging. For example, you'll have to deal with employees who are angry over changes in work conditions or who have been laid off. Human resources positions also entail administrative work that requires attention to detail and can sometimes be tedious. Although entry-level positions in human resources are highly competitive, the field is expected to grow faster than the average for all occupations through 2012 (Bureau of Labor Statistics, 2004), and human resources positions offer comfortable salaries, as shown in Table 8.1.

   If you're interested in pursuing a career in human resources, psychology offers a solid background in communication skills, statistics, research methods, presentation skills, and human behavior. Additional courses in communication, writing, business administration, labor law, and accounting will enhance your employability. Seek an internship to obtain experience and make contacts that can help you find a human resources position after graduation (Society for Human Resource Management, n.d.).

Commercial or Industrial Design Assistant

An assistant to a commercial or industrial designer helps in designing products and equipment, such as airplanes, cars, children's toys, computer equipment, furniture, home appliances, and medical, office, and recreational equipment. A designer combines artistic talent with research on customer needs, ways products are used, the consumer market, and production materials and methods to create a design that is functional, appealing, and competitive in the marketplace. Design assistants conduct research related to the designer's needs. They help the designer coordinate design concepts among engineering, marketing, production, and sales departments in order to produce a successful product. Depending on the particular field or industry, design assistants may help designers plan packaging and containers for products such as foods, beverages, toiletries, or medicine, or they might help create and design packaging, illustrations, or advertising for manufactured materials. Designers and design assistants are employed by manufacturers, corporations, and design firms. They tend to work regular 40-hour weeks in an office setting.

The market for design assistants will grow as fast as the average through the year 2012 (Bureau of Labor Statistics, 2004). In 2003, the median entry-level salary in design was $30,000 (American Institute of Graphic Arts, 2003). If you're interested in becoming a design assistant, creativity is essential and sketching ability will help you advance to design positions. Psychology's emphasis on research methods and problem solving will suit you well in this field. In addition, you should take courses in merchandising, business administration, marketing, and art—especially a course in computer-aided design (CAD).

Administrative Assistant

Because of office automatization and organizational restructuring, the role of the administrative assistant (also known as executive assistant or executive secretary) has expanded well beyond secretarial services in recent years. In addition to coordinating administrative and information management activities within an office, many administrative assistants train and orient new staff and conduct research on the Internet. Administrative assistants schedule meetings and appointments, maintain files, conduct research, manage databases, create reports, and manage projects.

Increasingly, administrative assistants are relieved from typing and instead support the executive staff (Bureau of Labor Statistics, 2004).

Employment of administrative assistants is expected to grow about as fast as the average for all occupations through 2012 (Bureau of Labor Statistics, 2004). An administrative assistant position offers several advantages, including an office environment, a 40-hour workweek, and the opportunity to help others solve practical problems. Salaries for administrative assistants are competitive. In 2005, the median salary for administrative assistants was $37,950; half of administrative assistants earn between $34,609 and $42,091 (Salary.com, 2005). Administrative positions can entail stress, especially when the office is trying to meet a deadline or a boss expects the assistant to run personal errands. Skills in organization, communication, research, and stress management, as well as an understanding of human behavior, leadership, and groups, make the psychology major competitive for administrative assistant positions.

OPPORTUNITIES WITH A GRADUATE DEGREE

Although a bachelor's degree in psychology prepares graduates for entry-level jobs, graduate degree holders have more opportunities for advancement. A master's degree offers a wide range of opportunities in human resources, usability, and marketing research careers. Doctoral degrees offer additional opportunities, especially in upper management, consulting, and product design and development careers; however, individuals with master's degrees and extensive experience often obtain positions comparable to those holding doctoral degrees.

Human Resources

Each of the human resources career tracks that is open to a bachelor's degree holder is also open to graduate degree holders, usually with additional responsibilities and compensation. A graduate degree enables the employee to engage in supervisory functions within human resources departments.

Human resource generalists with graduate degrees design and administer human resources policies, collect and analyze data, make recommendations to management, and take leadership roles on projects. Similarly, graduate degree holders who work in employment, recruitment, and placement design assessment techniques to select and place employees, collect data on the effectiveness of the assessments, and supervise other workers. Graduate degree holders who work in training and development create

TABLE 8.2 Salaries for Graduate Degree Holders in Human Resources	
Title	Median 2005 Salary
Advanced Human Resources Positions	
Employee Relations Specialist	$67,627
Employment Representative	$59,551
Human Resources Generalist	$64,986
Organizational Development Specialist	$69,387
Executive Recruiter	$68,884
Training Specialist	$61,881
Managerial Positions	
Employment Manager	$78,673
Employee Relations Manager	$80,141
Human Resources Director	$118,168
Human Resources Manager	$80,896
Organizational Development Manager	$88,329
Training Manager	$78,712

Source: Adapted from Salary.com, 2005.

training programs, conduct research on the effectiveness of those programs, and supervise other workers. Other human resources professionals emphasize the training and development needs of the organization as a whole; these professionals often are called organizational development specialists. With additional experience, graduate degree holders move on to managerial positions, as well as more advanced positions that entail overseeing all human resources functions within an organization, such as human resources manager or human resources director. Salaries for human resources positions for graduate degree holders are shown in Table 8.2.

Consultant

Consultant is an umbrella term for a variety of individuals who engage in problem solving within organizations. Consultants specialize in a variety of areas, including management and strategy development, training, organizational development, and recruitment. Consultants in each of these areas engage in the same basic task: They advise organizations on how to solve problems, such as researching a new market, reorganizing a company's structure, or hiring top executives. Consultants offer their clients perspective and insight (an understanding of the big picture and the problem at hand), analysis (an examination of potential solutions), and recommendations (a strategic plan to address the problem) (Boulakia, 1998; Kasserman, 2005). In other words, consultants solve business problems by applying a scientific approach: through testing hypotheses and analyzing data (McCracken, 1998).

There are many different types of consultants. Management consultants analyze ways to make an organization more competitive and efficient (Bureau of Labor Statistics, 2004). Search consultants are high-level recruiters, often called "headhunters," who use their knowledge of industrial psychology to recruit, assess, and place employees in top positions. Organizational development consultants help companies with team building, training, dealing with change, and professional development. Marketing consultants help companies advertise and market products and services. Mediation consultants help organizations solve interpersonal conflicts in the workplace, that is, conflicts among individuals and those within and between departments and teams; they also teach communication and conflict management skills. Some consultants emphasize developing leadership skills in executives; recently, these consultants have been referred to as executive coaches (Kilburg, 1996). An executive coach helps an executive identify personal strengths and weaknesses, and works to enhance an executive's skills and promote growth (Witherspoon & White, 1996).

Because they have advanced analytical skills, graduate degree holders in psychology are well suited to careers in consulting. They understand how to analyze data, manage databases, and present data simply and elegantly through the use of tables and graphs. Their knowledge of computer software and statistics is an asset to any organization, and their communication skills, honed through writing papers, theses, and dissertations, as well as making conference presentations, are valuable in the office setting (Sebestyen, 2000).

A career in consulting offers many advantages. It's a great way to learn about business, because most firms offer plenty of opportunities for professional development through training workshops, seminars, and mentoring programs (McCracken, 1998; Montell, 1999). As a consultant, you'll collaborate with talented colleagues from a variety of educational and experiential backgrounds. You'll be challenged to devise and implement useful solutions to real problems (P. M. Smith, 1997). The pace is quick, and the problems constantly change: One day you might analyze the potential market for a new product and the next day consider reorganizing the management structure of an organization. The main disadvantage of a career in consulting is that it often requires long hours and travel; however, the salary makes up for them. In 2005, the median annual salary for senior consultants, regardless of education, was $71,631; the median for consultants, regardless of education, was $55,125. The median income for all doctoral-level consultants in 2005 was $103,152 (Abbot, Langer, & Associates, 2005a). Among doctoral-level industrial/organizational psychologist consultants, the median starting salary in 2001 was $92,500, with 50 percent earning between $68,750 and $101,750. The median starting salary for psychologists from other subfields was $70,000, with 50 percent earning between $62,500 and $212,000 (Singleton, Tate, & Randall, 2003). Finally, consulting careers are expected to grow much faster than the average for all occupations through 2012 (Bureau of Labor Statistics, 2004); the field is expected to grow by 55 percent, making consulting fifth among the most rapidly growing industries.

Usability Specialist

Many psychologists with graduate degrees in industrial/organizational or human factors psychology obtain positions in product design and development. These psychologists specialize in promoting product *usability,* or ease and pleasure of use. Usable, or user friendly, products are easy for users to learn how to use, are efficient and memorable, minimize errors, and are pleasing or satisfying to use (Aamodt, 2004). Usability specialists ensure that product designs fit users. They work with all kinds of products: toys, computer hardware and software, electronic equipment, cars, and more.

Psychologists who work in product design and production use their expertise on human capabilities and limitations daily (Day, 1996). They serve as user advocates, in that their goal is to create products that meet the needs of the user. They research a product, create product prototypes, then test and modify them based on input from potential users. For example, in designing the interior of an automobile, a psychologist might create a life-size prototype in which all of the instruments and controls can be moved (for instance, by attaching them with Velcro). Potential users then provide feedback on the best location for each of the instruments and controls, moving them as necessary. Other psychologists conduct these types of usability studies to create aircraft that meet pilots' needs and thereby reduce pilot error (Lauber, 1997; Tyler, 2000).

Usability research also takes place in the computer software industry. For example, psychologists use their knowledge of cognitive psychology to explain why a particular software interface design is confusing for users (Chapman, 2005; Diddams, 1998). Psychologists record and analyze users' behaviors when they try to accomplish a task using a computer software product. They also interview users about their experience with the product: Was it easy to use? What confused them about the interface? The resulting knowledge is used to improve the software design.

Psychologists who choose careers in product design and development can engage in research that improves people's experiences with products. Their research has practical implications, and they get to see the results of their work. A regular 40-hour workweek, excellent opportunities for master's-level psychologists, and high rates of compensation are other advantages. The design and development industry is expected to grow as fast as the average through 2012 (Bureau of Labor Statistics, 2004). In 2003, the average entry-level salary for usability practitioners was $65,200; the average for all master's-level usability practitioners was $80,500 and for doctorates it was $104,000 (Human Factors International, 2003).

Environmental Designer

Psychologists with training in industrial/organizational psychology or human factors often work in environmental design. They study the interactive relationship between environments and human behavior and seek to understand why people find some spaces comfortable and others threatening, as well as why some spaces are easier to navigate than others. They then apply this information to designing and enhancing environments, such as the layout of offices, the design of office buildings and shopping malls, and even the design of neighborhoods and communities. Their aim is to reduce stress, create more efficiency, and minimize accidents (Winerman, 2004).

Psychologists with interest in environmental design work for corporations, local and federal governments, and consulting firms. Some participate in city and community planning, designing buildings, and enhancing the interior layout of existing structures. A career in environmental design requires good communication skills and the ability to work as part of a team. Environmental designers who are assigned to large projects work closely with professionals from many fields, including politicians, architects, urban planners, economists, and engineers, to complete projects. Working with many disciplines can be interesting but challenging. Good listening and research skills are essential to success in this field, because environmental designers spend a lot of time interacting with people—consumers and community members in addition to other professionals. For example, when a city plans to rebuild a run-down neighborhood, psychologists may interview people who live in the neighborhood, to obtain their ideas and perspectives about how to improve the area.

As you might imagine, an important advantage of a career in environmental design is the opportunity to be part of a large project and to make a difference. An environmental designer who participates in designing a new community housing project, for example, will find that the work influences residents' day-to-day lives. The teamwork needed to complete large-scale projects can sometimes lead to frustration, because when many people are involved, decisions can take a long time. Also, projects generally take a while to implement, which can be challenging for someone looking for more immediate results. Environmental designers who can take criticism well and who deal with pressure without becoming overly stressed have a distinct advantage in this often stressful field.

Careers in environmental design are expected to increase about as fast as average through the year 2012 (Bureau of Labor Statistics, 2004), and salaries are competitive. In 1999, the average salary for a doctoral-level psychologist in environmental design was over $65,000 ($77,613 adjusted for 2005) (Conaway, 2000). If you're interested in a career in environmental design, seek additional training in communications, research design and statistics, and related fields such as economics, urban planning, and architecture. Also, seek an internship with an environmental design firm, city planning office, or related placement to obtain hands-on experience in this exciting field.

As we've seen, there are many career opportunities for psychology students with business interests. Many entry-level positions are open to bachelor's degree holders in psychology who have taken coursework and obtained experience in relevant areas. Opportunities expand for graduate degree holders. Remember that we've offered a mere sampling of possible careers; more await your exploration. Finally, note that many other careers described in this book apply to students with interests in industrial, organizational, and human factors psychology. See Chapter 2 to learn about careers in research, publishing, and academia, as well as Chapter 10 for other career options for graduates with quantitative skills.

SUGGESTED READINGS

Aamodt, M. G. (2004). *Applied industrial/organizational psychology.* Pacific Grove, CA: Wadsworth.

Chapman, C. N. (2005). Software user research: Psychologist in the software industry. In R. D. Morgan, T. L. Kuther, & C. J. Habben (Eds.), *Life after graduate school in psychology: Insider's advice from new psychologists* (pp. 211–224). New York: Psychology Press.

Kasserman, J. (2005). Management consultation: Improving organizations. In R. D. Morgan, T. L. Kuther, & C. J. Habben (Eds.), *Life after graduate school in psychology: Insider's advice from new psychologists* (pp. 183–196). New York: Psychology Press.

Kuther, T. L. (2005). *Your career in psychology: Industrial/organizational psychology.* Belmont, CA: Wadsworth.

McKenzie, J. S., Drinan, H. G., & Traynow, W. J. (2001). *Opportunities in human resource management careers.* New York: McGraw-Hill.

Muchinsky, P. M. (2006). *Psychology applied to work.* Pacific Grove, CA: Wadsworth.

Naficy, M. (1997). *The fast track: The insider's guide to winning jobs in management consulting, investment banking, and securities trading.* New York: Broadway Books.

Nickerson, R. S. (Ed.). (1995). *Emerging needs and opportunities for human factors research.* Washington, DC: National Academy of Sciences. Available at http://www.nap.edu/catalog/4940.html

Pond, S. B. (1999). Industrial-organizational psychology: The psychology of people working together. *Eye on Psi Chi, 3*(3), 34–37.

Tenopyr, M. L. (1997). Improving the workplace: Industrial/organizational psychology as a career. In R. Sternberg (Ed.), *Career paths in psychology: Where your degree can take you* (pp. 185–196). Washington, DC: American Psychological Association.

Williams, S. (2005). Executive management: Helping executives manage their organizations through organizational and market research. In R. D. Morgan, T. L. Kuther, & C. J. Habben (Eds.), *Life after graduate school in psychology: Insider's advice from new psychologists* (pp. 225–238). New York: Psychology Press.

Wolgalter, M. S., & Rogers, W. A. (1998). Human factors/ergonomics: Using psychology to make a better and safer world. *Eye on Psi Chi, 3*(1), 23–26.

WEB RESOURCES

Society for Industrial and Organizational Psychology
   http://siop.org

Professional Industrial Organizational Psychologist Network
   http://www.piop.net

Academy of Management
   http://www.aomonline.org

Center for the Study of Work Teams
   http://www.workteams.unt.edu

Society for Human Resource Management
   http://www.shrm.org

Human Factors and Ergonomics Society
   http://hfes.org

International Institute for Environment and Development
   http://www.iied.org

Getting an Industrial Design Job
   http://new.idsa.org/webmodules/articles/articlefiles/GETIDJOB.pdf

Current Trends in Environmental Psychology
   http://www.ucm.es/info/Psyap/iaap/evans.htm

Careers in Industrial Organizational Psychology
  http://www.wcupa.edu/_ACADEMICS/sch_cas.psy/Career_Paths/Industrial/
    Career06.htm
Careers in Consulting
  http://www.careers-in-business.com/consulting/mc.htm
What Is Management Consulting?
  http://www.campusaccess.com/campus_web/career/c4job_cons.htm

CHECKLIST: IS WORK PSYCHOLOGY FOR YOU?

Do you:

☐ Have an interest in business?

☐ Want to understand how psychological methods can improve employee selection and placement?

☐ Want to help others gain skills?

☐ Want to devise methods to evaluate employees?

☐ Want to advise businesses and corporations on personnel policies?

☐ Want to promote teamwork in an office environment?

☐ Want to study leadership, understand the qualities of an effective leader, and help supervisors and managers to improve their leadership skills?

☐ Have an interest in helping organizations make transitions and changes?

☐ Have an interest in the way the environment shapes our behavior?

☐ Want to design and organize work environments to maximize efficiency?

☐ Have good communication skills?

☐ Feel comfortable working in groups?

☐ Enjoy conducting research?

☐ Have the ability to be flexible and deal with ambiguity?

Scoring: The more boxes you checked, the more likely it is that you're a good match for a career in work psychology.

Experimental, Cognitive, and Quantitative Psychology and Psychometrics

Chapter Guide

Number crunching, pocket protectors, lab rats, and IQ tests are just some of the things that come to mind when psychology students think of this chapter's career paths. As you'll see, experimental, cognitive, and quantitative psychology as well as psychometrics offer some of the most flexible career paths in psychology.

EXPERIMENTAL PSYCHOLOGY

All psychologists learn how to conduct research, but experimental psychologists specialize in it. *Experimental psychologists* tend to study research methodology in greater detail than do other psychologists. They then apply these methods to study a variety of topics, including learning, sensation, perception, human performance, motivation, memory, language, thinking, and communication. Some experimental psychologists study animals to apply what they learn to humans, or simply because animal behavior is interesting.

We usually identify experimental psychologists by the area in which they conduct research. For example, sensation and perception psychologists study the way we use our senses to become aware of the world around us; they might study vision, hearing, taste, smell, touch, or all of the senses. A learning psychologist studies processes of learning, such as classical and operant conditioning. There are a wide variety of experimental psychologists, because there are many areas in which to conduct research.

COGNITIVE PSYCHOLOGY

Cognitive psychologists study human cognition: how we take in, store, retrieve, and apply knowledge. They attempt to understand the nature of human thought. How do we attend to the world around us? How do we take in, learn, understand, remember, and make decisions? Cognitive psychologists are interested in topics such as attention, visual and auditory perception, memory, reasoning, retrieval and forgetting, and problem solving. They attempt to understand how we think, learn, remember, and use information to make decisions. They conduct research to extend our knowledge about the mind and to construct theories that explain why our minds work the way they do. Some cognitive psychologists conduct applied research to develop products that people find easy to use—for example, computer software, handheld computers, or remote controls—a task similar to the work of human factors psychologists. Other cognitive psychologists work to develop effective teaching methods by studying how people learn. Given the wide range of activities in which humans engage, cognitive psychologists have a great many kinds of decisions and cognitive activities to explain and improve—and a wide range of potential research topics.

QUANTITATIVE PSYCHOLOGY

Quantitative psychology, sometimes called mathematical psychology, is the study of research methodology, or methods and techniques for acquiring, analyzing, and applying information. Quantitative psychologists are specialists in designing, conducting, and interpreting experiments. They create new methods for analyzing data such as statistical tests. They also work to develop and test quantitative theories of cognition and behavior; they develop, for example, equations and formulas that can account for behavioral phenomena. Today there are mathematical theories of cognition, perception, social interactions, memory, decision making, abnormal behavior, and many other psychological phenomena.

PSYCHOMETRICS

Psychometrics is the science of measuring human characteristics. Psychometricians measure people's behavior, abilities, and potential in the intellectual, emotional, and social realms of functioning. Like quantitative psychologists, psychometricians are well versed in statistics; however, they specialize in measurement. That is, they answer the question "How do you design a survey that captures the behavior that you intend to study?" Psychometricians create and revise personality tests, intelligence tests, and aptitude tests. They also use these tests to assess people's abilities and level of functioning to assist other psychologists in the development of treatment plans.

OPPORTUNITIES WITH A BACHELOR'S DEGREE

If you're interested in experimental, cognitive, and quantitative psychology or in psychometrics, you'll find you have a variety of career options with a bachelor's degree. However, remember that, as with all areas of psychology, graduate degrees open doors to additional opportunities.

Insurance Underwriter

Before an insurance company takes on a new client, whether individual or organizational, an insurance underwriter evaluates the risk of loss, determines the appropriate premium rate, and writes the insurance policy to cover the individual's or organization's risks of loss. An underwriter analyzes the information that potential clients provide in insurance applications and supplements the analyses with information from loss control reports, medical reports, and other data to determine if a client is an acceptable risk. The underwriter then determines the appropriate insurance premium to charge.

A career as an underwriter offers several advantages: a standard 40-hour workweek, a quiet office environment, a competitive salary, and a measure of job security. Although insurance underwriting is not a growth field, employment of underwriters is expected to grow as fast as the average through 2012. However, because insurance is a necessity for both individuals and organizations, as a profession it is less vulnerable to economic recessions and layoffs than are other fields (Bureau of Labor Statistics, 2004). Finally, underwriting provides a comfortable salary. In 2005, an entry-level underwriter for life insurance plans earned a median salary of $37,791, whereas an entry-level underwriter for property and casualty plans earned $44,172 (Salary.com, 2005). According to the *Occupational Outlook Handbook*, the median salary for all insurance underwriters was $45,590 in 2002 (Bureau of Labor Statistics, 2004).

Psychology majors have a solid liberal arts background, computer skills, and quantitative abilities that are useful for a career as an insurance underwriter. If you're interested in this career, supplement your psychology major with additional courses in statistics, business administration, finance, or accounting. Also, consider seeking an internship with an insurance company to learn more about the field.

Computer Programmer

Computer programmers write the programs, or detailed instructions, that computers follow in performing their functions. They install, test, and debug programs to keep an organization's server and computer systems functional. If you're interested in computer programming and if you understand programming languages such as C++, COBOL, or JAVA, this career might be for you.

An important advantage of a career in programming is the opportunity to learn. New computer programs and languages rapidly emerge; programmers must continually reevaluate their skills and know the latest technologies. On the other hand, programmers must sometimes work long hours or weekends to meet deadlines or to fix bugs. Through 2012, employment of programmers is expected to grow about as fast as the average for all occupations. A typical entry-level programmer earned a median salary of $45,558 in 2003. Median annual earnings of computer programmers were $60,290 in 2002, with the middle 50 percent earning between $45,960 and $78,140 (Bureau of Labor Statistics, 2004).

Psychology students' experience with computers and critical thinking are useful in this field. The analytical approach that cognitive psychologists take toward understanding human problem solving is similar to the methodical approach that computer programmers take toward writing programs and solving bugs and glitches. If you'd like to become a programmer, seek a computer science minor and take courses in various programming languages to gain proficiency. Employers look primarily for programming knowledge, so a degree in computer science isn't necessary if you understand programming languages and have hands-on experience. Seek internship or summer employment opportunities in the field to gain experience and contacts.

Computer Support Specialist

A computer support specialist provides technical assistance to clients and users of hardware, software, and computer systems. There are at least two types of computer support specialists: help desk technicians and technical support specialists (or technical support analysts). Help desk technicians answer telephone calls and e-mail inquiries from customers seeking technical assistance for a given hardware or software product. They help the user by listening, asking questions to diagnose the problem, and walking the user through steps to solve it. Technical support specialists or analysts provide an organization's computer users with technical assistance to solve computer problems. They install, repair, and modify computer systems (hardware and software) as well as provide e-mail and telephone assistance to an organization's users.

Advantages to careers in computer support include an office environment as well as excellent job outlooks and high starting salaries. Computer support specialists are projected to increase faster than the average through 2012 (Bureau of Labor Statistics, 2004). In 2005, a typical help desk technician earned a median salary of $42,329; a technical support analyst earned a median salary of $47,882 (Salary.com, 2005). Psychology majors have computer knowledge, interpersonal skills, and communication skills that are useful for careers in computer support. Completing additional computer classes may increase your marketability.

Budget Analyst

Budget analysts develop, analyze, and execute budgets to allocate an organization's financial resources. They seek to improve efficiency and increase an organization's profits. Budget analysts provide advice and technical assistance to managers and department heads in preparing their annual budgets. They examine budgets for accuracy, completeness, and conformance with organizational procedures, objectives, and budgetary limits (Bureau of Labor Statistics, 2004). Throughout the year, budget analysts monitor the budget to avoid financial deficits and overspending.

Advantages of a career in budget analysis include a comfortable office setting, relative independence, and a good salary. However, long hours and tight, stressful deadlines are common. In 2005, a typical entry-level budget analyst earned a median base salary of $43,858 (Salary.com, 2005). Starting salaries of budget and other financial analysts in small firms tend to range from $29,750 to $36,250; in large organizations, compensation tends to range from $33,500 to $41,250. Employment of budget analysts is expected to grow at the average rate for all occupations through 2012 (Bureau of Labor Statistics, 2004). A bachelor's degree in psychology is sufficient for entry-level positions in budget analysis, because psychology majors are skilled in communication, quantitative analysis, and computer use. Additional courses in business, accounting, and statistics are helpful.

OPPORTUNITIES WITH A GRADUATE DEGREE

A graduate degree in experimental psychology, cognitive psychology, quantitative psychology, or psychometrics opens doors to careers outside of academia and laboratories. In these next sections, we'll examine alternative business careers for graduate degree holders in each of these areas.

Operations Research Analyst

Operations research (sometimes called management science) is a scientific approach to analyzing problems and making decisions. It entails using mathematics, statistics, and computer science to quantify situations and decide how to deal with them. If you choose a career in operations research analysis, you'll use mathematical modeling on computers to predict potential solutions to a problem in order to determine the best outcome.

Operations research analysts examine how to make products more efficiently, solve problems, and control inventory and distribution of products. They engage in problem solving by studying the problem, gathering data, analyzing it, and coming up with practical solutions. For example, operations research analysts might conduct research to determine the most efficient amount of inventory a business must keep on hand; they would do this by talking with engineers about production levels, discussing purchasing levels and arrangements, and examining data on storage costs (Bureau of Labor Statistics, 2004).

Operations research analysts are found in all work settings (military, government, business and industry) and under various titles (operations analyst, management analyst, policy analyst). As an operations research analyst, you can expect an office environment and high salary, but also stressful deadlines and long hours. Opportunities in operations research are good, especially for individuals with graduate degrees in quantitative areas (Bureau of Labor Statistics, 2004). In 2005, the median entry-level salary for operations analyst was $52,730 (Salary.com, 2005). Graduate degree holders tend to enter the field at a more advanced level.

A graduate degree in the quantitative areas of psychology discussed in this chapter offers the mathematical, statistical, and analytical expertise needed for a career in operations research. In addition to quantitative skills, operations research analysts need excellent communication and computer skills, including the use of statistical software packages and programming. An understanding of how the human mind works (for instance, how people think and solve problems) is always useful for operations research analysts who want to minimize the effects of human error on their work. That is, understanding the kinds of mistakes that workers might make can help operations research analysts make useful decisions.

Systems Analyst

A systems analyst (also called a systems developer, systems architect, or applications systems analyst) plans and develops an organization's computer systems, solves computer problems, and adapts computer technology to meet the needs of an organization. Systems analysts discuss system problems with users to determine the nature of the problems and find solutions, as well as to plan improvements to the system by using a variety of quantitative and mathematical techniques such as data modeling, mathematical model building, and information engineering. Because an organization typically uses a variety of software applications, systems analysts work to make the computer systems within an organization compatible in order to share information.

Systems analysts work in offices with a standard 40-hour workweek, but evening and weekend work is sometimes needed to meet deadlines or solve problems. Graduate degree holders in experimental, quantitative, and cognitive psychology typically gain experience in computer programming, understand the use of databases, think analytically, and know how to concentrate and pay attention to detail, which are prerequisites for a position as a systems analyst. Additional courses in management information systems or the use of specific computer software, such as C++, are recommended. Employment of systems analysts is expected to increase much faster than the average for all occupations through 2012; systems analysis is one of the fastest-growing occupations (Bureau of Labor Statistics, 2004). Salaries for systems analysts are very competitive, with a 2005 median annual entry-level salary of $48,502 (Salary.com, 2005). In 2002, the median annual salary for all systems analysts, regardless of experience, was $62,890; the middle 50 percent earned between $49,500 and $78,350 a year (Bureau of Labor Statistics, 2004).

Database Administrator

A database administrator determines how to organize and store data by using database management software. After determining the needs of organizations and users, they design, implement, update, test, and repair computer databases. Database administrators are responsible for ensuring database performance, backing up and archiving information, and ensuring database security.

Advantages of a career in database administration include intellectual challenge and never-ending learning, because technology is constantly changing. Like systems analysts, database administrators work in an office environment, but they often put in long hours to solve problems and debug database software. Database administration is a hot growth field. Employment of database administrators is expected to increase much faster than the average for all occupations through 2012 (Bureau of Labor Statistics, 2004). It also offers a high salary. In 2005, database administrators earned a median salary of $82,050 (Salary.com, 2005).

Graduate degrees in quantitative and cognitive areas of psychology offer the experience with computer systems and analytical skills that employers demand. If you're interested in a career in database administration, seek experience with popular programs such as Oracle, SQL, or Sybase. Most colleges and universities offer courses in these programs, but if yours does not, you can seek certification from courses developed by software manufacturers or else explore the software and related books on your own.

Actuary

Actuaries, found in insurance companies and consulting firms, use statistics and mathematical models to estimate the statistical probability of particular types of risk, such as death, injury, or property loss. They gather and analyze data to determine who will and will not receive insurance coverage, as well as which price to charge in order to cover claims and ensure profitability.

A career as an actuary offers a comfortable office environment, a standard 40-hour workweek, and the ability to work autonomously. The employment of actuaries is expected to grow as fast as the average for all occupations through 2012 (Bureau of Labor Statistics, 2004), and actuarial careers have been rated among the top 10 careers by the *Wall Street Journal* because they offer high salaries, pleasant working environments, a reasonable job outlook, job security, and reasonable levels of stress (Lee, 2002). According to Salary.com (2005), the typical entry-level actuary earned a median base salary of $47,198 in 2005, with the middle 50 percent earning between $41,976 and $50,796. Graduate degree holders are likely to enter the field with a more advanced title. Median annual earnings of all actuaries were $69,970 in 2002 (Bureau of Labor Statistics, 2004).

The strong background in mathematics and statistics that graduate degree holders obtain in experimental, cognitive, and quantitative psychology and in psychometrics provides an excellent base for a career as an actuary. Actuaries also require strong communication and computer skills, including experience with spreadsheets, databases, and statistical analysis software. Additional courses in business will improve your application. If you seek a career as an actuary, be prepared to pass a series of examinations to become certified by the Society of Actuaries (BeAnActuary.org, n.d.).

Financial Analyst

Financial analysts, (also called security analysts and investment analysts) provide organizations—such as banks, insurance companies, mutual and pension funds, and securities firms—with investment analysis and guidance. They build mathematical models and help organizations avoid financial risks and make the most of opportunities. They gather and analyze financial information by combining data from financial statements, commodity prices, sales, costs, expenses, and tax rates. They then make recommendations on how best to manage an organization's financial assets and avoid risk.

Advantages of a career in financial analysis include intellectual challenge, a comfortable office, and a high salary. Financial analysts also face long hours, stressful deadlines, and sometimes frequent travel (Attfield, 1999). Employment of financial analysts is expected to grow faster than average for all occupations through 2012. In 2002, the median annual earnings of financial analysts were $57,100 (Bureau of Labor Statistics, 2004). In 2005, a typical entry-level financial analyst earned $42,820, with 50 percent earning between $38,598 and $47,823 (Salary.com, 2005). A graduate degree may result in a more advanced title and higher entering salary. Annual bonuses may increase the salary substantially.

The broad background in statistics that graduate education in experimental psychology, quantitative psychology, cognitive psychology, and psychometrics provides is an asset to a career in financial analysis. Psychologists in these areas understand how to use mathematics and statistics to arrive at a practical solution. As a financial analyst, your knowledge of the scientific method will come in handy, because financial analysis entails developing hypotheses and designing tests to validate them by using available data and drawing conclusions (Attfield, 1999). Graduate training offers other benefits to this career, such as experience in giving presentations, strong communication skills, and the ability to work independently. If you're interested in a career in financial analysis, take some courses in business and finance to strengthen your credentials and confirm your interest.

Data-Mining Professional

Graduate degree holders in quantitative and experimental psychology and psychometrics are especially prepared for careers in data mining. *Data mining* is the extraction of useful information, or "nuggets," from large databases of information with the use of statistical methods and computational algorithms. It's akin to finding a needle in a haystack, where the needle is critical information that an organization needs and the haystack is the large database with information stored over a long time. Data mining entails using statistical analysis to examine large databases for patterns and trends that shed light on consumer habits and potential marketing strategies.

All industries use data mining. For example, discovering new patterns and trends through data mining can help banking executives "predict with increasing precision how customers will react to interest rate adjustments, which customers will be most receptive to new product offers, which customers present the highest risk for defaulting on a loan and how to make each customer relationship more profitable" (Fabris, 1998). Data-mining professionals, sometimes called data-warehousing professionals or database analysts, are in high demand to develop highly targeted marketing pro-grams, analyze economic trends, detect credit fraud, and forecast financial markets. This challenging career requires analytical thinking and problem-solving skills. If you're interested in a career in data mining, learn about the most popular database programs, such as SQL, DB2, and Oracle. The main challenges of a career in data mining and data warehousing are the stresses of meeting goals, rolling out database upgrades, learning new analysis tech-niques, long hours, and analyzing data and drawing conclusions on tight deadlines and with limited budgets and staffs (L. Smith, 2002). According to Information Week (2005), a typical person working in the data-mining and warehousing field earned a median base salary of $86,000 in 2005. An entry-level database analyst earned $48,185 in 2005, with the middle 50 percent earning between $43,117 and $57,076 (Salary.com, 2005). The training in statistics and research that a graduate degree in psychology provides tends to result in a higher entry-level salary and title than does a bachelor's degree.

As you can see, there are a variety of careers for bachelor's and graduate degree holders that require the statistical expertise of experimental, cogni-tive, and quantitative psychology and psychometrics. In addition to the careers discussed in this chapter, remember that many individuals with these interests seek careers in research (Chapter 2), teaching (Chapter 4), consulting (Chapter 8), human factors and business (Chapter 8), and mar-keting research (Chapter 10). Quantitative skill is one of the hottest skills in the workplace today. Regardless of your career interests, the statistical and methodological knowledge provided by a either a bachelor's or a graduate degree in psychology is excellent preparation for entry-level and more advanced quantitative careers, respectively.

SUGGESTED READINGS

Fitch, T. (2002). *Career opportunities in banking, finance, and insurance.* New York: Facts on File.

Hillier, F. S., & Lieberman, G. L. (2000). *Introduction to operation research.* New York: McGraw-Hill.

Liberty, J. (1999). *Complete idiot's guide to a career in computer programming.* New York: Alpha Books.

Mannila, H., Smyth, P., & Hand, D. J. (2001). *Principles of data mining.* Cambridge, MA: MIT.

Stair, L., & Stair, L. B. (2002). *Careers in computers.* New York: McGraw-Hill.

Wise, S. (2002). The assessment professional: Making a difference in the 21st century. *Eye on Psi Chi, 6*(3), 20–21.

WEB RESOURCES

Insurance: Overview
   http://www.careers-in-finance.com/in.htm
Is a Career in Operations Research/Management Science Right for You?
   http://www.informs.org/Edu/Career/booklet.html
Be an Actuary
   http://www.beanactuary.org
Data Mining: What Is Data Mining?
   http://www.anderson.ucla.edu/faculty/jason.frand/teacher/technologies/palace/
      datamining.htm
Data Warehousing Information Center
   http://www.dwinfocenter.org
Budget Analysis as a Career
   http://www.budgetanalyst.com/careers.htm
Insurance Information Institute
   http://www.iii.org
America's Health Insurance Plans
   http://www.ahip.org
Association of Computer Support Specialists
   http://www.acss.org
System Administrators Guild
   http://www.sage.org
Institute for Operations Research and the Management Sciences
   http://www.informs.org

CHECKLIST: ARE EXPERIMENTAL OR QUANTITATIVE AREAS OF PSYCHOLOGY FOR YOU?

Do you:

☐   Enjoy conducting research?

☐   Like working with numbers?

☐   Enjoy problem solving?

☐   Like science?

☐   Find computers fun to work with?

☐   Take an analytical approach to understanding problems?

☐   Know how to use a computer programming language?

☐   Pay attention to detail?

☐   Enjoy writing research reports?

☐   Enjoy intellectual challenges?

☐   Like "fixing" computer problems?

☐   Like math?

☐   Find research methodology courses fun?

☐   Like statistics?

☐   Enjoy using new computer programs?

Scoring: The more boxes you checked, the more likely it is that you're a good match for a career in the experimental or quantitative areas of psychology.

SOCIAL AND CONSUMER PSYCHOLOGY

CHAPTER GUIDE

What causes social problems such as interpersonal violence, prejudice, and stereotyping? How do we change people's attitudes? What influences purchasing patterns? Why do people buy what they buy? Social and consumer psychology address a variety of interesting and important questions. Whereas consumer psychology is an applied discipline, social psychologists traditionally find careers in academia, teaching, and conducting research. Nonetheless, the increasing emphasis on application within psychology has translated into a variety of new career options.

Social Psychology

Social psychology is the study of how people interact with each other and the social environment. Among other goals, it tries to answer the question "Why do we act the way we do?" Social psychologists study personality, attitude formation and change, and interpersonal relations such as attraction, prejudice, group dynamics, and aggression. Like many of the other psychologists you've read about, social psychologists engage in both basic and applied research. Basic research centers on fundamental questions, such as "How does culture and our social environment shape us?" The goal of basic research is to advance scientific knowledge; whether or not we can apply the findings does not define their worth. In other words, basic research results in knowledge for its own sake. Applied research, on the other hand, is conducted to gain insight into and solve actual problems. For example, applied social psychologists conduct research on practical questions, such as "How can we reduce aggression among schoolchildren?" or "How can we reduce the effects of prejudice in the classroom or office environment?" Social psychologists who emphasize basic research are found in academic and research settings, as described in Chapter 2. Social psychologists who are interested in applied questions can be found in the settings described in this chapter as well as in social policy settings (Chapter 11) and business and organizational settings (Chapters 8 and 9).

Consumer Psychology

If you're interested in understanding subliminal suggestions and why some commercials and marketing campaigns find more success than do others, consumer psychology may be for you. Consumer psychologists study how we process information and make decisions about purchasing products and services (Beall & Allen, 1997). They use this information to help businesses and organizations improve their marketing and sales strategies (J. Carpenter, 2000). A consumer psychologist might design a study to evaluate which type of ketchup container (glass or squeezable plastic, round or square) consumers are more likely to purchase. They study consumer behavior to aid companies in their marketing strategies. For example, a consumer psychologist might study factors that contribute to the effectiveness of fast-food commercials, conclude that people are more receptive to such commercials when they are hungry, and therefore suggest that fast-food companies place their commercials in the late afternoon, before dinnertime. Consumer psychologists study the effectiveness of different types of sales techniques and use that research to provide advice to businesses. They train salespeople, conduct consumer satisfaction surveys, and study the growth of consumers' emotional attachments to products.

In other words, consumer psychologists attempt "to understand the processes by which consumers search for goods and services, decide which goods and services to purchase, and consume the items they purchase" (Beall & Allen, 1997, p. 199). They try to understand changing needs of consumers and help companies adapt their products and services accordingly. Consumer psychologists are found in business, government, and nonprofit agencies, where they work as consultants and employees in departments of market research.

OPPORTUNITIES WITH A BACHELOR'S DEGREE

Advertising

Many students interested in social and consumer psychology seek careers in advertising, a field that helps companies market their products. Entry-level positions in advertising are typically in the account management and media departments.

Account Manager   The account management department serves as the link between agency and client; it brings the client to the agency and is responsible for ensuring that the various components of the agency work smoothly to meet the client's advertising needs. The entry-level position is assistant account manager (also called account coordinator; he or she helps the account manager complete these tasks). Account managers identify and solicit new clients, determining client needs and communicating them to those who create advertisements. Account managers create schedules, enforce deadlines, and help creative staff and management understand client needs (Wetfeet, 2005a). Social psychological principles underlie much of their work because account managers must have good interpersonal and sales skills and understand persuasion and attitude formation in order to attract new clients and assist them in developing marketing plans to advertise their products.

Media Planner   The media department places advertisements and is responsible for placing the right ad at the right time in order to reach the appropriate audience cheaply and effectively. Entry-level positions in media departments include assistant media planners and assistant media buyers. Assistant media planners help media planners examine the public's reading and viewing preferences, study the demographics of various types of media (what consumers read and watch), and evaluate the content of newspapers, magazines, and television programs to determine where to place advertising. Assistant media buyers help media buyers purchase advertising time and space, make sure that ads appear as planned, and create advertising budgets. Psychology students bring a host of useful skills to media planning, including a firm grasp of research methods and statistical analysis, plus an understanding of attitude formation and change, which are all essential to studying the public's preferences and designing effective ads. The average beginning salary for a media buyer in 2005 was between $31,250 and $42,250 (College Journal, n.d.).

Evaluating Careers in Advertising   Careers in advertising are fast paced and exciting. They offer opportunities to exercise creativity, solve problems, engage in research, and advance in the field. To prepare for a career in advertising, take classes in social psychology, consumer psychology, marketing, accounting, advertising, business management, communications, and design. Hone your communication, creative, and organizational skills. The ability to handle stress, work in a team environment, and use technology (such as doing Internet research and designing websites) are essential to this career path.

Seek an advertising internship to gain hands-on experience as well as contacts in the field because entry-level positions in advertising are competitive. Despite the competitive nature of entry-level positions, there is plenty of room for growth. Employment in advertising is expected to grow faster than the average for all occupations through the year 2012. Finally, careers in advertising offer comfortable salaries. In 2003, the average starting salary in advertising was $29,495 (Bureau of Labor Statistics, 2004).

Real Estate

How does psychology relate to a career in real estate? Believe it or not, psychological principles underlie much of the work. Real estate agents bring buyers and sellers together and act as intermediaries in the sale of land and residential and commercial properties. They generate lists of available properties, learn as much as possible about them, market them through open houses and advertisements, show them to clients, and help clients obtain financing and draw up contracts to purchase properties. Real estate agents earn a commission on each property sold.

Sales techniques, persuasion, and attitude formation and change are important social psychological principles used daily by real estate agents in their interactions with clients as well as marketing and advertising. Effective real estate agents can "read" clients to determine which homes are appropriate fits. They use techniques of persuasion in describing the home and its benefits; for example, the home is "cozy," rather than cramped and tiny, or "lively," instead of next to a late-night pub.

Real estate agents must understand the neighborhoods and communities in which they sell properties. They must be both skilled at interpersonal relations and competent at number crunching, because they must be able to assess which neighborhoods best fit clients' needs and budgets. Real estate agents spend much of their time obtaining *listings*, or agreements from property owners to sell their properties through a particular agency. When a property is sold, the agent who sold the property and the one who obtained the listing both receive a commission.

An advantage to a career in real estate is flexibility. Much of the administrative work can be completed out of a home office. However, a great deal of time goes into showing properties to clients. Real estate agents often work long hours, often more than 40 per week. For example, in 2000, nearly 25 percent of real estate agents worked 50 hours per week or more (Bureau of Labor Statistics, 2002). In addition to long hours, real estate agents must be available to meet clients on evenings and weekends. As agents gain experience, they may earn higher commission rates as well as take on more business by becoming more efficient. With experience, some agents are promoted to supervisory positions or open their own businesses. The primary disadvantage to a career in real estate is the reliance on commission income. Income is irregular, and there are often months without income, especially for beginning agents (Evans, 1998). Real estate agents earned a median salary of $30,930 in 2002. Employment of real estate brokers and sales agents is expected to grow more slowly than the average for all occupations through 2012 (Bureau of Labor Statistics, 2004).

If you're considering a career in real estate, recognize that all real estate agents must be licensed. Each state has different requirements, but all include a written test with questions on basic real estate transactions and laws about the sale of property. Many states require 30–90 hours of classroom instruction. Licenses must be renewed every one or two years (without an exam), and continuing education is often required because zoning restrictions and laws change (Bureau of Labor Statistics, 2004). For more information about obtaining a real estate license, contact the Association of Real Estate License Law Officials (http://www.arello.org). Classes in real estate, finance, business administration, economics, or law will provide a helpful background for a career in real estate.

Retail

One-fifth of all workers in the United States in 2000 were employed by retail establishments (Bureau of Labor Statistics, 2002). Retail sales personnel sell goods, provide customer service, and help buyers make informed purchases. They must understand consumer behavior, sales techniques, and the given products, because success in retail requires a high level of service and expertise. Many large retail stores have management training programs in which an employee spends six months to three years learning about all aspects of the business and, after training, is placed as an assistant manager or store manager (Careers in Business, 2000). Store managers are responsible for the operation and activity of a store. They manage sales staff, order and track inventory, market products, design techniques to attract customers, and promote sales and good customer relations (Wetfeet.com, 2005b). Employed directly by a manufacturer or wholesaler, sales representatives travel often to visit clients. They develop relationships with clients, discuss the clients' needs, suggest how their merchandise can meet those needs, and show samples and catalogs of the products they sell (Bureau of Labor Statistics, 2004).

Retail careers are busy, people oriented, and exciting, and they provide opportunities for advancement. If you choose a career in retail, you'll meet many people from different walks of life, use your psychology skills every day, and even travel (if you become a sales representative). Retail careers usually require unusual work hours, often during evenings and weekends. Psychology majors' understanding of human behavior, motivation, and attitudes suit this career well. Strong communication skills, friendliness, decisiveness, enthusiasm, and the ability to manage stress are essential. Management careers also require leadership skills, self-direction, and interpersonal skills, such as the ability to soothe angry customers.

TABLE 10.1 Salaries in Retail	
Title	**Median 2005 Salary**
Assistant Retail Store Manager	$34,042
Retail Store Manager	$42,597
Retail Sales Person	$23,960
Sales Representative	$50,539

Source: Adapted from Salary.com, 2005.

Prepare for a career in retail by taking additional courses in business, marketing, accounting, and communications. Retail positions are expected to grow about as fast as the average for all occupations through the year 2012 (Bureau of Labor Statistics, 2004). As shown in Table 10.1, retail careers offer a range of salaries, depending on the position.

Public Relations

Public relations specialists work to improve an organization's communication with the community; consumer, employee, and public interest groups; and the media. They build and maintain positive relationships with the public by informing the community and media about an organization's policies, activities, and accomplishments (Bureau of Labor Statistics, 2004). Public relations specialists write and distribute press releases to media contacts for distribution to the public. By arranging speaking engagements, they keep organization representatives in contact with the community. Further, they often prepare and edit speeches for company leaders.

Public relations specialists anticipate, analyze, and interpret public opinions about organizations, in order to inform an organization's future decisions and business practices. They keep an organization's management and administrative personnel aware of the attitudes and concerns of the public and special interest groups. They give advice to management about the public ramifications of policy decisions and communications and how to build good public relations, which are critical to an organization's success (Public Relations Society of America, n.d.). Public relations also entails research—on the public's attitudes and opinions, as well as on the effectiveness of an organization's fundraising, marketing, community relations, and other programs. The employment settings of this career include businesses, government, universities, hospitals, schools, and other organizations. Titles include public relations specialist, information officer, press secretary, communications specialist, public affairs specialist, and others.

A career in public relations offers exciting and varied work. Psychology majors are well suited to careers in public relations because of their interpersonal skills, writing skills, background in survey research, and understanding of human behavior, attitude formation, and attitude change. Some of the disadvantages of a career in public relations include long hours, irregular work schedules that are frequently interrupted, and stress resulting from high-pressure deadlines. Unlike advertising professionals, who pay for media coverage and therefore control the advertisement's message and distribution, public relations professionals must face the frustration of earning their media coverage and having little control over how the message is ultimately conveyed (Bergen, n.d.).

Because entry-level positions in public relations are competitive, preparation matters. Take courses in communication, journalism, and business to enhance your marketability. Perhaps most important is hands-on experience, through internships with public relations firms, corporate departments, or nonprofit organizations (Public Relations Society of America, n.d.). Despite the competitive nature of entry-level positions, overall employment of public relations specialists is expected to increase much faster than the average for all occupations through 2012 (Bureau of Labor Statistics, 2004). A final advantage of a career in public relations is the salary. In 2000, the average starting salary for new graduates entering public relations positions was $31,547 (National Association of Colleges and Employers, n.d.). Looking at data from 2002, we see that the median salary for a public relations specialist was $41,710, with half of the people employed as public relations specialists earning between $31,300 and $56,180 (Bureau of Labor Statistics, 2004).

OPPORTUNITIES WITH A GRADUATE DEGREE

As is probably clear by now, your employment opportunities dramatically expand with a graduate degree in psychology. The following sections explore a range of new opportunities for graduate degree holders in social and consumer psychology who are interested in applying their skills to solve real-world problems.

Market Research

Market researchers are found in a variety of organizations, including public relations firms, advertising agencies, and corporations. They conduct research on the sale of a product or service. Market researchers design methods of gathering information on products or services, as well as consumers' needs, tastes, purchasing power, and buying habits. They also examine consumer reactions to products and services. Through research, they identify advertising needs; measure the effectiveness of advertising and other promotional techniques; gather data on competitors' products, services, and locations; and analyze their marketing methods and strategies (Careers in Business, 2000). Market researchers who work for public relations firms or in government positions often conduct opinion research to determine public attitudes on various issues, which may help political and business leaders evaluate public support for their positions or advertising policies (Bureau of Labor Statistics, 2004).

Careers in market research are fast paced and exciting. Market researchers work on a variety of projects, and project turnover is fast. Clients making business decisions often need research to be done quickly (Yund, 1998). In addition to conducting research with practical implications, another advantage of this career is that it is a growth field. Employment of market researchers is expected to grow faster than the average for all occupations through 2012. Finally, salaries in market research are very competitive. In 2002, a typical market research analyst earned a median base salary of $53,810; half of the people in this job earn between $38,760 and $76,310 (Bureau of Labor Statistics, 2004). Market research directors on the other hand, earn between $75,000 and $200,000 (Careers in Business, 2000).

Product Development

Psychologists use their knowledge about human development, interpersonal relations, and attitude formation and change to provide organizations with research-based information to assist them in providing goods and services that meet people's needs. In other words, psychologists often work as consultants in product development. They examine people's reactions to particular products, as well as their needs, tastes, purchasing power, and buying habits. The resulting knowledge is used to improve both the product and the advertising and promotional campaigns for that product.

Product development consultants work for companies, for consulting firms, and in private practice. An important reward of a career as a consultant in product development is that you'll engage in work with practical implications and then get to see the results of your work. You'll work on a variety of projects with a fast turnover. A regular 40-hour workweek and high rates of compensation are other advantages. In 2002, a typical product development consultant or manager earned a median base salary of $68,698 (Salary.com, 2005).

Management

A degree in social or consumer psychology prepares graduates for management careers in advertising, marketing, public relations, and sales. Managers in these fields coordinate the market research, marketing strategy, sales, advertising, promotion, pricing, product development, and public relations activities of large companies.

Advertising Manager   Advertising managers oversee advertising and promotional activities within a firm. If a firm contracts an advertising agency to handle promotions, then the advertising manager may serve as a liaison between the firm and the advertising agency (Bureau of Labor Statistics, 2004). Larger companies have their own advertising staff, overseen by advertising managers.

Marketing Manager   Marketing managers coordinate the work of market researchers in order to determine the demand for products and services offered by the firm and develop a marketing strategy (Bureau of Labor Statistics, 2004). They also develop pricing strategies that maximize profits while ensuring customer satisfaction. Marketing managers confer with advertising managers and market researchers to promote products and services and devise strategies to attract new customers.

Public Relations Manager   Public relations managers supervise the work of public relations specialists and direct publicity programs. They determine the target of publicity programs and evaluate their effectiveness. In a large company, public relations managers may examine the compatibility of the advertising and public relations programs and suggest changes, when needed, to the company's top management. Public relations managers keep abreast of social, economic, and political trends and make recommendations on how to enhance the company's visibility and positive image in light of current trends (Bureau of Labor Statistics, 2004).

Sales Manager   Sales managers direct a company's sales program. They hire sales representatives, devise programs to train them, and oversee their work. They also assign sales territories and set goals (Bureau of Labor Statistics, 2004). Sales managers determine the sales potential of products, assess inventory requirements, monitor customer preferences, and communicate this information to other departments to help develop and modify or maximize products.

Evaluating Managerial Careers   Like other careers, work in advertising, marketing, public relations, and sales presents a variety of benefits and challenges. Long hours, including evenings and weekends, are common. For example, approximately 44 percent of advertising, marketing, and public relations managers worked more than 40 hours per week in 2002 (Bureau of Labor Statistics, 2004). Managerial careers often entail substantial travel. For example, managers must attend many offsite meetings sponsored by associations or industries held at national, regional, and local offices or arranged with dealers, distributors, and clients. In addition, tight deadlines can make for stressful work.

According to the Bureau of Labor Statistics (2004), management positions in advertising, marketing, public relations, and sales are on the rise. Employment is expected to increase faster than the average for all occupations through 2012; however, such positions will remain competitive. Finally, management careers pay well. In 2002, the median base salary was $71,352 for advertising managers, $68,323 for marketing managers, and $69,690 for sales managers (Salary.com, 2005). According to the Bureau of Labor Statistics (2004), public relations managers earned a median salary of $60,640 in 2002.

If you're interested in a career as an advertising, marketing, public relations, or sales manager, take additional courses in business administration, marketing, business law, advertising, accounting, public speaking, and finance. Graduate degree holders' expertise with statistics is especially valuable. Finally, managerial careers require maturity, creativity, motivation, resistance to stress, flexibility, and the ability to communicate persuasively—all skills that graduate study in psychology develops.

Graduate degrees in social and consumer psychology are among the most marketable of psychology degrees. This chapter presented just a few of the opportunities for graduate degree holders in these areas. If you're interested in other alternatives to the traditional academic career of professor, consider writing and publishing careers (Chapter 2), trial consulting (Chapter 5), consulting (Chapter 8), and social policy careers (Chapter 11). With creative thinking and innovation, you'll design and achieve the career of your dreams.

Suggested Readings

Beall, A. E., & Allen, T. W. (1997). Why we buy what we buy: Consulting in consumer psychology. In R. Sternberg (Ed.), *Career paths in psychology: Where your degree can take you* (pp. 197–212). Washington, DC: American Psychological Association.

Branscombe, N. R., & Spears, R. (2001). Social psychology: Past, present, and some predictions for the future. In J. S. Halonen & S. F. Davis (Eds.), *The many faces of psychological research in the 21st century*. Retrieved June 5, 2002, from http://teachpsych.lemoyne.edu/teachpsych/faces/script/ChO7.htm

Edwards, K. W. (1997). *Your successful real estate career.* New York: Amacom.

Field, S. (2001). *Career opportunities in the retail and wholesale industry.* New York: Facts on File.

Field, S., & Rubenstein, H. J. (2001). *Career opportunities in advertising and public relations.* New York: Checkmark.

Friestad, M. (2001). What is consumer psychology? *Eye on Psi Chi, 6*(1), 28–29.

Lederman, E., & Lazarus, S. (1999). *Careers in advertising.* New York: Princeton Review.

Neidle, A. (2000). *How to get into advertising: A guide to careers in advertising, media, and marketing communications.* London: Cassell Academic.

Wagner, R. (2001). A hot market for social scientists in market research. *Chronicle of Higher Education.* Retrieved June 1, 2002, from http://chronicle.com/jobs/2001/01/2001011901c.htm

WEB RESOURCES

What Is a Personality/Social Psychologist?
 http://www.spsp.org/what.htm
Social Psychology
 http://www.trinity.edu/~mkearl/socpsy.html
Realty Times
 http://realtytimes.com
Association of Real Estate License Law Officials
 http://www.arello.org
The Psychology of Consumers: Consumer Behavior and Marketing
 http://www.consumerpsychologist.com
A Guide to Public Relations Education and Training
 http://www.martex.co.uk/prcareerdevelopment/il.htm
Careers in Public Relations: An Overview
 http://www.prsa.org/_Resources/profession/careeroverview.asp
Advertising
 http://careers.wlu.edu/web_exchange/adindex.htm
Marketing
 http://www.wetfeet.com/asp/careerprofiles_track.asp?careerpk=23
About Retail Careers
 http://retailindustry.about.com/library/blcareer.htm
Careers in Advertising
 http://arttech.about.com/library/bl_freelancing_help_advertising.htm

CHECKLIST: IS SOCIAL OR CONSUMER PSYCHOLOGY FOR YOU?

Do you:

☐ Like shopping and spending time in stores?

☐ Wonder what influences people's purchases?

☐ Have an interest in attitude formation and change?

☐ Like solving problems?

☐ Enjoy persuading others?

☐ Like watching the Super Bowl for the commercials?

☐ Like "reading" people?

☐ Find research enjoyable?

☐ Think quickly on your feet?

☐ Like working with numbers?

Scoring: The more boxes you checked, the more likely it is that a career in social or consumer psychology is for you.

DEVELOPMENTAL PSYCHOLOGY

CHAPTER GUIDE

How do we grow and change throughout our lives? Can the media influence children's behavior? How does exposure to violence influence children and adolescents? Developmental psychologists examine questions pertinent to our everyday lives. Historically, graduate training in developmental psychology has led to academic careers; however, today more developmental psychologists are entering applied careers. In this chapter, we'll explore careers for students who are interested in developmental psychology.

DEVELOPMENTAL PSYCHOLOGY

Developmental psychology is the study of how people grow, develop, and change across the lifespan. Developmental psychologists are concerned with the emotional, intellectual, and physical development of children, adolescents, and adults. Many developmental psychologists specialize in a particular age group, such as infants and young children, adolescents, young adults, or older adults. Perhaps the fastest-growing field within developmental psychology is *gerontology,* or the study of the aging process from middle age through later life. Gerontologists study physical, emotional, social, and psychological changes that older adults experience as they age. They also study how our society is changing as the population of the United States ages, as well as how to apply developmental knowledge in order to effect policies and programs for older adults and their families. Developmental psychologists conduct research on a diverse array of topics, such as the prevalence and causes of midlife crises, how infants learn language, and influences on antisocial activity during adolescence.

A growing number of psychologists are concerned with applied developmental psychology, which is part of the larger, multidisciplinary field of applied developmental science. Applied developmental psychologists conduct research on practical problems in real-world settings, such as the scope and nature of children's exposure to violence and how to promote resilience in children and adolescents reared in disenfranchised neighborhoods. Applied developmental psychologists develop and evaluate interventions that promote optimal cognitive, emotional, and social development. They disseminate knowledge about developmental processes to policy makers, businesses, industry, health-care professionals, and parents. Applied developmental psychologists also engage in direct service delivery by constructing, administering, and interpreting assessments of developmental strengths and vulnerabilities; by developing behavioral management programs for individuals and groups; and by delivering psychological services in various mental health settings (Fisher & Osofsky, 1997; Kuther, 1996; University of New Orleans, 2001).

OPPORTUNITIES WITH A BACHELOR'S DEGREE

Gerontology Aide

Gerontology aides are human service workers (also known as social and human service assistants) who specialize in working with older adults and provide direct and indirect services to clients. They develop programs such as health promotion, senior theater groups, and intergenerational activities for older people in senior centers, community agencies, and retirement communities. Gerontology aides also provide direct care to older adults in hospitals, clinics, and nursing homes, or through adult day-care or home-care programs. They monitor and keep records on clients' progress and report to supervisors and case managers. Gerontology aides may accompany clients to group meal sites, adult day-care centers, or doctors' offices; telephone or visit clients' homes to make sure services are being received; and help clients with daily living needs. Most gerontology aides work under the direction of professionals, who include psychologists, nurses, counselors, or social workers, depending on the setting. Gerontology aides are found in offices, clinics, hospitals, group homes, day programs, and clients' homes.

An important advantage to obtaining a position as a gerontology aide is the ability to help others and contribute to their welfare. Other advantages include a fairly standard 40-hour workweek—but working on weekends and evenings may be necessary, depending on the setting. Because social and human service assistant positions, including gerontology aides, are projected to grow much faster than the average for all occupations through 2012 (Bureau of Labor Statistics, 2004), the field will provide psychology students with many career choices. If you're interested in becoming a gerontology aide, your psychology curriculum will prepare you well. Take additional courses in communication, gerontology, and perhaps social work to round out your skills.

Although helping others is heartwarming, a position as a gerontology aide can be emotionally draining. It can be difficult to work with clients you cannot help, such as those who are dying. Human services careers are not for everyone, and turnover among staff tends to be high. Finally, gerontology aides earn a relatively low salary. In 2002, the median annual earnings of social and human service assistants, such as gerontology aides, were $23,370 ($25,536 adjusted for 2005, assuming 3 percent annual increases) (Bureau of Labor Statistics, 2004).

Careers in Nonprofit Organizations

The nonprofit sector offers new graduates a broad range of job opportunities. In the last 20 years alone, the nonprofit sector has grown at a rate surpassing both government and private business (Cornell Career Services, n.d.). What is a nonprofit organization? As the name suggests, nonprofit organizations do not operate to earn a profit; in other words, their income does not go to stockholders, directors, or any other people with interests in the organization. Instead, income is funneled back into the organization to help it meet its goals. Most of the great variety of nonprofit organizations work to advance a cause or interest. For example, some nonprofits promote educational, scientific, cultural, civic, or social welfare causes. Many psychology graduates work for nonprofit organizations that try to improve the lives of individuals, families, and children.

Nonprofit organizations offer opportunities for both program and administrative positions. Students interested in applied developmental psychology often seek program positions within organizations that focus on the needs of children, youth, and families. If you seek a program position, you might help provide health services, counseling, crisis intervention, therapy, education, and research activities (Rowh & Suchorski, 2000). Bachelor's degree holders in psychology are competitive for entry-level positions as program assistants in each of these areas. In this position, you'll help the program director and work on analyzing issues and implementing programs. Tasks might include data entry and analysis, report writing, and office work. The average annual base salary for such a position is $23,768 (College Journal, 2005). Other psychology graduates with applied developmental psychology interests are hired in direct service program positions in which they work with an organization's clients by leading support groups for children, youth, and parents, conducting education and training sessions for parents, or providing education and support to families in their homes. In 2004, the typical direct service outreach worker earned a median salary of $25,814 (Abbott, Langer, & Associates, 2005c). For more information about direct service positions for baccalaureate degree holders in psychology, see Chapter 4.

Administrative positions within nonprofit organizations include public relations specialists (Chapter 10), administrative assistants (Chapter 8), computer staff (Chapter 9), and other office support workers. Here, we discuss another administrative position critical to nonprofits. Because nonprofit organizations rely heavily on contributions and grants, their survival depends on fund-raising. Psychology students offer many skills that serve this position, including an understanding of interpersonal behavior, principles of persuasion, and attitude formation and change.

Fund-raising positions also require strong communication, public relations, and organizational skills in order to mobilize public support, as well as an appreciation for how people respond to solicitations and requests for help. As a fund-raiser for a nonprofit organization, you'll plan and organize programs to raise money to support the organization and its work. This involves designing programs and activities to encourage contributions and financial support; soliciting donations from individuals, foundations, and corporations; and working to achieve and maintain positive relationships with donors. Fund-raising positions also entail writing proposals for grants or donations, conducting research on prospective donors, and coordinating special fund-raising events (Rowh & Suchorski, 2000). The psychology major's people skills, problem-solving ability, understanding of social psychological principles, and critical analysis skills match a career in fund-raising well. Courses in marketing, accounting, communication, and business administration will broaden your skills. Depending on experience, the average fund-raising salary starts at about $40,000 per year (Herbst, 2005). In 2003, the median salary for all fund-raisers was $72,050 (Blum, 2005).

An important advantage to a career in a nonprofit organization is the opportunity to help individuals and to improve the health and welfare of people in general. The work is interesting, and you'll be able to influence pressing social issues. With experience, you'll find opportunities for advancement within an organization, either by taking on additional supervisory and administrative tasks or by moving to larger nonprofit organizations. Disadvantages to a career in the nonprofit sector include low pay relative to skills and education. In addition, most nonprofits depend on a variety of unstable funding activities including grants, public donations, and fund-raising events. Because the financial stability of many nonprofits is uncertain, workers sometimes face layoffs. The overall lack of funding can contribute to a stressful work environment because of inadequate resources for staff development, quality equipment, and office space.

Careers in child-care, gerontology services, and nonprofit organizations are just some of the opportunities available to students interested in developmental psychology. Also consider careers in teaching (Chapter 4), corrections (Chapter 5), and public relations (Chapter 10).

OPPORTUNITIES WITH A GRADUATE DEGREE

Your employment opportunities dramatically expand with a graduate degree in developmental psychology. The following sections explore a range of new opportunities for graduate degree holders in developmental psychology who are interested in applying their skills to solve real-world problems.

Scientist-Practitioner Careers

Applied developmental psychologists merge science with practice. They work in medical facilities, schools, social service agencies, and private practice. Some serve as consultants who provide teachers with information about behavioral management and instructional techniques appropriate for individuals with a wide range of developmental needs, including those with developmental disabilities (Fisher & Osofsky, 1997). Others conduct developmental assessments of children who have suffered injuries or who are suspected of having a developmental delay. After diagnosing a developmental delay or learning disability, an applied developmental psychologist discusses treatment and intervention alternatives with parents and provides teachers and parents with information about the child's condition and how to promote development. In cases of severe developmental delays, applied developmental psychologists in hospital and service settings work with a multidisciplinary team of physicians, social workers, physical therapists, and other professionals to determine the best course of treatment or intervention. As you can see, applied developmental psychologists engage in activities similar to those of clinical and counseling psychologists. However, the applied developmental psychologist differs from other clinicians in at least two important ways: (1) Applied developmental psychologists do not conduct individual therapy; (2) Applied developmental psychologists are oriented toward promoting development across the lifespan by helping individuals develop skills to optimize their capacities.

Applied developmental psychologists design and empirically evaluate programs provided by hospitals, social service agencies, mental health clinics, and schools (Bruzzese, 2005). For example, they might evaluate the impact of a behaviorally oriented program administered in a hospital or clinic setting, such as the effect of maternal prenatal care and education on infant health outcomes. In school settings, they might design and evaluate remedial education programs or determine the effectiveness of mainstreaming practices. In residential care settings, they might evaluate the effectiveness of a program to help improve feelings of self-efficacy (or control) in older adults.

Applied developmental psychologists may also work in social service agencies and court settings, where they evaluate families who wish to provide foster parenting, determine parental fitness for regaining child custody, or participate as part of a multidisciplinary team to assist abused children during the subsequent investigation and court process. Applied developmental psychologists conduct evaluations of children and families during divorce and child custody cases, determine the developmental status of adolescents in criminal cases in which they might be tried as adults, and serve as expert witnesses in child abuse, custody, and trials in which the defendants are children and adolescents.

If you're interested in a career in applied developmental psychology, recognize that a master's degree will prepare you for engaging in developmental assessment activities under the supervision of a licensed psychologist. A master's degree will also prepare you for many positions in program design and evaluation. A doctoral degree will enable you to engage in more advanced activities, but it will also impose additional responsibilities, such as seeking licensure.

Applied developmental psychologists who plan careers as scientist-practitioners must seek state licensure in order to offer psychological services to the public (Goldstein, Wilson, & Gerstein, 1983). State licensure aims at ensuring at least a minimum level of competency in practitioners. It provides a standard of professionalism in psychology and protects consumers from the consequences of unprofessional conduct by licensed professionals (Fisher & Koocher, 1990; Kuther, 1996). Licensure has personal, professional, and economic implications for applied developmental psychologists. By providing statutory recognition, licensure has a legitimizing and enhancing effect on any profession. A license offers public recognition that a psychologist is competent, and it is required for psychologists who wish to be reimbursed by health insurers for providing mental health services. Typically, licensure eligibility requires two years of supervised field experience, with at least one year of postdoctoral work in addition. It also requires passing a written national examination and a written examination covering ethical and legal issues within a particular state, as well as an oral examination in some states. Note that the requirements for licensure vary from state to state. Licensure offers scientist-practitioners additional employment and professional advancement opportunities. In 2001, licensed scientist-practitioner psychologists working in direct human services positions earned a median salary of $71,000; those with two to four years of experience earned $62,000 (Singleton, Tate, & Randall, 2003).

Although this discussion has emphasized the applied and practice activities of applied developmental psychologists, recognize that many of these professionals conduct applied research in university, hospital, government, and private settings. For example, a researcher in a university might study risk factors for adolescent delinquency and then develop a prevention and intervention program to help at-risk adolescents. For more information about research careers in a variety of settings, see Chapter 2.

Product Development and Media Consultant

Psychologists use their knowledge about human development, interpersonal relations, and attitude formation and change to provide organizations with research-based information to assist them in providing goods and services that meet people's needs. Developmental psychologists offer organizations special assistance in designing and marketing developmentally appropriate toys, learning products, television programs, and more.

Psychologists often work as consultants in product development and marketing. They determine the developmental appropriateness of toys and provide insight into children's abilities and styles of play. They test prototypes of toys with children and modify them based on their input. Consultants conduct focus groups with parents and children to determine their views about specific products and to get feedback on toy designs. The resulting knowledge is used to improve the product. They also conduct market research by examining children's and parents' reactions to particular toys, advertising, and promotional techniques, as well as their needs, tastes, purchasing power, and buying habits. The next time you're in a toy store and pick up a particular toy, notice the label describing the toy's age appropriateness; it's probably the work of a developmental psychologist.

Other developmental psychologists assist companies in developing and marketing products appropriate for older adults. They apply gerontological knowledge to improve the design of products and environments (such as a residential home). For example, a consultant might suggest modifying the design of product packaging by using contrasting colors and larger print that older adults can more easily read. Through focus groups and research, consultants determine older adults' needs and preferences and provide organizations with the information to design better products and marketing techniques.

Psychologists also provide developmental and educational advice to the media, especially creators of children's programming. For example, they conduct and interpret research on children's attention spans that inform creative guidelines for television programs such as *Sesame Street*. As in product development, focus groups and market research form the information base that is used to target television and radio audiences.

Product development and marketing consultants work for companies, for consulting firms, and in private practice. An important reward of a career as a consultant in product development and marketing is that you'll engage in work with practical implications and get to see the results of your work. You'll work on a variety of projects with a rapid turnover. Because clients must make swift business decisions, they often need the research done quickly. A regular 40-hour weekly schedule and high rates of compensation are other advantages. In 2005, a typical market research analyst earned a median base salary of $51,157 (Salary.com, 2005); however, higher salaries are likely for psychologists because of their scientific background and specialized knowledge about human development and psychological principles.

Social Policy Research

Developmental psychologists often find satisfying careers in social policy. Social policy work typically is conducted within government positions (as in the National Institutes of Mental Health or the National Institute on Drug Abuse) and at think tanks or policy-oriented organizations that resemble academia. We've already discussed the nature of research positions in Chapter 2. Even so, research careers in social policy–oriented organizations deserve special mention within this chapter, because many social and developmental psychologists are interested in using the psychological knowledge base to promote public welfare by educating legislators and lobbying for social change. If you choose a career in social policy, much of your time will be spent writing grants, conducting research, analyzing the impact of various policies, and writing, presenting, and publishing your work in various formats to ensure that your findings are accessible to the public and to policy makers.

Perhaps the best way to gain perspective on research careers in think tanks is to explore three prominent policy-oriented organizations. Remember that these are just a small sampling of the policy centers that abound.

- RAND (a contraction of *research and development*) is the oldest U.S. think tank, created in 1946. The mission of RAND, like other think tanks, is to apply research and analysis to improve policy and decision making. A very large think tank, RAND conducts policy research in a variety of areas. Projects have included creating a nationwide drug prevention program for schoolchildren, evaluating the quality of health care for older adults, and assessing the impact of Indonesia's economic crisis on its citizens. For more information about RAND, see http://www.rand.org.
- The Families and Work Institute is a research center that provides data about the interaction of work and family to inform decision making. Researchers at the Families and Work Institute conduct research on "work-life issues and concerns confronting workers and employers in order to inform decision-makers in government, business, communities, and families" (Families and Work Institute, n.d.). Sample projects include longitudinal studies with nationally representative samples of U.S. workers to learn about the changing nature

of work, longitudinal studies of employers to understand how U.S. employers are responding to employee work-life needs, and interviews with children to understand how they make sense of their world and the implications of this for schools, programs, and policies. For more information about the Families and Work Institute, visit http:// www.familiesandwork.org.

- Manpower Demonstration Research Corporation (MDRC) is dedicated to learning what works to improve the well-being of low-income people and actively communicating findings to enhance the effectiveness of public policies and programs. Researchers at MDRC conduct evaluations of welfare reforms and other supports for the working poor as well as research on how programs affect children's development and their families' well-being. Other projects examine the effectiveness of school reform policies designed to improve academic achievement and access to college, and still others look at community approaches to increasing employment in low-income neighborhoods. For more information about MDRC, visit http:// www.mdrc.org.

How do you prepare for a career in policy research? Although graduate training provides a knowledge base about research methodology, a career in policy-related research requires you to learn how to formulate research questions in ways that can inform policy; you must also learn how to communicate findings to a wide and varied audience (Susman-Stillman et al., 1996). If you're interested in this career, seek a policy-related undergraduate, predoctoral, or postdoctoral fellowship and get hands-on learning to supplement your graduate training. Researchers in think tanks and policy-oriented organizations earn salaries similar to those in academia. In 2001, doctoral degree holders with two to four years of experience earned a median salary of $57,000 in nonprofit research settings (Singleton, Tate, & Randall, 2003).

Suggested Readings

Acuff, D. S., & Reiher, R. H. (1997).*What kids buy and why: The psychology of marketing to kids.* New York: Free Press.

Berk, L. (2001). Trends in human development. In J. S. Halonen & S. F. Davis (Eds.), *The many faces of psychological research in the 21st century.* Retrieved June 5, 2002, from http://teachpsych.lemoyne.edu/teachpsych/faces/script/Ch10.htm

Eberts, M., & Gisler, M. (1999). *Careers for kids at heart and others who adore children.* New York: McGraw-Hill.

Giacobello, J. (2001). *Choosing a career in the toy industry.* New York: Rosen.

Krannich, R. L., & Krannich, C. R. (1998). *Jobs and careers with nonprofit organizations: Profitable opportunities with nonprofit.* Manassas Park, VA: Impact.

Kuther, T. L. (1996). Doctoral training in applied developmental psychology: Matching graduate education and accreditation standards to student needs, career opportunity, and licensure requirements. In C. B. Fisher, J. P. Murray, & I. E. Sigel (Eds.), *Applied developmental science: Graduate training for diverse disciplines and educational settings* (pp. 53–74). Norwood, NJ: Able.

Rowh, M., & Suchorski, J. (2000). *Opportunities in fund-raising careers.* New York: McGraw-Hill.

Susman-Stillman, A. R., Brown, J. L., Adam, E. K., Blair, C., Gaines, R., Gordon, R. A., et al. (1996). Building research and policy connections: Training and career options for developmental scientists. *Social Policy Report, 10*(4), 1–19.

WEB RESOURCES

National Child Care Association
http://www.nccanet.org

National Association for the Education of Young Children
http://www.naeyc.org

National Network for Child Care
http://www.nncc.org

Society for Research in Child Development
http://www.srcd.org

Careers in Aging: Consider the Possibilities
http://www.careersinaging.com/careersinaging

Careers in Aging
http://www.careersinaging.com

Careers in Gerontology
http://www.geron.org/StudentOrg/careers.htm

Toy Inventor Designer Guide
http://www.toy-tia.org/Content/NavigationMenu/Press_Room/Publications_Resources1/Toy_Inventor_Designer_Guide/Toy_Inventor_Designer_Guide.htm

Sesame Workshop
http://www.sesameworkshop.org

Children's Advertising Review Unit
http://www.caru.org

Society for Research on Adolescence
http://www.s-r-a.org

Moving Ideas: Electronic Policy Network
http://movingideas.org

Families and Work Institute
http://www.familiesandwork.org

American Geriatrics Society
    http://www.americangeriatrics.org
American Association of Fundraising Counsel
    http://www.aafrc.org
Association of Fundraising Professionals
    http://www.afpnet.org
Association for Gerontology in Higher Education
    http://www.aghe.org
RAND
    http://www.rand.org/about
MDRC
    http://www.mdrc.org

CHECKLIST: IS DEVELOPMENTAL PSYCHOLOGY FOR YOU?

Do you:

- ☐ Want to know how people change as they age?
- ☐ Like solving problems?
- ☐ Like learning about older adulthood?
- ☐ Have the ability to consider multiple perspectives?
- ☐ Like working with theories?
- ☐ Find infants interesting?
- ☐ Have the ability to tolerate ambiguity?
- ☐ Want to do work that helps people?
- ☐ Like children?
- ☐ Not want to be a clinician?
- ☐ Have interest in social policy?
- ☐ Think adolescents are interesting?
- ☐ Wonder how we change as we progress through adulthood?
- ☐ Enjoy conducting research?
- ☐ Find all ages interesting?
- ☐ Enjoy reading books about developmental issues (for example, what to expect the first year or during the toddler years)?

Scoring: The more boxes you checked, the more likely it is that you're a good match for a career in developmental psychology.

CHAPTER 12

GETTING A JOB AFTER GRADUATION

CHAPTER GUIDE

Each year, psychology ranks consistently among the top five most popular bachelor's degrees awarded (U.S. Department of Education, NCES, 2003). Most students who graduate with a psychology degree do not go to graduate school (Borden & Rajecki, 2000); instead, they enter the world of work—and find success. You've already learned about the wealth of career paths that you can enter with your psychology degree. Let's take a closer look at why your degree is so valuable. Education in psychology offers broad training in skills that are critical to nearly every workplace, such as communication, problem solving, writing, and critical thinking. In this chapter, we'll show you how to recognize the general skills that enhance your employability. We'll also give an overview of the hiring process so you can present your skills in their best light.

SKILLS AND ABILITIES SOUGHT BY EMPLOYERS

What exactly do employers seek in new hires? Several research studies have examined this question. Table 12.1 is a compilation of the conclusions of research studies investigating the skills employers seek in prospective employees (Appleby, 2000; Edwards & Smith, 1988; Grocer & Kohout, 1997; Lloyd & Kennedy, 1997; National Association of Colleges and Employers, 2005; Sheetz, 1995). Do you notice any similarity between the skills employers seek and those that a major in psychology develops? You may be better prepared for the career world than you think! As we've seen, psychology majors are especially valued for their interpersonal skills, including the ability to communicate, influence others, and work in groups, as well as their research skills. The "people skills" and research knowledge typical of psychology majors, honed through course work, practica, and extracurricular activities, provide an upper hand in the job market. Your major has helped you develop a host of skills that employers want.

So, you've decided to put your psychology education to work and enter the job market after graduation—but where do you start? Just how do you obtain a "real" job? In the next sections, we'll provide an overview of the job-seeking process. Remember that this is simply an overview. There are many books and Internet sites devoted to job seeking, and we encourage you to explore the resources listed at the end of this chapter for additional, more-detailed information.

TABLE 12.1   Skills Employers Value in New Hires

Reading and Writing Skills

- Ability to extract important ideas through reading

- Writing skills to document ideas

- Ability to write reports, proposals, and summaries

Problem-Solving Skills

- Good judgment and decision-making skills

- Ability to apply information to solve problems and analyze them on the basis of personal experience and psychological principles

Career-Related Work Experience

- Hands-on practical experience through cooperative education, internships, practica, part-time jobs, or summer work experience

- A real-world work orientation and the ability to apply school-based knowledge in practical settings

Data Analysis Skills

- Computational skills; the ability to reason numerically and to identify problems in data

- Ability to collect, record, and report statistical information

Computer Skills

- Knowledge of software applications, including word-processing, spreadsheet, and database software

- Familiarity with the Internet and e-mail

Communication and Interpersonal Skills

- Good listening skills

- Ability to communicate orally in a clear, concise, accurate and logical fashion

- Sensitivity to social signals

- Group skills including discussion, team building, and conflict management

- Tolerance for, and an understanding of, individual differences

Psychological Knowledge

- Specific psychological knowledge, such as how attitudes are formed and changed or how people think, solve problems, and process information

- Understanding of group dynamics

- Knowledge about how people perceive and sense their environment

Self-Management

- Personal qualities and traits such as self-esteem, confidence, and social skills

- Tolerance for stress and ambiguity

- Ability to set and pursue goals, control one's emotions, and engage in appropriate behavior

TABLE 12.1	*(Continued)*

Information Acquisition and Use

- Understanding of how to absorb and retain information

- Understanding of how to learn, where to find information, and how to evaluate and use it

Adaptability

- Adaptability, flexibility, and ability to handle multiple tasks

- Broad knowledge base outside of the field of psychology

- Ability to use resources in order to complete tasks effectively (for example, creating a schedule, writing a budget, assigning space, and managing others)

LOCATING POSITIONS

Your first stop in the job-hunting process should be the career services office at your college or university, where you'll find skilled professionals who can help you with all aspects of the job search. The career services office can also help you locate available positions, as employers seeking to hire current students and recent graduates often contact colleges. Examine advertisements in your local paper and on the Internet for leads on jobs. Contact the human resources department of major businesses, corporations, and agencies in your area to inquire about job openings. Finally, remember that most jobs aren't advertised, so it's important that you use your personal networks to locate "hidden" positions. Through school, friends (and their parents), part-time jobs, and internships, you've already made many connections. Tap into these professional connections when scouting for positions—you may get leads on jobs not advertised to the general public.

PREPARING A RESUME

A well-written resume is the ticket to getting an interview—and possibly a job offer. A *resume* is a summary of your educational history, skills, and work experience. Employers always expect applicants to include resumes in their applications—even if they don't explicitly say so in their advertisement. Your resume introduces you to the employer; its purpose is to convince an employer to interview you. It's a chance to present yourself: your strengths, skills, and unique fit to the position to which you're applying. Therefore, your task is to showcase your skills. There are many types of

TABLE 12.2	Sample Chronological Resume

CHRISTINE JONES

Student Dorms #321 Your University Purchase, NY 11234 (914) 555-1414 Jones@yourstateu.edu	77 Pleasant Street Pleasantville, NY 11245 (914) 555-6677 Fax (914) 555-9999
EDUCATION:	Your University, Purchase, NY Bachelor of Arts in Psychology, May 2001 Minor: Communications
EXPERIENCE:	Resident Assistant, Your University, Purchase, NY, May, 1999–Present Assisted the director of a 360-resident living unit on campus. Assisted in creating and implementing policies and procedures for managing the residence. Developed and presented programs on a variety of subjects including alcohol awareness, career development, leadership, and safety.
	Intern, *Purchase Daily News,* Purchase, NY August, 1998–May, 1999
	Researched and wrote weekly articles on breaking news. Interviewed and researched local residents for weekly "Local Profile" articles.
	Cashier, Purchase Delicatessen, Purchase, NY June, 1997–August, 1999
	Assisted customers in locating products, operated computerized cash register, handled large sums of cash, stocked shelves, and monitored store inventory.
ACTIVITIES:	Theater Society, active member, two years, chorus member in three plays.
	Psychology Club, active member, three years, organized fundraisers, participated in tutoring groups, and invited local speakers to club meetings.
REFERENCES:	Available upon request

Source: Adapted from Kuther, 2006.

resumes, but the two most common are the chronological and the functional resume.

Chronological Resume

The chronological resume presents your education and career in a chronological framework, which is easy for employers to understand and read. A brief description of the content of each section of the chronological resume follows; a sample chronological resume appears in Table 12.2.

- **Contact information** Include your name, permanent address, phone and fax numbers, and e-mail address. Be sure to use a professional e-mail address, not a nickname such as HotTamale101, which will be poorly received. Similarly, include your website only if it looks professional and is relevant to your career goal.

- **Education** Include the name of the degree you'll receive, the institution and date, and your major and GPA (but only if it's higher than 3.0). Also include any academic honors that you've received.
- **Experience** Present all relevant employment experiences: part-time, internships, cooperative education or self-employment. List your most recent job first and work backward in time. Include all relevant experiences, regardless of whether they were paid. Include the title, company, address, and dates of employment. Briefly describe your duties and responsibilities as they relate to the position you're seeking, and emphasize specific skills and achievements. Use active words to describe your duties and the results that you produced.
- **Activities and affiliations** List professional affiliations and activities that are relevant to your specific employment goals.

The main disadvantage of a chronological resume is that applicants who are just starting out usually do not have many professional experiences to list, resulting in a resume that may appear skimpy. Employers may not easily recognize your skills when your work-related experiences are presented chronologically, especially if you have few such experiences. In these cases, a functional resume is often recommended.

Functional Resume

The functional resume presents all of your accomplishments. It organizes your experiences and work history by highlighting skills and accomplishments that might not be obvious in a chronological resume. Like the chronological resume, the functional resume begins with contact information as the heading. Table 12.3 illustrates the functional resume.

Rearrange your employment, volunteer, and internship history into sections that highlight areas of skills and accomplishments. Each skill or accomplishment section must contain statements relating to your experience in that category (as well as employer and work dates). Organize accomplishments in their order of importance with regard to the position that you seek. The education section is identical to the one in the chronological resume, but because it appears toward the bottom of the page, it's less important visually.

Take great care in crafting your resume, because most employers glance at a resume for 20–30 seconds (Krannich, 1991). If the first few lines of your resume don't catch the employer's attention, your opportunity is lost. Make it past the 20-second test by considering the main

TABLE 12.3	Sample Functional Resume

CHRISTINE JONES

Student Dorms #321   77 Pleasant Street
Your University   Pleasantville, NY 11245
Purchase, NY 11234   (914) 555-6677
(914) 555-1414;   Fax (914) 555-9999
Jones@yourstateu.edu

Interpersonal Experience

Resident Assistant, Your University, Purchase, NY, May, 1999–Present

Assisted the director of a 360-resident living unit on campus. Assisted in creating and implementing policies and procedures for managing the residence. Developed and presented programs on a variety of subjects including alcohol awareness, career development, leadership, and safety.

Cashier, Purchase Delicatessen, Purchase, NY June, 1997–August, 1999 Assisted customers in locating products, operated computerized cash register, handled large sums of cash, stocked shelves, and monitored store inventory.

Leadership and Organizational Experience

Psychology Club, active member, three years, organized fund raisers, participated in tutoring groups, and invited local speakers to club meetings.

Writing Experience

Intern, *Purchase Daily News,* Purchase, NY August, 1998–May, 1999 Researched and wrote weekly articles on breaking news. Interviewed and researched local residents for weekly articles.

Public Speaking

Theater Society, active member, two years, chorus member in three plays.

Education

Your University, Purchase, NY

Bachelor of Arts in Psychology, Minor: Communications, May 2001

References available upon request

Source: Adapted from Kuther, 2006.

question that employers ask themselves as they read resumes: Why should I read this or contact this person for an interview? Keep this question in mind as you prepare your resume, make sure that you answer it, and you'll have a unique resume. All of this hard work is essential; a good resume gets you to the next stage, whereas a poor resume stops you from going anywhere.

Make your resume look professional. Use a laser printer and understand that typos and grammatical errors may cost you an interview. See Table 12.4 for more resume tips. Also, many books and Internet resources provide advice for writing resumes. See the recommended readings and websites at the end of this chapter for more information.

TABLE 12.4	Resume Checklist

- ☐ Clearly communicate your purpose and value.
- ☐ Communicate your strongest points first.
- ☐ Don't make statements that you can't document.
- ☐ Be direct, succinct, and expressive with language.
- ☐ Don't use lengthy sentences and descriptions; this is the only time that sentence fragments are acceptable, but use them judiciously.
- ☐ Don't use the passive voice.
- ☐ Don't change the tense of verbs throughout the resume.
- ☐ Confine your information to one page.
- ☐ Use space to organize your resume; it should not appear cramped.
- ☐ Aim for overall visual balance on the page.
- ☐ Use a font size of 10 to 14 points.
- ☐ Choose a simple typeface and stick to it (i.e., don't change fonts).
- ☐ Use ample spacing and bold for emphasis (but don't overdo it).
- ☐ Don't fold or staple your resume.
- ☐ Check spelling, grammar, and punctuation.
- ☐ Proofread.
- ☐ Ask someone else to proofread.
- ☐ Get outside help. Get feedback from two or three people, including someone who regularly evaluates resumes and hires employees.
- ☐ Do not include your reference information on your resume (see Tables 12.2 and 12.3).
- ☐ Before giving their names to a potential employer, ask your references if they are willing to serve as references.

Source: Kuther, 2006, pp. 151–152.

COVER LETTER

Your resume highlights your skills, but you must also explain why you are well suited to a particular job. The cover letter is an introduction to your resume that enables you to tailor your application to a prospective employer. Your cover letter must be concise and explain who you are and what you can offer an employer. Usually, three paragraphs will suffice. First, explain your reason for writing (for example, "to apply to the research assistant position advertised in the *Daily News*"). Demonstrate interest in the employer and position. Then, discuss what you can offer an employer. Highlight the most important aspects of your background that are relevant to the position and/or organization. Show that you've done some homework and learned about the employer. Finally, summarize

TABLE 12.5	Cover Letter Checklist

☐ Address the letter to an individual, using the person's name and title. If answering a blind newspaper advertisement, use the following address: "To Whom It May Concern."

☐ Indicate the position for which you are applying and explain why you are qualified to fill it.

☐ Include a phone number where you can be reached.

☐ Ask someone to proofread your letter for spelling, grammar, and punctuation errors.

☐ Indicate how your education and work skills are transferable and relevant to the position for which you are applying.

☐ Keep a copy of each cover letter for your records; write notes from any phone conversations that might occur on your copy of the cover letter.

☐ Make a connection to the company through a person you know, some information you've researched, or a specific interest.

Source: Kuther, 2006, pp. 154–155.

your main points, provide contact information, thank the reader, and reiterate your interest in the position.

Your cover letter should motivate the reader to examine your resume. Keep your audience in mind and address their needs. Continually ask yourself, "What is the purpose of this letter? What are the needs of the reader? What benefits will an employer gain from me? How can I maintain the reader's interest? How can I end the letter persuasively, so that the reader will want to examine my resume and contact me?" Communicate what you can do for the employer, not what the job will do for you. Table 12.5 presents a cover letter checklist.

REFERENCES

Nearly all positions that you pursue will require you to provide the names of several references—people who can verify your qualifications and abilities. Whom should you use as a reference? Employers are interested in your potential as an employee, so your references should be able to comment on your professional abilities and personal characteristics that directly relate to job performance, such as dependability, resourcefulness, and attitude. Professors, supervisors for your practica or other applied experiences, and former employers are good choices for references. As you choose your references, remember that you must ask their permission before listing them on your resume or application. When a prospective employer contacts one of your references, you don't want that person to ask, "Who?" Don't surprise your references—ask them first so that you make a good impression and ensure that they feel comfortable recommending you for a job.

THE INTERVIEW

If your resume shows a good fit to the position, you may be invited for an interview. The interview is the most important criterion for hiring; it beats out grades, related work experience, and recommendations (Krannich, 1991). The interview helps companies identify which applicants they'd like to take a closer look at. Often, second and sometimes even third interviews occur. This is your chance to impress the prospective employer. How do you do it? Present a professional image, good communication skills, clearly defined professional goals, honesty, and cheerfulness. Be sure to prepare beforehand, because your interviewer wants to understand why you want to work for them, what you're suited for, and what your qualifications are. Although interviews are stressful, you can increase your confidence by being thoroughly prepared.

Be Prepared

Keep the purpose of the interview and the interviewer's objectives in mind. From your perspective, the purpose of the job interview is to get a second interview or job offer; for employers, however, its purpose is to whittle down the list of applicants to one or two finalists. The interviewer seeks to learn the following:

- Why does this person want to work for us?
- What position is this person suited for?
- What are his or her qualifications?
- Why should I hire him or her?
- Does this person meet my employment needs?
- Is he or she trustworthy?

The interviewer looks for your weaknesses, trying to uncover any reasons you should not be hired. Your job is to communicate your strengths. To do so, you need to understand yourself and the company or organization to which you're applying.

Conduct research to understand the needs of the organization. What is the relative size and growth of the industry? What product lines or services are offered? Where are headquarters located? Identify the competition. Be familiar with any recent items in the news. Try to predict what will be asked during the interview, and prepare answers. Table 12.6 presents common questions asked during interviews. Be prepared to talk about your experiences, interests, and fit to the position and organization. You'll also be judged on the questions that you ask. Ask thoughtful and intelligent questions about the company and position. Table 12.7 provides sample questions that an applicant might ask on an interview.

TABLE 12.6

Common Interviewing Questions

- What do you hope to be doing five or ten years from now?
- Why did you apply for this job?
- What can you tell me about yourself?
- What are your strengths and weaknesses?
- What can you offer to us and what can we offer to you?
- What are the two or three accomplishments in your life that have given you the greatest satisfaction?
- Do you work well under pressure?
- Have you ever held any supervisory or leadership roles?
- What do you like to do in your spare time?
- What other jobs are you applying for?
- Is there anything else we should know about you?
- Why do you feel that you will be successful in this position?
- What courses did you like best? Least? Why?
- What did you learn or gain from your part-time and summer job experience?
- What are your plans for graduate study?
- Why did you choose your major?
- What can a psychology major do for this organization?
- How did you finance your education?
- If you could do it all again, what would you change about your education?
- Did you do the best you could in school? Why or why not?
- Why did you leave your last employer?
- What job did you like the most? The least? Why?
- Have you ever been fired?
- Why do you want to join our organization?
- Why should we hire you?
- When will you be ready to work?
- What do you want to do with your life?
- Do you have any actual work experience?
- How would you describe your ideal job?
- Are you a team player? Explain.
- What motivates you?

TABLE 12.6	(Continued)

- What are some of your recent goals, and what did you do to achieve them?
- Have you ever had a conflict with a boss or professor? How did you resolve it?
- If I were to ask one of your professors to describe you, what would he or she say?
- Why did you choose to attend your college?
- What qualities do you feel a successful manager should have?
- What do you know about our company?
- What kind of salary are you looking for?

Source: Adapted from Kuther, 2006, pp. 156–157.

Dress Appropriately

Because your appearance communicates messages about your level of seriousness and professionalism dress appropriately for your interview. During the first five minutes of an interview, your appearance and demeanor strongly affect interviewers' initial judgments and expectations about your professionalism and "fit" for a position. Use this to your advantage. Even if you're applying to a company with a casual dress code, dress up for the interview to communicate your enthusiasm for the position.

Whether you're a man or a woman, you can't go wrong with a classic navy or gray suit. Men should wear a white or blue oxford shirt with an understated tie. Women should wear a modest blouse, with understated hair and makeup. Keep jewelry to a minimum: a watch, simple earrings

TABLE 12.7	Questions to Ask During an Interview

What are the duties and responsibilities of this job?

How long has this position been in the company?

What would be the ideal type of person for this position?

What kinds of skills or personality characteristics are ideal for this position?

Whom would I be working with?

What am I expected to accomplish during the first year?

How will I be evaluated?

Are promotions and raises tied to performance criteria?

What is unique about working for this company?

What does the future look like for this company?

Source: Adapted from Kuther, 2006, p. 157.

(for women only), and a ring. Remember that these are merely general rules. Look to others in your field for cues about appropriate attire. Dress codes vary by employment setting and employer; some settings permit more creativity and self-expression. However, during an interview it's best to err on the side of conservatism.

Present Yourself Well

During the interview, be enthusiastic. Remember that your interviewer is committed to his or her position and the company and wants to hire someone who is similarly committed. Discuss what you've learned from your research and preparation. Ask questions to fill any gaps in your understanding. Convey a sense of long-term interest by asking about opportunities for further professional education and advancement.

Throughout the interview, be aware of your body language and keep fidgeting to a minimum. Lean slightly toward the interviewer to communicate your interest in what he or she is saying (Krannich, 1991). Maintain eye contact to convey interest and trustworthiness. Smile to convey your positive attitude. Don't forget that your tone of voice can indicate how interested you are in the interview and the organization. Here are some other helpful tips for interviewing success:

- Bring a copy of your resume. It comes in handy if you have to fill in applications and provides initial information for your interviewer.
- Allow the interviewer to direct the conversation.
- Answer questions in a clear and positive manner.
- Never speak negatively about former employers or colleagues, no matter what.
- Let the interviewer lead the conversation toward salary and benefits. Try not to focus your interest on these issues (at least not during the initial interview).
- When discussing salary, be flexible.
- If the employer doesn't say when you'll hear about the decision, ask about when you can call to follow up.
- Thank the employer for the interview.

THE JOB OFFER

Usually job offers are made over the phone or in person (for example, toward the end of an interview). No matter how the offer is delivered, you're likely to be surprised. The most appropriate response to an offer in person or by phone is to ask any questions that come to mind and then request a day or two to think about the offer.

Before accepting an offer, be sure that you understand the conditions and elements of the job. In many cases, salaries for entry-level positions leave little room for negotiation. Take your lead from the employer as to whether the salary is negotiable. If it isn't, you must decide whether you're still willing to accept the position and what, if anything, would make it more attractive. As you think about whether to accept the job offer, consider the scope of the position, how it fits your career goals, opportunities for professional growth, and pragmatics (geographic location, benefits, salary, work hours, and so forth). If you decide to accept the offer, be sure to inform any employers still actively considering you. Also contact your references to inform them of your new job as well as to thank them for their assistance.

If you decide not to accept the job, notify the employer as soon as possible, by telephone. Timeliness is important, because other applicants also are waiting for a response. Be polite, thank the employer for the offer, and wish him or her success. Follow up with a polite letter as well.

SUGGESTED READINGS

Bolles, R.N., & Bolles, M. E. (2004). *What color is your parachute? A practical manual for job-hunters and career-changers*. Berkeley, CA: Ten Speed Press.

DeGalan, J., & Lambert, S. (2000). *Great jobs for psychology majors*. Chicago: VGM Career Horizons.

Farr, M. J. (1995). *The quick interview and salary negotiation book*. Indianapolis, IN: Jist Works.

Fry, R. (2001). *Your first resume: For students and anyone preparing to enter today's tough job market*. New York: Thomson.

Greene, B. (2004). *Get the interview every time: Fortune 500 hiring professionals' tips for writing winning resumes and cover letters*. New York: Kaplan.

Kuther, T. L. (2006). *The psychology major's handbook* (2nd ed.). Belmont, CA: Wadsworth.

WEB RESOURCES

Job Hunter's Bible
    http://www.jobhuntersbible.com
Quintessential Careers
    http://www.quintcareers.com

College Grad Job Hunter
    http://www.collegegrad.com

JobWeb
    http://www.jobweb.com

MonsterTrak.com
    http://www.monstertrak.monster.com

Careerbuilder
    http://careerbuilder.com

MonsterTrak
    http://www.monstertrak.monster.com

GETTING INTO GRADUATE SCHOOL IN PSYCHOLOGY

CHAPTER GUIDE

If you're a psychology major, the possibility of attending graduate school after graduation has probably crossed your mind. You've learned throughout this book that although many opportunities exist for bachelor's degree holders in psychology, many more opportunities become available with graduate study. During the 1999–2000 school year, more than 12,500 students enrolled in psychology graduate programs (Pate, 2001). Why do students pursue graduate degrees? Is graduate study right for you and your goals? The following sections will help you answer these questions.

Do You Need to Go to Graduate School?

Why do students attend graduate school? First and foremost, students enter graduate study in psychology and related fields because of a deep interest in understanding human behavior. Successful graduate students have a love of learning; they thirst for knowledge and thrive on discovery. Graduate study provides a unique opportunity to contribute to the discipline and enhance our knowledge base of the causes and correlates of human behavior. Many students pursue graduate study in order to contribute to society, help others in need, and improve people's quality of life. As you've learned, a graduate degree in psychology will enable you to teach in high schools, colleges, universities, or medical schools; conduct research in a university or private organization in industry or business; practice psychology in applied settings; and/or engage in a variety of consulting and applied roles. Unquestionably, graduate degrees offer prestige and opportunities for career and economic advancement, but graduate school isn't required for success in many fields.

A decision to attend graduate school should reflect your interests, goals, dreams, and abilities. This requires careful self-analysis or soul searching, the kind that can be uncomfortable because it forces you to face uncertainty, which is stressful. However, uncertainty about your educational and career goals is one stressor that you don't want to avoid. Careful consideration is vital to making a decision that you can live with for the next two to seven years and beyond.

What kind of career do you want? Is it really necessary for you to go to graduate school to achieve your goals? Are there alternative ways of achieving them? As we've discussed throughout this book, if your main goal is to work with people, you can find many alternatives to a doctoral degree in psychology.

Why do you want to go to graduate school? Is it for the right reasons? Some students pursue graduate degrees because of intellectual curiosity, career advancement, or a desire to help others. Others may want the prestige associated with a doctoral degree. What are your reasons? How will a master's or doctoral degree help you to attain your goals? Discuss this decision with your advisor, other faculty, family, and friends. Choose the level of education that offers the training and course work to prepare you for the career to which you aspire.

Why question whether graduate school is the right thing for you? Questioning your intentions is important because graduate school is a full-time commitment and a long-term investment. Graduate school will differ greatly from your days as an undergraduate student. Graduate students frequently spend 50–60 hours each week on studies and research. Graduate school can also be expensive, with student loan debts in some cases reaching $100,000 or more (Clay, 2000b). Thus, the decision to attend graduate school should be carefully considered and discussed with significant others in your life. Then, if you still plan to attend graduate school, be prepared for some of the most exciting times in your life as you meet prominent psychologists and enter a new world of information and research activity. But what type of program are you looking for?

SORTING OUT THE LETTERS: MA, PhD, AND PsyD

Lots of misinformation circulates about graduate study and the various graduate degrees. In this section, we'll briefly explore the different types of graduate degrees that a psychology student may pursue.

Master's Degree

A master's degree is a graduate degree typically requiring two years of full-time study. Of the many different types of master's degrees, the most common is the standard MA (Master of Arts) or MS (Master of Science) degrees in service-oriented fields such as clinical, counseling, and school psychology. These usually include additional practical experience in an applied setting. Most master's degree programs require a master's thesis based on a research project; however, some programs offer alternatives to the research thesis in the form of qualifying examinations or a written project slightly less rigorous than the thesis.

What's the difference between an MA and an MS? Nothing much, in terms of program curricula. Whether a university offers the MA or MS degree depends on the policies of the university, not the characteristics of the program. Many students are unaware that the degrees are interchangeable and become needlessly concerned that the one set of letters (MA or MS) is better or worse than the other. (This also holds true at the undergraduate level; BA and BS degrees are usually indistinguishable in terms of content.)

Myths abound about the master's degrees in psychology and related fields, as students and advisors often know little about them. Despite possible biases against, and lack of discussion about, the master's degree in psychology, it remains a very popular degree (Actkinson, 2000). Between 1973 and 1993, the number of master's programs quadrupled from 178 to 931 (Norcross, Haynch, & Terranova, 1996). More students enter master's programs than doctoral programs (Briihl & Wasieleski, 2004). About 13,000 students receive master's degrees in psychology each year (Hays-Thomas, 2000), and the master's degree is now the degree of choice for practitioners (American Psychological Association Research Office, 2003). Studies have been inconclusive regarding therapeutic outcomes and level of training of the practitioner (see, for example, Christensen & Jacobson, 1994; Seligman, 1995; Stein & Lambert, 1995). Further, economic changes have led to the hiring of more master's-level practitioners (Humphreys, 1996). Most states recognize licensed professional counselors. Many psychologists argue that a form of licensure should be extended to master's-level psychologists (Hays-Thomas, 2000) in order to permit their independent or unsupervised practice (North American Association of Masters in Psychology, 2005).

What can you do with a master's degree? Depending on the program and curriculum, a master's degree enables graduates to (1) teach psychology in high school (other certification may be needed) and junior colleges; (2) become more competitive for jobs in government and industry; (3) practice clinical, counseling, or school psychology under supervision; (4) obtain certification or licensure for school psychology (depending on the state) and practice industrial/organizational psychology; and (5) pursue alternative careers in counseling such as marriage and family therapy, alcohol and substance abuse counseling, or social work. If you're considering a master's in clinical or counseling psychology with the intention of setting up an independent practice, carefully research your options beforehand, because requirements for licensure as counselors or marriage and family therapists vary by state (Levant, Moldawsky, & Stigall, 2000). Be sure to do your homework so that you get the experiences you need for your chosen field and so that you're not disappointed later. Master's degree recipients in research-oriented fields such as quantitative psychology, developmental psychology, general psychology, and experimental psychology have developed useful methodological and quantitative skills. They are often employed in research positions in university research centers, government, business, and private organizations. Others seek entry into doctoral programs.

Some master's degree programs serve as springboards to doctoral programs. These programs may be slightly more rigorous because they prepare students to pursue their education further. If you plan to obtain a doctoral degree but you lack the undergraduate credentials to get accepted directly into your desired doctoral programs, two years at a reputable and rigorous master's degree program (requiring a thesis) may elevate your credentials enough to allow you to succeed in your doctoral application. In fact, many students may not be serious about psychology until their junior or senior years of college and may not have the GPA or research experience desired by doctoral programs. When one of the authors experienced this problem, this route allowed him to obtain the desired degree.

Doctoral Degrees

Although a master's degree may allow you to work in some settings, a doctoral degree is essential if you're planning on conducting research or teaching at the college level. A doctoral degree provides a greater range of flexibility and autonomy than a master's, but it usually requires five to seven years of graduate work to complete. In clinical or counseling psychology, the requirement for the doctoral degree generally includes one year of internship or supervised experience.

Psychology offers two types of doctoral degrees: the PhD and the PsyD. The PhD refers to the Doctor of Philosophy. This is a research degree that culminates in a dissertation based on original research. In clinical or counseling psychology, the PhD is flexible, because it trains people for research, teaching, writing, and clinical practice. The PsyD refers to the Doctor of Psychology. It is offered only in clinical and counseling psychology and is considered a professional degree, much like a JD (a lawyer's degree).

How do the PsyD and the PhD compare? Both are doctoral degrees and both allow you to practice psychology. They differ in their emphases, however. The PhD has a long historical tradition. Most of your college professors hold this degree as it is conferred in nearly all academic fields. The PhD in psychology provides training in research and methodology as well as specialized knowledge in a particular area. PhD recipients may find employment at universities, medical centers, and mental health centers, as well as in industry and government.

Sought by those who want to practice, the PsyD is a practitioner degree that emphasizes clinical training or the professional model of training. The PsyD degree often is offered at private or professional schools, is generally more expensive than a PhD, and is offered in larger programs than are traditional scientist-practitioner PhD programs (Mayne, Norcross, & Sayette, 1994). Most funding for PhD students comes from faculty research grants; however, because PsyD programs typically involve less research, they offer fewer opportunities for research assistantships and other funding to support graduate education. Professional programs train students to be educated consumers of research rather than generators of research. Because there is less emphasis on research, PsyD students tend to earn their degrees a little more quickly than do PhD students (Gaddy, Charlot-Swilley, Nelson, & Reich, 1995; Norcross & Castle, 2002).

Practice-oriented students often find the curricula of professional programs to be better aligned with their own interests and career aspirations than are those of traditional scientist-practitioner programs. Although some have argued that the PhD is more prestigious than the PsyD (Buskist & Shurburne, 1996), you should choose the degree that will prepare you for the career you desire. If you're interested in practicing psychology and do not want to teach in a university setting or conduct research, the PsyD may be for you. The only time graduates from professional schools suffer a disadvantage is when they apply for positions in research or academic settings. For more information about PsyD and PhD training opportunities, see Chapter 3.

SKILLS AND ABILITIES SOUGHT BY GRADUATE PROGRAMS

What do graduate programs look for in applicants? Surveys of faculty members who participate in selecting graduate students have found the following to be "very important" criteria in evaluating applicants (Bonifazi, Crespi, & Rieker, 1997; Keith-Spiegel, Tabachnick, & Spiegel, 1994):

- The extent to which the applicant's interests and skills match the program's goals
- Research experience, conference presentations, and publications
- Interest by a member or members of the selection committee in working with a particular applicant
- The clarity, focus, and content of the applicant's admission essays

The overall fit or match between the student, program, and faculty is essential, as revealed in the focus on the admissions essay and prior research. Surveys of faculty have classified the following criteria as "generally important" in selecting applicants (Bonifazi et al., 1997; Keith-Spiegel et al., 1994):

- Experience as research assistant
- Writing skills
- Knowledge about, and interest in, the program
- Number of statistics, research methodology, and hard science courses taken
- Prestige and status of faculty in undergraduate department, especially of those who are writing letters of recommendation
- Potential for success as judged by interview
- Honors and merit scholarships

Generally speaking, graduate programs look for interest in the program, research experience, and a background in statistics, methodology, and science.

APPLYING TO GRADUATE SCHOOL

Applying to graduate school is a long and arduous process. The application entails so many components that simply completing your application and mailing it off can feel like a huge accomplishment. Let's examine the various components of the graduate school application. Remember that this is simply an overview of the admissions process; many books, such as those suggested at the end of this chapter, specialize in this topic.

The Application

The most obvious part of the application is the application form itself. This form asks for your demographic information: your name, address, and so on. Remember that neatness counts, so make copies of each application before you begin. Instead of typing each one, scan your applications into the computer so that you can prepare professional-looking forms. If you don't have a scanner at home, plan on spending time in the computer lab at school.

GRE General Test

The Graduate Record Exam (GRE) General Test is a standardized test that measures a variety of skills that are thought to predict success in graduate school. The GRE General Test yields three scores: verbal ability, quantitative ability, and analytical-writing ability. The verbal section tests your ability to understand and analyze written material through the use of analogies, antonyms, sentence completions, and reading-comprehension questions. The quantitative section tests basic math skills and your ability to understand and apply quantitative skills to solve problems. Types of questions include quantitative comparisons, problem solving, and data interpretation. The analytical-writing section examines your ability to compose and defend a cohesive argument. This section consists of two tasks: "Present Your Perspective on an Issue," in which you address an issue from your perspective, and "Analyze an Argument," in which you critique an argument and discuss how well reasoned you find it.

Graduate schools consider the verbal and quantitative sections to be particularly important in making decisions about applicants. Therefore, the total GRE score usually refers to the quantitative and verbal scores (each ranging from 200 to 800) summed to a total of 1,600 possible points. The GRE General Test is administered by computer year-round, but plan to take it in the spring or summer before you apply to graduate school.

GRE Psychology Test

About half of doctoral programs require that applicants take the Graduate Record Exam Psychology Test (Matlin & Kalat, 2001). The GRE Psychology Test consists of about 215 questions that tap information from the core psychology courses required in most undergraduate programs. About 40 percent of the test consists of experimental and natural science questions from the areas of learning, language, memory, thinking, perception, ethology, sensation, comparative psychology, and physiological psychology. Social and social science areas of psychology account for an additional 43 percent of the test, including clinical, abnormal, developmental, personality, and social psychology. The remaining 17 percent consists of history, industrial/organizational and applied psychology, measurement, research methodology, and statistics (Matlin & Kalat, 2001). Unlike the General Test, the GRE Psychology Test is administered only three times a year: in April, November, and December.

Admissions Essays and Personal Statements

The personal statement or admissions essay is your chance to communicate directly with the admissions committee. Here you can present yourself as an individual, the person behind the GPA and GRE scores. Your essays will tell the admissions committee about your ability to write, to stick to the task at hand, and to persuade readers. It's the place where you can make yourself stand out, because you can talk about your interests, career aspirations, and values. Usually programs provide a question or a specific topic on which to write. Most questions posed by graduate programs fall into one of several categories, as identified by Keith-Spiegel and Wiederman (2000):

- **Career plans** What are your long-term career goals? Where do you see yourself 10 years from now?
- **General interest areas** What academic or professional areas interest you?
- **Research experiences** Discuss areas in which you might like to do research, research experiences you have had, or both. Describe your research interests.
- **Academic objectives** Why are you undertaking graduate study? Describe how graduate training is necessary for your goals.
- **Clinical or other field experience** Describe your clinical experience. How have your field experiences shaped your career goals?
- **Academic background and achievements** Discuss your academic background.
- **Personal** Is there anything in your background that you think would be relevant in our evaluation of applicants? Describe your life up to now: family, friends, home, school, work, and particularly those experiences most relevant to your interests in psychology and you. Write an autobiographical sketch.
- **Personal and professional development** Describe your values and your approach to life.

Although essay topics are often similar, you should not write a generic essay to send to all programs. Tailor your essay to the specific question and the program, because the admissions committee is interested in how well your interests and abilities match the program and faculty. As you write your essay, occasionally stop to make sure that you're answering the question posed by the admissions committee (and not digressing). Although many students use the personal essay as an opportunity to explain how they became interested in psychology, remember that your essay will be used by the admissions committee to determine whether you're suitable for graduate study. Do not disclose personal information that might be construed negatively. Certainly, your essay is a personal statement and you should feel comfortable expressing yourself; however, this is not the time to explain that your interest in psychology stems from your dysfunctional family or your own history of pathology. Remember that this is your chance to present your strengths and really shine, so take advantage of the opportunity to discuss your accomplishments, describe valuable experiences, and emphasize the positive.

Letters of Recommendation

Most graduate programs require applicants to submit three letters of recommendation. The letter of recommendation is a letter, written by a faculty member or supervisor, that discusses the personal qualities, accomplishments, and experiences that make you unique and perfect for the programs to which you've applied. As you might imagine, these letters are crucial parts of your application.

In most cases, faculty in your department write these letters. Make sure that the people you ask to write your letters

- Know you well and have known you for a long time
- Know your work and describe it positively
- Have a high opinion of you
- Know where you are applying as well as your educational and career goals
- Can favorably compare you with your peers
- Can write a good letter

Aim for a set of letters covering the range of your skills, including discussion of your academic and scholastic skills, research abilities and experiences, and applied experiences (such as co-operative education, internships, related work experience). When you approach potential recommenders, ask them if they know you well enough to write a meaningful letter. Pay attention to their demeanor. If you sense reluctance, thank them for considering it and say that you'll ask someone else. Remember that asking early in the semester is best. As the end of the semester approaches, faculty may hesitate because of time constraints.

Provide your letter writers with all the necessary information so they don't have to work at remembering the details that they should include. Make an appointment to speak with each of your recommenders and give them plenty of time to write your letter (at least three to four weeks). Provide a file with the following:

- Your transcript
- Résumé or vita
- GRE scores
- Courses you've taken with them and grades you've earned
- Research experiences
- Internship and other applied experiences
- Honor societies to which you belong

- Awards you've won
- Work experience
- Professional goals
- Due date for the application
- Information about the programs to which you're applying
- Copy of each of the application recommendation forms

The Interview

Once you've submitted your application, the waiting begins. Some graduate programs conduct phone interviews, some conduct on-site interviews, and some don't interview at all. If you're invited for an interview, remember the purpose: The interview gives admission committees an opportunity to meet candidates and see the people behind the GPAs and GRE scores. It's a chance for them to meet you, to see how you react under pressure, and to assess your verbal and nonverbal communication skills. The interview might range from half an hour with one or two faculty to a full day or more filled with meetings with students and faculty, and include small-group discussions, larger group interviews, and even social hours or parties.

To prepare for a graduate admissions interview, learn as much about the program as possible. Review the program description, department website, and faculty websites. Understand the program's emphasis, and be aware of the faculty's research interests. Consider how you will answer common interview questions, such as those in Table 13.1. See also Chapter 4 for more tips on interviewing.

In addition to answering questions, you must also ask questions. Admissions committees *expect* you to ask them, so prepare some thoughtful questions about the program, faculty, and students. Use this opportunity to learn about the program and whether it meets your needs. During your visit, try to get a sense of the department's emotional climate. What do graduate students call professors—"Doctor," or do they use first names? Are students competitive with one another? Try to get a sense of whether the atmosphere matches your personality. Is it formal or informal? Would you be happy there? Table 13.2 presents sample questions to help you determine what you'd like to ask.

After the interview, another period of waiting begins. Most programs inform applicants of their acceptance from March through early April. In most cases, your decision on whether to accept an offer is due by April 15. Accepting an offer of admission to graduate school may seem like a happy ending, but it's only the beginning of the next phase of your career.

Whatever path you choose, we hope you find the right career for you. Psychology is one of the best ways to find fulfilling work, and we wish you the best as you explore your options.

TABLE **13.1**   **Common Questions Asked by a Graduate School Admissions Interviewer**

- Why are you interested in our program?
- What do you know about our program?
- What are your career goals?
- Why did you choose a career in psychology?
- What are your research interests? Describe your research experience. What are your research strengths and weaknesses?
- What are your academic strengths? What were your favorite courses, and why?
- What do you like best about yourself?
- Whom would you like to work with? Why?
- Describe the accomplishments you feel proudest about.
- If you were to begin a research project now, what would be the topic?
- Describe your theoretical orientation.
- Discuss your experiences in clinical settings. Evaluate your clinical abilities. What are your strengths and weaknesses?
- What can you tell us about yourself?
- How would your professors describe you?
- How will you be able to make a contribution to this field? How do you hope to contribute?
- What are your hobbies?
- What is your greatest academic accomplishment? Your greatest personal one?
- Tell me about your experience in psychology thus far. What is the most challenging aspect? What is the most rewarding?
- What are your career goals? How will this program help you achieve your goals?
- How do you intend to finance your education?
- What skills do you bring to the program? How will you help your mentor in his or her research?
- Are you motivated? Explain and provide examples.
- What do you plan to specialize in? Why?
- If you're not accepted into graduate school, what are your plans?
- Why did you choose this career?
- What do you know about our program?
- Why did you choose to apply to our program?
- What other schools are you considering?
- In what ways have your previous experiences prepared you for graduate study in our program?
- Do you have any questions?
- What do you believe your greatest challenge will be if you are accepted into this program?

TABLE 13.2	Questions to for Interviewees to Ask During a Graduate School Admissions Interview

- What distinguishes this program from others?

- Where are recent alumni employed? What do most students do after graduation?

- What types of financial aid are offered? What criteria are used for choosing recipients of aid?

- Are there any scholarships or fellowships available? How do I apply?

- Are there teaching opportunities, such as teaching assistantships and adjunct positions, for current students?

- Do most students publish an article or present a paper before graduation?

- What planned practical experiences are included in the program? Do you have any examples of internship placements?

- What is the relative importance of admissions test scores, undergraduate grades, recommendations, statements on applications, experience, and other requirements?

- Does the department prefer applicants immediately out of undergraduate programs or applicants with work experience? If the department prefers or requires experience, what kind of experience is the department looking for?

- How do graduate students obtain research experience? Are they assigned to labs, or do they choose labs on their own?

- How are mentors assigned to students?

SUGGESTED READINGS

American Psychological Association. (1994). *Getting in: A step-by-step plan for gaining admission to graduate school in psychology.* Washington, DC: Author.

American Psychological Association. (2006). *Graduate study in psychology: 2006.* Washington, DC: Author.

Keith-Spiegel, P., & Wiederman, M. W. (2000). *Complete guide to graduate school admissions: Psychology, counseling, and related professions.* Mahwah, NJ: Erlbaum.

Kuther, T. L. (2006). *The psychology major's handbook* (2nd ed.). Belmont, CA: Wadsworth.

Mayne, T. J., Norcross, J. G., & Sayette, M. A. (2006). *Insider's guide to graduate programs in clinical and counseling psychology.* New York: Guilford.

WEB RESOURCES

PsiChi Articles on Applying to Graduate School
   http://psichi.org/pubs/search.asp?category1=7
Suggested Plan for Grad School Admission
   http://www.uwstout.edu/programs/bap/pgs.html

About Graduate School
  http://gradschool.about.com
American Psychological Association of Graduate Students (APAGS)
  http://www.apa.org/apags
Psychology Graduate Applicants' Portal
  http://www.psychgrad.org

CHECKLIST: IS GRADUATE SCHOOL FOR YOU?

Do you:

☐ Feel ready to live at or near poverty for the next two to seven years?

☐ Like the thought of studying all the time?

☐ Enjoy writing term papers?

☐ Feel at ease speaking in public?

☐ Read psychology books or articles even if they are not assigned?

☐ Manage time well when you study for tests or write papers?

☐ Enjoy reading and studying?

☐ Like library research?

☐ Sometimes give up a social event (like a party) to study for a test or to finish a paper?

☐ Still like the thought of going to school?

☐ Concentrate and study for hours at a time?

☐ Get mainly Bs or higher?

☐ Read recent issues of psychology journals?

☐ Feel that psychology is the only career you'd like to explore?

☐ Have an A or a B in statistics?

☐ Like doing research?

☐ Feel up to working long hours?

☐ Feel able to incur significant student loan debt?

☐ Hand in assignments and do them on time?

Scoring: The more boxes you checked, the more likely it is that you're a good match for graduate work in psychology.

Source: Adapted from Kuther, 2006.

References

Aamodt, M. G. (2004). *Applied industrial/organizational psychology*. Pacific Grove, CA: Wadsworth.

Abbott, Langer, & Associates. (2005a). *Compensation in consulting firms*. Retrieved November 4, 2005, from http://www.abbott-langer.com/conssumm.html

Abbott, Langer, & Associates. (2005b). *Compensation in the publishing field*. Retrieved November 4, 2005, from http://www.abbott-langer.com/pubsumm.html

Abbott, Langer, & Associates. (2005c). *Pay rates in nonprofit organizations*. Retrieved November 3, 2005, from http://www.abbott-langer.com/snosumm.html

Ackerman, M. J. (1999). *Essentials of Forensic Psychological Assessment*. New York: Wiley.

Actkinson, T. R. (2000). Master's and myth: Little-known information about a popular degree. *Eye on Psi Chi, 4*(2), 19–21, 23, 25.

American Association of Marriage and Family Therapy. (2002). *Advancing the professional interests of marriage and family therapists*. Retrieved October 3, 2005, from http://www.aamft.org/index_nm.asp

American Counseling Association. (2002). *Welcome*. Retrieved October 3, 2005, from http://www.counseling.org//AM/Template.cfm?Section=Home

American Institute of Graphic Arts. (2003). *Salary survey, 2003*. Retrieved December 20, 2005, from http://www.aiga.org/content.cfm?Alias=2000salarysurvey

American Psychological Association. (2001). *Preparing Future Faculty Program*. Retrieved January 18, 2002, from http://www.apa.org/ed/pff.html

American Psychological Association. (2004). Accredited doctoral programs in professional psychology: 2004. *American Psychologist, 59*, 930–944.

American Psychological Association. (2005). *APA congressional fellowship program*. Retrieved October 15, 2005, from http://www.apa.org/ppo/funding/congfell.html

American Psychological Association. (n.d.a). *Employed Psychology PhDs by Setting: 1997*. Retrieved July 20, 2001, from http://research.apa.org/doc10.html

American Psychological Association. (n.d.b). *Introduction to military psychology: An overview*. Retrieved January 18, 2001, from http://www.apa.org/about/division/div19intro.html

American Psychological Association Division 16. (2005). *Goals and objectives*. Retrieved October 15, 2005, from http://www.indiana.edu/~div16/G&O.htm

American Psychological Association Division 22. (n.d.). *What is rehabilitation psychology?* Retrieved July 19, 2002, from http://www.apa.org/divisions/div22/Rpdef.html

American Psychological Association Division 38. (n.d.). *What a health psychologist does and how to become one.* Retrieved October 3, 2005, from http://www.health-psych.org/whatis.html

American Psychological Association Division 47. (2003). *Graduate training and career possibilities in exercise and sport psychology.* Retrieved October 27, 2005, from http://www.psyc.unt.edu/apadiv47/gradtrain.htm

American Psychological Association Division 47. (2004). *Becoming a sports psychologist.* Retrieved October 27, 2005, from http://www.psyc.unt.edu/apadiv47/about_becomingsportpsych.html

American Psychological Association Division of Clinical Neuropsychology. (1989). Definition of a clinical neuropsychologist. *The Clinical Neuropsychologist, 3,* 22. Retrieved July 18, 2002, from http://www.div40.org/def.html

American Psychological Association Research Office. (2001). *PhDs and PsyDs by major degree field: 2001 new doctorates in psychology.* Retrieved October 15, 2005, from http://research.apa.org/doctoraled03.html

American Psychological Association Research Office. (2003). *Type of degree awarded and major field: 2001 new doctorates in psychology.* Retrieved February 13, 2006, from http://research.apa.org/doc01.html

American Psychological Association Society of Clinical Psychology. (2002). *What is clinical psychology?* Retrieved June 24, 2002, from http://www.apa.org/divisions/div12/about.shtml

American Psychology-Law Society. (2004). *Careers in psychology and law: A guide for prospective students.* Retrieved October 15, 2005, from http://www.ap-ls.org/students/careers%20in%20psychology.pdf

American Psychology-Law Society. (2005). *Careers in psychology and law: Subspecialties in psychology and law: A closer look.* Retrieved October 15, 2005, from http://www.unl.edu/ap-ls/student/careers_closerlook.html

Amsel, J. (1996). An interesting career in psychology: Acquisitions editor. *Psychological Science Agenda.* Retrieved January 18, 2002, from http://www.apa.org/science/ic-amsel.html

Anderson, M. B. (Ed.). (2000). *Doing sport psychology.* Champaign, IL: Human Kinetics.

Andrews, C. K. (2005). Trial consulting: Moving psychology into the courtroom. In R. D. Morgan, T. L. Kuther, & C. J. Habben (Eds.), *Life after graduate school in psychology: Insider's advice from new psychologists* (pp. 257–274). New York: Psychology Press.

Andrews, D. A., & Bonta, J. (1994). *The psychology of criminal conduct.* Cincinnati, OH: Anderson.

Andrews, D. A., Zinger, I., Hoge, R. D., Bonta, J., Gendreau, P., & Cullen, F. T. (1990). Does correctional treatment work? A clinically relevant and psychologically informed meta-analysis. *Criminology, 28,* 369–404.

Anson, R. H., & Bloom, M. E. (1988). Police stress in an occupational context. *Journal of Police Science and Administration, 16,* 229–235.

Appleby, D. (2000). Job skills valued by employers who interview psychology majors. *Eye on Psi Chi, 4*(3), 17.

Attfield, C. (1999). Stock market: Making the transition from acids to assets. *Next Wave.* Retrieved June 16, 2002, from http://nextwave.sciencemag.org/cgi/content/full/1999/03/02/2

Augenbraun, E., & Vergoth, K. (1998). Broadcast science journalism: Working in television, cable, radio, or electronic media. In C. Robbins-Roth (Ed.), *Alternative careers in science: Leaving the ivory tower* (pp. 49–62). San Diego, CA: Academic Press.

Ax, R. K., & Morgan, R. D. (2002). Internship training opportunities in correctional psychology: A comparison of settings. *Criminal Justice and Behavior, 29*, 332–347.

Balster, R. L. (1995). An interesting career in psychology: A research psychologist in a medical school. *Psychological Science Agenda.* Retrieved February 1, 2002, from http://www.apa.org/science/ic-balster.html

Bardon, J. I. (1989). The school psychologist as an applied educational psychologist. In R. C. D'Amato & R. S. Dean (Eds.), *The school psychologist in nontraditional settings: Integrating clients, services, and settings* (pp. 1–32). Hillsdale, NJ: Erlbaum.

Bartholomew, D. (2001a). Academia or industry: Finding the fit. *Next Wave.* Retrieved February 1, 2002, from http://nextwave.sciencemag.org/cgi/content/full/2000/08/10/6

Bartholomew, D. (2001b). Academia or industry: Where would I fit in? *Next Wave.* Retrieved February 1, 2002, from http://nextwave.sciencemag.org/cgi/content/full/2000/06/15/1

Bartol, C. R. (1996). Police psychology then, now, and beyond. *Criminal Justice and Behavior, 23*, 70–89.

Baskin, M. L. (2005). Public health: Career opportunities for psychologists in public health. In R. D. Morgan, T. L. Kuther, & C. J. Habben (Eds.), *Life after graduate school in psychology: Insider's advice from new psychologists* (pp. 241–256). New York: Psychology Press.

Bat-Chava, Y. (2000). *An interesting career in psychology: Research director for a nonprofit organization.* Retrieved February 1, 2001, from http://www.apa.org/science/ic-bat-chava.html

Beall, A. E., & Allen, T. W. (1997). Why we buy what we buy: Consulting in consumer psychology. In R. Sternberg (Ed.), *Career paths in psychology: Where your degree can take you* (pp. 197–212). Washington, DC: American Psychological Association.

BeAnActuary.org. (n.d.). *About actuarial examinations.* Retrieved June 16, 2002, from http://www.beanactuary.org/examprocess/)

Belar, C. D. (1997). Clinical health psychology: A specialty for the 21st century. *Health Psychology, 16*, 411–416.

Belar, C. D., Brown, R. A., Hersch, L. E., Hornyak, L. M., Rozensky, R. H., Sheridan, E. P., Brown, R. T., & Reed, G. W. (2001). Self-assessment in clinical health psychology: A model for ethical expansion of practice. *Professional Psychology: Research and Practice, 32*, 135–141.

Belar, C. D., & Deardorff, W. W. (1995). *Clinical health psychology in medical settings: A practitioner's guidebook.* Washington, DC: American Psychological Association.

Bergen, J. (n.d.). *Public relations careers.* Retrieved June 5, 2002, from http://www.prfirms.org/career/career_info/prcareer.asp

Berry, M. P. (2005). Interdisciplinary medical setting: The multiple roles of a health psychologist. In R. D. Morgan, T. L. Kuther, & C. J. Habben (Eds.), *Life after graduate school in psychology: Insider's advice from new psychologists* (pp. 45–58). New York: Psychology Press.

Birmingham, D., & Morgan, R. D. (2001, August). *Helping police manage Type III stress.* In Shelia Holton (Chair), Law Enforcement and Stress: Crossing the Blue Line.

Symposium presented at the annual convention of the American Psychological Association, San Francisco.

Blum, D. E. (2005). Fund raisers' pay hits new high, compensation survey finds. *Chronicle of Philanthropy, 17*(14), 31.

Boothby, J. L., & Clements, C. B. (2001). A national survey of correctional psychologists. *Criminal Justice and Behavior, 27,* 716–732.

Bonifazi, D. Z., Crespi, S. D., & Rieker, P. (1997). Value of a master's degree for gaining admission to doctoral programs in psychology. *Teaching of Psychology, 24,* 176–182.

Borden, V. M. H., & Rajecki, D. W. (2000). First-year employment outcomes of psychology baccalaureates: Relatedness, preparedness, and prospects. *Teaching of Psychology, 27,* 164–168.

Boulakia, C. (1998). What is management consulting? *Science's Next Wave.* Retrieved July 5, 2002, from http://nextwave.sciencemag.org/cgi/content/full/1998/03/29/262

Brigham, J. C. (1999). What is forensic psychology, anyway? *Law and Human Behavior, 23,* 273–298.

Briihl, D. S., & Wasieleski, D. T. (2004). A survey of master's level psychology programs: Admissions criteria and program policies. *Teaching of Psychology, 31*(4), 252–256.

Brodsky, C. M. (1982). Work stress in correctional institutions. *Journal of Prison and Jail Health, 2,* 74–102.

Bruzzese, J. M. (2005). Medical schools and centers: The merger of developmental psychology and pediatric asthma education. In R. D. Morgan, T. L. Kuther, & C. J. Habben (Eds.), *Life after graduate school in psychology: Insider's advice from new psychologists* (59–70). New York: Psychology Press.

Bureau of Labor Statistics. (2002). *Occupational outlook handbook.* Retrieved June 6, 2002, from http://stats.bls.gov/oco/ocoiab.htm

Bureau of Labor Statistics. (2004). *Occupational outlook handbook.* Retrieved September 27, 2005, from http://stats.bls.gov/oco/ocoiab.htm

Buskist, W., & Shurburne, T. R. (1996). *Preparing for graduate study in psychology: 101 questions and answers.* Needham Heights, MA: Allyn and Bacon.

Butcher, J. N., & Miller, K. B. (1999). Personality assessment in personal injury litigation. In A. K. Hess & I. B. Weiner (Eds.), *Handbook of forensic psychology* (2nd ed., pp. 104–126) Wiley: Hoboken, NJ.

Callan, J. R. (2004). An interesting career in psychology: Engineering psychology in research and development. *Psychological Science Agenda.* Retrieved February 22, 2006, from http://www.apa.org/science/psa/ic-callan.html

Careers in Business. (2000). *Careers in business.* Retrieved June 5, 2002, from http://www.careers-in-business.com

Carpenter, C. (2002). An interesting career in psychology: Becoming a science writer. *Psychological Science Agenda.* Retrieved November 4, 2005, from http://www.apa.org/science/ic-carpenter.html

Carpenter, J. (2000). *Careers in consumer psychology.* Retrieved June 5, 2002, from http://www.wcupa.edu/_ACADEMICS/sch_cas.psy/Career_Paths/Consumer/Career05.htm

Carpenter, S. (2001). National Science Foundation boosts cognitive neuroscience. *Monitor on Psychology, 32*(4). Retrieved January 13, 2002, from http://www.apa.org/monitor/apr01/nsf.html

Carter, J. E. (2005). Sport psychology: Locker room confessions. In R. D. Morgan, T. L. Kuther, & C. J. Habben (Eds.), *Life after graduate school in psychology: Insider's advice from new psychologists* (pp. 275–288). New York: Psychology Press.

Chapman, C. N. (2005). Software user research: Psychologist in the software industry. In R. D. Morgan, T. L. Kuther, & C. J. Habben (Eds.), *Life after graduate school in psychology: Insider's advice from new psychologists* (pp. 211–224). New York: Psychology Press.

Cheek, F., & Miller, M. (1983). The experience of stress for correction officers: A double-blind theory of correctional stress. *Journal of Criminal Justice, 11,* 105–120.

Christensen, A., & Jacobson, N. S. (1994). Who (or what) can do psychotherapy; The status and challenge of nonprofessional therapies. *Psychological Science, 5,* 8–12.

Chronicle of Higher Education. (2005). *Average salaries for full time faculty members, 2004–2005.* Retrieved November 4, 2005, from http://chronicle.com/weekly/v51/i33/33a01201.htm

Clay, R. A. (2000a). Often, the bells and whistles backfire. *Monitor on Psychology.* Retrieved June 5, 2002, from http://www.apa.org/monitor/apr00/usability.html

Clay, R. (2000b, May). The postdoc trap. *Monitor on Psychology, 31*(5), 20–24, 26.

Cobb, H. C., Reeve, R. E., Shealy, C. N., Norcross, J. C., Schare, M. L., Rodolfa, E. R., Hargrove, D. S., Hallz, J. E., & Allen, M. (2004). Overlap among clinical, counseling, and school psychology: Implications for the profession and Combined-Integrated training. *Journal of Clinical Psychology, 60,* 939–955.

Cohen, J. (2002). I/Os in the know offer insights on Generation X workers. *Monitor on Psychology.* Retrieved June 5, 2002, from http://www.apa.org/monitor/feb02/genxwork.html

College Journal (2005). Nonprofits. Retrieved February 16, 2006, from http://www.collegejournal.com/salarydata/nonprofits/

College Journal. (n.d.). Salary data. Retrieved February 16, 2006, from http://www.collegejournal.com/salarydata/

Condelli, W. S., Bradigan, B., & Holanchock, H. (1997). Intermediate care programs to reduce risk and better manage inmates with psychiatric disorders. *Behavioral Sciences and the Law, 15,* 459–467.

Copper, C. (1997). An interesting career in psychology: Social science analyst in the public sector. *Psychological Science Agenda.* Retrieved January 19, 2002, from http://www.apa.org/science/ic-copper.html

Cornell Career Services. (n.d.). *Jobs at not-for-profit organizations.* Retrieved July 2, 2002, from http://www.career.cornell.edu/students/search/nonprofit/np-UDel.html

D'Amato, R. C., & Dean, R. S. (Eds.). (1989). *The school psychologist in nontraditional settings: Integrating clients, services, and settings.* Hillsdale, NJ: Erlbaum.

Danish, S., Petitpas, A. J., & Hale, B. D. (1993). Life development interventions for athletes: Life skills through sports. *Counseling Psychologist, 21,* 352–385.

Day, M. C. (1996). An interesting career in psychology: Human-computer interface designer. *Psychological Science Agenda.* Retrieved June 5, 2002, from http://www.apa.org/science/ic-day.html

DeLeon, P. H. (1988). Public policy and public service: Our professional duty. *American Psychologist, 43,* 309–315.

Diddams, M. (1998). An interesting career in psychology: Cognitive and I/O psychologists in the technology industry. *Psychological Science Agenda.* Retrieved June 5, 2002, from http://www.apa.org/science/ic-diddams.html

Ditton, P. M. (1999). *Mental health and treatment of inmates and probationers* (Bureau of Justice Statistics Special Report, NJC 174463). Washington, DC: U.S. Department of Justice.

Edwards, J., and Smith, K. (1988). What skills and knowledge do potential employers value in baccalaureate psychologists? In P. J. Woods (Ed.), *Is psychology for them? A guide to undergraduate advising.* Washington, DC: American Psychological Association.

Evans, B. (1998). Why do realtors really leave the profession? *Realty Times.* Retrieved July 2, 2002, from http://realtytimes.com/rtnews/rtapages/19981012_leaving.htm

Fabris, P. (1998). *Data mining: Advanced navigation.* Retrieved June 16, 2002, from http://www.cio.com/archive/051598_mining.html

Families and Work Institute. (n.d.) *Work-life research.* Retrieved July 2, 2002, from http://www.familiesandwork.org/announce/workforce.html

Ferguson, S. A. (1997). An interesting career in psychology: Highway safety research analyst. *Psychological Science Agenda.* Retrieved February 16, 2006, from http://www.apa.org/science/ic-ferguson.html

Ferrell, S. W., Morgan, R. D., & Winterowd, C. L. (2000). Job satisfaction of mental health professionals providing group psychotherapy in state correctional facilities. *International Journal of Offender Therapy and Comparative Criminology, 44,* 232–241.

Fisher, C. B., & Koocher, G. (1990). To be or not to be? Accreditation and credentialing in applied developmental psychology. *Journal of Applied Developmental Psychology, 11,* 381–394.

Fisher, C. B., & Osofsky, J. (1997). Training the applied developmental scientist for prevention and practice: Two current examples. *Social Policy Report, 11*(2), 1–18.

Fowler, R. D. (1996). Psychology, public policy, and the Congressional Fellowship program. In R. P. Lorion, I. Iscoe, P. H. DeLeon, & G. R. VandenBos (Eds.), *Psychology and public policy: Balancing public service and professional need* (pp. ix–xiv). Washington, DC: American Psychological Association.

Gaddy, C. D., Charlot-Swilley, D., Nelson, P. D., & Reich, J. N. (1995). Selected outcomes of accredited programs. *Professional Psychology: Research and Practice, 26,* 507–513.

Garrett, C. (1985). Effects of residential treatment on adjudicated delinquents: A meta-analysis. *Journal of Research in Crime and Delinquency, 22,* 287–308.

Gelso, C., & Fretz, B. (2001). *Counseling Psychology* (2nd ed.). Orlando, FL: Harcourt.

Gendreau, P., & Andrews, D. (1990). Tertiary prevention: What the meta-analyses of the offender treatment literature tells us about "what works." *Canadian Journal of Criminology, 32,* 173–184.

Gendreau, P., & Ross, R. (1979). Effective correctional treatment: Bibliotherapy for cynics. *Journal of Research in Crime and Delinquency, 25,* 463–489.

Gendreau, P., & Ross, R. (1981). Offender rehabilitation: The appeal of success. *Federal Probation, 45,* 45–48.

Goetnick, S. (1998). Science writing: Communicating with the masses. In C. Robbins-Roth (Ed.), *Alternative careers in science: Leaving the ivory tower* (pp. 21–33). San Diego, CA: Academic Press.

Golden, C. J., Zillmer, E., & Spiers, M. (1992). *Neuropsychological assessment and intervention.* Springfield, IL: Thomas.

Goldstein, D., Wilson, R. J., & Gerstein, A. I. (1983). Applied developmental psychology: Problems and prospects for an emerging discipline. *Journal of Applied Developmental Psychology, 4,* 341–348.

Grocer, S., & Kohout, J. (1997). *The 1995 APA survey of 1992 psychology baccalaureate recipients.* Retrieved August 21, 2000, from http://research.apa.org/95survey/homepage.html

Harris, G. (1983). *Stress in corrections.* Boulder, CO: National Institute of Corrections.

Hart, S. (1996). Producing a great textbook with the help of a developmental editor. *Bioscience, 46.* Retrieved January 18, 2001, from http://www.aibs.org/biosciencelibrary/vol46/oct.96.hart.html

Hart, S. G. (2002). *A safe and secure system.* Retrieved June 5, 2002, from http://www.apa.org/ppo/issues/safesecure.paper.html

Hassine, V. (1996). *Life without parole.* Los Angeles: Roxbury.

Hawk, K. M. (1997). Personal reflections on a career in correctional psychology. *Professional Psychology: Research and Practice, 28,* 335–337.

Hayes, N. (1996). What makes a psychology graduate distinctive? *European Psychologist, 1,* 130–134.

Hays-Thomas, R. L. (2000). The silent conversation: Talking about the master's degree. *Professional Psychology: Research and Practice, 31,* 339–345.

Health—psychiatric technician. (2002). *Career explorations: The personal side of work.* Retrieved July 22, 2002, from http://www.jobprofiles.org/heapsytech.htm

Herbst, A. C. (2005, June 19). Fund-raising: Well-paid jobs that sometimes go begging. *New York Times, 154*(53250), S10, pp. 1–3.

Herrman, D. (1997). Rewards of public service: Research psychologists in government. In R. J. Sternberg (Ed.), *Career paths in psychology: Where your degree can take you* (pp. 151–164). Washington, DC: American Psychological Association.

Himelein, M. J. (1999). *A student's guide to careers in the helping professions.* Office of Teaching Resources in Psychology: Retrieved January 3, 2001, from http://www.lemoyne.edu/OTRP/otrpresources/helping.html.

Hodgins, S. (1995). Assessing mental disorder in the criminal justice system: Feasibility versus clinical accuracy. *International Journal of Law and Psychiatry, 18,* 15–28.

Holland, J. L. (1959). A theory of vocational choice. *Journal of Counseling Psychology, 6,* 35–45.

Holland, J. L. (1994). *Self-Directed Search.* Retrieved July 5, 2001, from http://www.self-directed-search.com

Human Factors International. (2003, September 26). *HFI Usability Salary Survey.* Retrieved November 5, 2005, from http://www.humanfactors.com/salarysurveyresults.htm

Humphreys, K. (1996). Clinical psychologists as psychotherapists: History, future, and alternatives. *American Psychologist, 51,* 190–197.

Huss, M. T. (2001). Psychology and law, now and in the next century: The promise of an emerging area of psychology. In J. S. Halonen & S. F. Davis (Eds.), *The many faces of psychological research in the 21st century* (Chapter 11). Society for the Teaching of

Psychology: retrieved from http://teachpsych.lemoyne.edu/teachpsych/faces/text/Ch11.htm

Information Week. (2005). *2005 Information week: IT salary adviser.* Retrieved November 1, 2005, from http://www.informationweek.com/advisor/

Inwald, R. E. (1982). Research problems in assessing stress factors in correctional institutions. *International Journal of Offender Therapy and Comparative Criminology, 26,* 250–254.

Irwin, J. (1996). The march of folly. *Prison Journal, 76,* 489–494.

Kaplan, R. M., Sallis, J. F., Jr., & Patterson, T. L. (1993). *Health and human behavior.* New York: McGraw-Hill.

Kasserman, J. (2005). Management consultation: Improving organizations. In R. D. Morgan, T. L. Kuther, & C. J. Habben (Eds.), *Life after graduate school in psychology: Insider's advice from new psychologists* (pp. 183–196). New York: Psychology Press.

Keith-Spiegel, P., Tabachnick, B. G., & Spiegel, G. B. (1994). When demand exceeds supply: Second order criteria used by graduate school selection committees. *Teaching of Psychology, 21,* 79–81.

Keith-Spiegel, P., & Wiederman, M. W. (2000). *The complete guide to graduate school admission: Psychology, counseling, and related professions.* Mahwah, NJ: Erlbaum.

Kierniesky, N. C. (1992). Specialization of the undergraduate major. *American Psychologist, 47,* 1146–1147.

Kilburg, R. R. (1996). Toward a conceptual understanding and definition of executive coaching. *Consulting Psychology Journal: Practice and Research, 48,* 134–144.

Kirkland, K., & Kirkland, K. L. (2001). Frequency of child custody evaluation complaints and related disciplinary action: A survey of the Association of State and Provincial Psychology Boards. *Professional Psychology: Research and Practice, 32,* 171–174.

Kolb, B., & Whishaw, I. Q. (1995). *Fundamentals of human neuropsychology.* New York: Bedford, Freeman, & Worth.

Krannich, R. I. (1991). *Careering and re-careering for the 1990's: The complete guide to planning your future.* Woodbridge, VA: Impact.

Kuther, T. L. (1996). Doctoral training in applied developmental psychology: Matching graduate education and accreditation standards to student needs, career opportunity, and licensure requirements. In C. B. Fisher, J. P. Murray, & I. E. Sigel (Eds.), *Applied developmental science: Graduate training for diverse disciplines and educational settings* (pp. 53–74). Norwood, NJ: Ablex.

Kuther, T. L. (2002). Ethical conflicts in the teaching assignments of graduate students. *Ethics and Behavior, 12,* 197–204.

Kuther, T. L. (2004). *Your career in psychology: Psychology and the law.* Belmont, CA: Wadsworth.

Kuther, T. L. (2005). *Your career in psychology: Industrial/organizational psychology.* Belmont, CA: Wadsworth.

Kuther, T. L. (2006). *The psychology major's handbook* (2nd ed.). Belmont, CA: Wadsworth.

Landrum, E., Davis, S., & Landrum, T. (2000). *The psychology major: Career options and strategies for success.* Upper Saddle River, NJ: Prentice-Hall.

Landwehr, H. (2001). An interesting career in psychology: Aviation human factors psychologist. *Psychological Science Agenda.* Retrieved November 2, 2005, from http://www.apa.org/science/ic-landwehr.html

Lauber, J. K. (1997). An interesting career in psychology: Human factors psychologists in aviation. *Psychological Science Agenda.* Retrieved June 5, 2002, from http://www.apa.org/science/ic-lauber.html

Lee, T. (2002). Rating the nation's best and worst jobs. *Career Journal.* Retrieved June 16, 2002, from http://www.careerjournal.com/jobhunting/change/20020507-lee.html

Levant, R. F., Moldawsky, S., & Stigall, T. T. (2000). The evolving profession of psychology: Comment on Hays-Thomas' (2000) "The silent conversation." *Professional Psychology Research and Practice, 31,* 346–348.

Levant, R. F., Reed, G. M., Ragusea, S. A., DiCowden, M., Murphy, M. J., Sullivan, F., Craig, P. L., & Stout, C. E. (2001). Envisioning and accessing new roles for professional psychology. *Professional Psychology: Research and Practice, 32,* 79–87.

Levine, L. (2002). Biotechnology. *Microsoft Encarta Online Encyclopedia.* Retrieved July 22, 2002, from http://encarta.msn.com/find/Concise.asp?z=17pg=2&ti=761575885

Lezak, M. D. (1995). *Neuropsychological assessment* (3rd ed.). New York: Oxford University Press.

Lindquist, C. A., & Whitehead, J. T. (1986). Burnout, job stress, and job satisfaction among southern correctional officers: Perceptions and causal factors. *Journal of Offender Counseling, Services, and Rehabilitation, 10,* 5–26.

Lipsey, M. (1992). Juvenile delinquency treatment: A meta-analytic inquiry into the variability of effects. In T. Cook, H. Cooper, D. Cordray, H. Hartmann, L. Hedgews, R. Light, T. Louis, & F. Mosteller (Eds.), *Meta-analysis for explanation* (pp. 83–127). New York: Russell Sage.

Liss, M. B. (1992). Psychology and law courses: Content and materials. *Law and Human Behavior, 16,* 463–471.

Lloyd, M. A. (2000). *Master's- and doctoral-level careers in psychology and related areas.* Retrieved February 1, 2000, from http://www.psychwww.com/careers/masters.htm

Lloyd, M. A., & Kennedy, J. H. (1997). *Skills employers seek.* Retrieved August 20, 2000, from http://www.psywww.com/careers/skills.htm

Martinson, R. (1974). What works? Questions and answers about prison reform. *Public Interest, 35,* 22–54.

Matlin, M. W., & Kalat, J. W. (2001). Demystifying the GRE Psychology Test: A brief guide for students. *Eye on Psi Chi, 5*(1), 22–25.

Max, D. T. (2000, December). The cop and the therapist. *The New York Times Magazine,* p. 94.

Mayne, T. J., Norcross, J. C., & Sayette, M. A. (1994). Admission requirements, acceptance rates, and financial assistance in clinical psychology programs. *American Psychologist, 12,* 806–811.

McCracken, P. (1998). The path of a scientist's job search. *Science's Next Wave.* Retrieved June 5, 2002, from http://nextwave.sciencemag.org/cgi/content/full/1998/03/29/265

McGovern, T. V., Furumoto, L., Halpern, D. F., Kimble, G. A., & McKeachie, W. J. (1991). Liberal education, study in depth, and the arts and sciences major—psychology. *American Psychologist, 46,* 598–605.

Melton, G. B., Petrila, J., Poythress, N. G., & Slobogin, C. (1997). *Psychological evaluations for the courts: A handbook for mental health professionals and lawyers* (2nd ed.). New York: Guilford Press.

Meyers, A. W., Coleman, J. K., Whelan, J. P., & Mehlenbeck, R. S. (2001). Examining careers in sport psychology: Who is working and who is making money? *Professional Psychology: Research and Practice, 32,* 5–11.

Montell, G. (1999). Another career choice for Ph.D.'s: Management consulting. *Chronicle of Higher Education.* Retrieved June 5, 2002, from http://chronicle.com/jobs/99/11/99111203c.htm

Morgan, R. D., Van Haveren, R. A., & Pearson, C. A. (2002). Correctional officer burnout: Further analyses. *Criminal Justice and Behavior, 29,* 144–160.

Morgan, R. D., Winterowd, C. L., & Ferrell, S. W. (1999). A national survey of group psychotherapy services in correctional facilities. *Professional Psychology: Research and Practice, 30,* 600–606.

MSU Career Placement and Services. (2005a). *Recruiting trends 2004–2005.* East Lansing: Michigan State University.

MSU Career Placement and Services. (2005b). *Twelve essentials for success.* East Lansing: Michigan State University.

Muchinsky, P. M. (2006). *Psychology applied to work.* Pacific Grove, CA: Wadsworth.

Murray, B. (2000). From brain scan to lesson plan. *Monitor on Psychology, 31*(3). Retrieved January 13, 2002, from http://www.apa.org/monitor/mar00/brainscan.html

Murray, B. (2002). Psychologists help companies traverse the minefields of layoffs. *Monitor on Psychology.* Retrieved June 6, 2002, from http://www.apa.org/monitor/apr02/layoffs.html

Myers, D. G. (2001). *Psychology* (6th ed). New York: Worth.

National Association of Colleges and Employers. (2001). *Summer 2001 salary survey.* Washington, DC: Author.

National Association of Colleges and Employers. (2005). *Job outlook 2005 survey.* Washington, DC: Author

National Association of Colleges and Employers. (n.d.). *Network into marketing, advertising, and public relations careers.* Retrieved June 5, 2002, from http://www.jobweb.com/Resources/Library/Careers_In/Network_Into_45_01.htm

National Association of School Psychologists. (2003). *What is a school psychologist?* Retrieved October 15, 2005, from http://www.nasponline.org/about_nasp/whatisa.html

National Association of Science Writers. (n.d.) *The science writer.* Retrieved January 18, 2001, from http://nasw.org/csn/sciwri.htm

National Association of Social Workers. (2005). *The power of social work.* Retrieved October 5, 2005, from http://www.naswdc.org/

National Center for Education Statistics. (2003). *Degrees and other awards conferred: 2003.* Retrieved September 19, 2005, from http://nces.ed.gov/programs/digest/d03/

National Rehabilitation Counseling Association. (2001). *NCRA.* Retrieved October 5, 2005, from http://nrca-net.org/

Norcross, J. C., & Castle, P. H. (2002). Appreciating the PsyD: The facts. *Eye on Psi Chi, 7*(1), 22–26.

Norcross, J. C., Castle, P. H., Sayette, M. A., & Mayne, T. J. (2004). The PsyD: Heterogeneity in practitioner training. *Professional Psychology: Research and Practice, 35,* 412–419.

Norcross, J. C., Hanych, J. M., & Terranova, R. D. (1996). Graduate study in psychology: 1992–1993. *American Psychologist, 51,* 631–643.

Norcross, J. C., Karg, R. S., & Prochaska, J. O. (1997). Clinical psychologists in the 1990's: Part I. *Clinical Psychologist, 50,* 4–9.

Norcross, J. C., Prochaska, J. O., & Gallagher, K. M. (1989a). Clinical psychologists in the 1980s: I. Demographics, affiliations, and satisfactions. *Clinical Psychologist, 42,* 29–39.

Norcross, J. C., Prochaska, J. O., & Gallagher, K. M. (1989b). Clinical psychologists in the 1980s: II. Theory, research, and practice. *Clinical Psychologist, 42,* 29–39.

Norcross, J. C., Sayette, M. A., Mayne, T. J., Karg, R. S., & Turkson, M. A. (1998). Selecting a doctoral program in professional psychology: Some comparisons among PhD counseling, PhD clinical, and PsyD clinical psychology programs. *Professional Psychology: Research and Practice, 29,* 609–614.

North American Association of Masters in Psychology. (2005). Licensure information. Retrieved February 16, 2006, from http://enamp.org

Pate, W. E. (2001). *Analyses of data from graduate study in psychology: 1999–2000.* Retrieved July 5, 2002, from http://research.apa.org/grad00contents.html

Pate, W. E., Frincke, J. L., & Kohout, J. L. (2005). Salaries in psychology 2003: Report of the 2003 APA salary survey. Retrieved February 13, 2006, from http://research.apa.org/03salary/homepage.html

Pate, W. E., & Kohout, J. (2004). *Report of the 2003 medical school/academic medical center psychologists employment survey.* Retrieved September 19, 2005, from http://research.apa.org/amsp/2003/index.html

Patterson, F. (2001). Developments in work psychology: Emerging issues and future trends. *Journal of Occupational and Organizational Psychology, 74,* 381–390.

Perry, C., Jr., & Marsh, H. W. (2000). Listening to self-talk, hearing self-concept. In M. B. Anderson (Ed.), *Doing sport psychology* (pp. 61–76). Champaign, IL: Human Kinetics.

Peters, R. L. (1992). *Getting what you came for: The smart student's guide to earning a master's or a Ph.D.* New York: Noonday Press.

Preparing Future Faculty. (n.d.) *Preparing future faculty.* Retrieved January 18, 2002, from http://www.preparing-faculty.org/PFFWeb.Resources.htm

Public Relations Society of America. (n.d.). *About public relations.* Retrieved June 5, 2002, from http://www.prsa.org/_resources/profession/index.asp

Randall, C. R. (1998). Technical writing: Making sense out of manuals. In C. Robbins Roth (Ed.), *Alternative careers in science: Leaving the ivory tower* (pp. 11–21). San Diego, CA: Academic Press.

Resnick, J. H. (1991). Finally, a definition of clinical psychology: A message from the President, Division 12. *Clinical Psychologist, 44,* 3–11.

Roediger, H. (1997). Teaching, research, and more: Psychologists in an academic career. In R. J. Sternberg (Ed.), *Career paths in psychology: Where your degree can take you* (pp. 7–30). Washington, DC: American Psychological Association.

Romans, J. S. C., Boswell, D. L., Carlozzi, A. F., & Ferguson, D. B. (1995). Training and supervision practices in clinical, counseling, and school psychology programs. *Professional Psychology: Research and Practice, 26*, 407–412.

Rowh, M., & Suchorski, J. (2000). *Opportunities in fund-raising.* New York: McGraw-Hill.

Salary.com. (2002). *Salary wizard.* Retrieved June 5, 2002, from http://www.salary.com

Salary.com. (2005). *Salary wizard.* Retrieved June 5, 2005, from http://www.salary.com

Salzinger, K. (1995). The academic life. *Psychological Science Agenda.* Retrieved January 18, 2002, from http://www.apa.org/psa/janfeb95/acad.html

Sarafino, E. P. (2002). *Health psychology: Biopsychosocial interactions* (4th ed.). New York: Wiley.

Scrader, B. (2001). Industrial/organizational psychology 2010: A research odyssey. In J. S. Halonen & S. F. Davis (Eds.), *The many faces of psychological research in the 21st century.* Retrieved June 5, 2002, from http://teachpsych.lemoyne.edu/teachpsych/faces/text/Ch03.htm

Sebestyen, G. (2000). Watching the consultants. *Science's Next Wave.* Retrieved June 5, 2002, from http://nextwave.sciencemag.org/cgi/content/full/2000/07/26/1

Seligman, M. E. P. (1995). The effectiveness of psychotherapy: The *Consumer Reports* study. *American Psychologist, 50*, 965–974.

Sheetz, P. I. (1995). *Recruiting Trends: 1995–1996.* East Lansing: Collegiate Employment Research Institute, Michigan State University.

Sherman, C. P., & Poczwardowski, A. (2000). Relax! . . . It ain't easy (or is it?). In M. B. Anderson (Ed.), *Doing sport psychology* (pp. 47–60). Champaign, IL: Human Kinetics.

Simmons, J. (2000). Doing imagery in the field. In M. B. Anderson (Ed.), *Doing sport psychology* (pp. 77–92). Champaign, IL: Human Kinetics.

Singleton, D., Tate, A. C., & Kohout, J. L. (2003). 2002 Master's, specialist's, and related degrees employment survey. Retrieved February 3, 2006, from http://research.apa.org/mes2002contents.html

Singleton, D., Tate, A., & Randall, G. (2003). *Salaries in psychology, 2001: Report of the 2001 APA salary survey.* Washington, DC: American Psychological Association. Retrieved September 15, 2005, from http://research.apa.org/01salary/index.html

Smith, L. (2002). Working extra hours pays off. *Information Week.* Retrieved June 16, 2002, from http://www.informationweek.com/story/IWK20020426S0002

Smith, P. M. (1997). An interesting career in psychology: Organizational development consultant. *Psychological Science Agenda.* Retrieved June 5, 2002, from http://www.apa.org/science/ic-smith.html

Society for Human Resource Management. (n.d.). *Careers in human resource management.* Retrieved June 5, 2002, from http://www.shrm.org/students/careers.html

Steadman, H. J., Morris, S. M., & Dennis, D. L. (1995). The diversion of mentally ill persons from community-based services: A profile of programs. *American Journal of Public Health, 85*, 1630–1635.

Stein, D. M., & Lambert, M. J. (1995). On the relationship between therapist experience and psychotherapy outcome. *Journal of Consulting and Clinical Psychology, 63*, 182–196.

Sullivan, M. J. (2005). Psychologists as legislators: Results of the 2004 elections. *Professional Psychology: Research and Practice, 36*, 32–36.

Sundberg, N. D., Winebarger, A. A., & Taplin, J. R. (2002). *Clinical psychology: Evolving theory, practice, and research* (4th ed.). Upper Saddle River, NJ: Prentice-Hall.

Susman-Stillman, A. R., Brown, J. L., Adam, E. K., Blair, C., Gaines, R., Gordon, R. A., et al. (1996). Building research and policy connections: Training and career options for developmental scientists. *Social Policy Report, 10*(4), 1–19.

Taylor, E. D., Dobbins, D. R., & Woodruff, D. W. (2005). Research consultation: Psychologists as research consultants. In R. D. Morgan, T. L. Kuther, & C. J. Habben (Eds.), *Life after graduate school in psychology: Insider's advice from new psychologists* (pp. 307–320). New York: Psychology Press.

Taylor, S. E. (1999). *Health psychology* (4th ed.). Boston: McGraw-Hill.

Tenopyr, M. L. (1997). Improving the workplace: Industrial/organizational psychology as a career. In R. Sternberg (Ed.), *Career paths in psychology: Where your degree can take you* (pp. 185–196). Washington, DC: American Psychological Association.

Toch, H. (1992). *Mosaic of despair: Human breakdowns in prison* (Rev. ed.). Washington, DC: American Psychological Association.

Torrey, E. F. (1995). Editorial: Jails and prisons—America's new mental hospital. *American Journal of Public Health, 85,* 1611–1613.

Trull, T. J., & Phares, E. J. (2001). *Clinical psychology.* Belmont, CA: Wadsworth.

Turner, J. (1998). Technical writing: Writing for dollars. *Science's Next Wave.* Retrieved February 1, 2002, from http://nextwave.sciencemag.org/cgi/content/full/1998/09/03/9

Tyler, R. R. (2000). An interesting career in psychology: Aviation human factors practitioner. *Psychological Science Agenda.* Retrieved June 5, 2002, from http://www.apa.org/science/ic-tyler.html

U.S. Department of Education, NCES. (2003). *Digest of Education Statistics 2002* (NCES 2003-060), table 252. Data from U.S. Department of Education, NCES, Integrated Postsecondary Education Data System, "Completions Survey" (IPEDS-C:90-01), 1990–91, 1995–96, and 2000–01.

University of New Orleans. (2001). *Applied developmental psychology: Departmental program brochure.* Retrieved July 2, 2002, from http://www.uno.edu/~psyc/adbroch2001.pdf

Van Haveren, R., Habben, C. J., & Kuther, T. L. (2005). New psychologists online: Changing the face of psychology through technology. In R. D. Morgan, T. L. Kuther, & C. J. Habben (Eds.), *Life after graduate school in psychology: Insider's advice from new psychologists* (pp. 321–328). New York: Psychology Press.

Vesilind, P. A. (2000). *So you want to be a professor? A handbook for graduate students.* Thousand Oaks, CA: Sage.

Watkins, C. E., Lopez, F. G., Campbell, V. L., & Himmell, C. D. (1986). Contemporary counseling psychology: Results of a national survey. *Journal of counseling psychology, 33,* 301–309.

Weiner, I. B., & Hess, A. K. (2006). *The handbook of forensic psychology* (3rd ed.). New York: Wiley.

Weinstein, M., & Rossini, E. D. (1999). Teaching group treatment in doctoral programs in counseling psychology. *Psychological Reports, 85,* 697–700.

Wetfeet.com. (2005a). *Account management.* Retrieved October 27, 2005, from http://www.wetfeet.com/asp/careerprofiles_overview.asp?careerpk=2

Wetfeet.com. (2005b). *Retail: Career overview.* Retrieved June 5, 2002, from http://www.wetfeet.com/asp/careerprofiles_overview.asp?careerpk=35

Whitebrook, M., & Phillips, D. (1999). Child care employment: Implications for women's self sufficiency and for child development. *Foundation for Child Development Working Paper Series.* Retrieved July 2, 2002, from http://www.ffcd.org/wbwp2txt.pdf

Williams, S. (2005). Executive management: Helping executives manage their organizations through organizational and market research. In R. D. Morgan, T. L. Kuther, & C. J. Habben (Eds.), *Life after graduate school in psychology: Insider's advice from new psychologists* (pp. 225–238). New York: Psychology Press.

Williams, S., Wicherski, M., & Kohout, J. L. (2000). *Salaries in psychology 1999: Report of the 1999 APA salary survey.* Washington, D.C.: American Psychological Association. Retrieved June 5, 2002, from http://research.apa.org/99salaries.html

Winerman, L. (2004). Designing psychologists. *Monitor on Psychology, 35*(7), 30–31.

Wiskoff, M. F. (1997). Defense of the nation: Military psychologists. In R. J. Sternberg (Ed.), *Career paths in psychology: Where your degree can take you* (pp. 245–268). Washington, DC: American Psychological Association.

Witherspoon, R., & White, R. P. (1996). Executive coaching: A continuum of roles. *Consulting Psychology Journal: Practice and Research, 48,* 124–133.

Woods, D. (2002). *Behind human error: Human factors research to improve patient safety.* Retrieved June 5, 2002, from http://www.apa.org/ppo/issues/shumfactors2.html

Yund, M. A. (1998). Market research analyst, among other things. *Science's Next Wave.* Retrieved June 5, 2002, from http://nextwave.sciencemag.org/cgi/content/full/1998/06/04/8

Index

Aamodt, M. G., 105, 107, 115
Abbott, Langer, & Associates, 115, 149
Academia, 18–23
  advantages of, 20–21
  biopsychology in, 96–97
  clinical neuropsychology in, 96–97
  cognitive neuropsychology in, 96–97
  competition in, 22
  disadvantages of, 21
  health psychology in, 83
  research in, 22–23
  sport psychology in, 86
Account managers, 135–136
Ackerman, M. J., 69
Acquisitions editor, 28
Actkinson, T. R., 176
Actuaries, 128
Adam, E. K., 155
Adaptability, 12, 161
Addictions, APA division of, 4
Administration, 46–47
  nonprofit, 149
  salaries in, 47
Administrative assistants, 111–112
Adult Development and Aging, APA
    Division of, 4
Advertising
  account managers in, 135–136
  competition in, 136
  evaluating careers in, 136
  job outlook for, 136
  management in, 142
  media planners in, 136
  salaries in, 136
Allen, M., 40
Allen, T. W., 134–135

American Association of Marriage and
    Family Therapy, 37
American Counseling Association, 37
American Occupational Therapy
    Association, 82
American Psychological Association (APA).
    See also individual divisions
  congressional fellowship program of, 73
  Preparing Future Faculty Program of,
    11, 20
  programs accredited by, 41, 43
  Research Office of, 34, 41, 51, 176
American Psychological Law Society, 62
American Psychology–Law Society (APA
    Division), 4, 70, 71–73
American School Counselor Association,
    59
American Society for the Advancement of
    Pharmacotherapy Applied (APA
    Division), 4
Amsel, J., 28
Anderson, M. B., 78, 87
Andrews, C. K., 6, 71–72
Andrews, D. A., 66
Anson, R. H., 64–65, 71
APA. *See* American Psychological Association
Appleby, D., 159
Applied developmental psychology, 147,
    151–152
Artistic personality type, 8–9
Assessments, 5, 34
  in clinical psychology, 34, 37, 40
  in forensic examination, 68–69, 70
  in health psychology, 84
  neuropsychological, 98–99
  in police psychology, 70

Rogerian theoretical orientation.
See Person-centered theoretical
orientation
Romans, J. S. C., 41
Rorschach test. See Thematic
Apperception Test
Ross, R., 66
Rossini, E. D., 41
Rowh, M., 149–150
Rozensky, R. H., 83

Salaries
of actuaries, 128
in administration, 47
of administrative assistants, 112
in advertising, 136
of biopsychologists, 97, 99
of budget analysts, 125
of child-care workers, 53–54
of clinical laboratory technicians, 95
of computer programmers, 124
of computer support specialists, 124
of consultants, 114–115
of correctional psychologists, 67–68
of database administrators, 127
of data-mining professionals, 130
of design assistants, 111
of environmental designers, 117
of financial analysts, 129
of fitness instructors, 79
of forensic examiners, 70
of gerontology aides, 148
of health psychologists, 83–85
of human resources professionals, 113
in management, 143
in market research, 141, 154
in military, 26–27
negotiating, 171
in nonprofit organizations, 149–150
of occupational therapy assistants, 82
of operations research analysts, 126
of parole officers, 65
of pharmacy technicians, 96
of police officers, 64
of police psychologists, 71
of politicians, 73
of practicing psychologists, 45
of probation officers, 65
in product development, 141

of professoriate, 21
in program development, 46
of psychiatric technicians, 94
in public relations, 140
of real estate agents, 137
of recreational therapists, 81
of recreational workers, 79
in research, 25
in retail, 139
of school counselors, 58
of school psychologists, 57
of science technicians, 93–94
of scientist-practitioners, 152
in social policy research, 155
of social workers, 38
of sport psychologists, 86–87
of substance abuse counselors, 39
of system analysts, 127
of teachers, 52
of trial consultants, 72
of usability assistants, 116
of writers, 30
Salary.com, 112, 123–127, 130,
141, 143
Sales manager, 142
Sallis, J. F., 84
Salzinger, K., 21
Sarafino, E. P., 83, 85
Sayette, M. A., 40, 42–43, 178
Schare, M. L., 40
School counselors, 58–59
School psychology
assessment in, 55
bachelor's degree, opportunities with,
51–54
checklist for, 60
consultation in, 54–55
educational services in, 55
employment settings for, 57–58
graduate degree, opportunities with,
54–59
intervention strategies in, 56
introduction to, 50–60
prevention strategies in, 55
private practice in, 56–57
program development in, 56
research in, 56
salaries in, 57
school settings of, 55–56